German Reading Skills for Academic Purposes

German Reading Skills for Academic Purposes allows researchers and learners with no prior understanding of German to gain an understanding of written German at CEFR C2/ACTFL Intermediate-High level that will allow them to read a variety of German texts, including research articles and monographs.

This is achieved by looking closely at the elements of German grammar required for the understanding of written German along with practical advice and observations.

One of the main themes running through the textbook is that it uses a toolkit approach that puts deductive reasoning and decoding skills at its heart to allow learners to engage with a wide variety of texts.

Alexander Burdumy is Assistant Professor of German at the University of Durham, UK.

German Reading Skills for Academic Purposes

Alexander Burdumy

Routledge
Taylor & Francis Group

LONDON AND NEW YORK

First published 2019
by Routledge
2 Park Square, Milton Park, Abingdon, Oxon OX14 4RN

and by Routledge
52 Vanderbilt Avenue, New York, NY 10017

Routledge is an imprint of the Taylor & Francis Group, an informa business

© 2019 Alexander Burdumy

British Library Cataloguing-in-Publication Data
A catalogue record for this book is available from the British Library

Library of Congress Cataloging-in-Publication Data
A catalog record has been requested for this book

ISBN: 978-0-367-18662-3 (hbk)
ISBN: 978-0-367-18663-0 (pbk)
ISBN: 978-0-429-19748-2 (ebk)

Typeset in Sabon
by Deanta Global Publishing Services, Chennai, India

Contents

Foreword

This book represents in many ways a labour of love and is dedicated to those who want to learn how to read German.

When I started working at the University of Durham, I had not yet encountered courses that were focused solely on learning how to read a German text. Over the years I have been fortunate to meet many learners from different disciplines and at different stages in their education who wished to learn how to read German texts, sometimes for their research, sometimes for professional purposes, sometimes as a cross-disciplinary skill and sometimes for personal reasons such as further education.

With this book I try to support these learners the best that I can. In this book I combine a very hands-on approach by teaching students strategies and techniques to decode German texts with the help of a dictionary, an approach that I call the "toolkit approach." When someone wants to build a house, they need the raw materials: the stones, mortar, timber, roof tiles and so on. In a language, this is the vocabulary. In order to build the house one needs tools and machines; in languages these are the grammatical rules that are used to bind the words together and lock them into a meaning. Yet there is one more important thing needed to build a house: the technical know-how. This is where this book differs from a typical grammar book. It provides a pathway to acquiring the know-how by building up rules and advice, and practice. Grammar points are ordered in a logical order, exercises strengthen understanding, and advice and tips help to make the process of understanding German easier.

I wish to thank especially Dr Gaby Wright, Mr Mark Critchley and Mrs Florelena Galvis for taking the time to help me with this book and for their helpful advice. I also want to thank all the students who over the years have given me valuable experience on the matter as well as feedback and advice on earlier versions of this book.

How to use this book

This book can be used for self-study, as a reference and as a course book.

The chapters are organised in a linear manner. For the most part there is no need to switch to other sections of the book and one can focus on advancing through all 16 chapters. There are four additional parts to the book; these are a section with additional practice texts, an appendix, an answer key and a vocabulary section. The appendix includes information that does not fit into any specific chapter, for example an explanation of grammatical terminology, a list of tricky words and constructions, advice on dictionaries and other helpful information.

Every chapter has at least one practice text attached to it in some form. For the most part, these are authentic text materials or based on authentic text material, and some of the recurring themes in texts, exercises and examples involve works by Schiller and Goethe, academia, the former GDR, Theology and Classicism. The answer key provides answers for self-study and there is also occasional additional advice in the answer key. Many texts and exercises have vocabulary sections directly beneath; as you progress through the book, these will become less comprehensive and frequent, but most words can still be found in the vocabulary section of the book.

One important piece of advice is to not rush through the early chapters. Most of the earlier chapters that cover a large deal of different content have summaries at the end – be sure to review these. German has a high initial learning curve that gradually levels off, and as a result the early chapters 1–6 contain a lot of vital core information that first needs to be understood before the later chapters can be tackled. There is a little overlap of topics/content here and there (for example, for cases, sentence structure and for prepositions), to allow more advanced learners to jump to specific sections they want to work on. In general, when a topic is repeated, the first entry is simpler and more general, and the second one is more complex and in-depth.

Throughout the book you will see several monkey wrenches. These mark the most important practice advice in the book on how to deal with central aspects of the German language. Pay close attention to these; they form the core part of your toolkit when it comes to decoding a German-language text.

There are a few conventions that have been used throughout the book.

- German words have been put in italics when they occur in English sentences or in examples.
- Single letters such as sounds, prefixes or suffixes have not been put in brackets, to make for a clearer typeface.
- The abbreviation lit. means literally. This is used when it makes sense to explain how a German word/phrase/sentence would be translated literally into English, as opposed to a more idiomatic translation.

Acknowledgements

I would like to thank the following publishers and authors for permission to reproduce the following copyright texts:

"Hintergründe zum Weltbevölkerungswachstum," an adapted selection of texts from the website of the charity organisation *Deutsche Stiftung Weltbevölkerung*, found at https://www.dsw.org.

"Die Zäsur des Mauerbaus 1961," excerpt from: Burdumy, Alexander (2013). *Sozialpolitik und Repression in der DDR. Ost-Berlin 1971–1989.* Klartext Verlag. pp. 81–82.

"Glück im Unglück," an adapted excerpt from: Bönisch, Georg (2008). "Glück im Unglück". In *SPIEGEL SPECIAL Geschichte. Der Kalte Krieg. Wie die Welt das Wettrüsten überlebte.* 3/2008. Spiegel Verlag. pp. 24–33.

"Ablasshandel," from the website *Der Luther-Tetzel-Weg*, found at www.luther-tetzel-weg.de; originally published by Kirchengemeinde St. Nikolai Jüterbog & Pfarrer Bernhard Gutsche.

"Wenn die Haifische Menschen wären," from: Brecht, Bertolt (1995). *Werke. Große kommentierte Berliner und Frankfurter Ausgabe,* Band 18: Prosa 3. Bertolt-Brecht-Erben/Suhrkamp Verlag.

"Ich habe doch nichts zu verbergen," excerpt from: Morozov, Evgeny (2015). "Ich habe doch nichts zu verbergen". In *Aus Politik und Zeitgeschichte, 11-12/2015.* BPB. pp. 3-7.

The original can be found here:
http://www.bpb.de/shop/zeitschriften/apuz/202251/big-data (accessed 10/02/2019).

"Von den 95 Thesen zum Augsburger Religionsfrieden," excerpt from: Kaufmann, Thomas (2016). "Meilensteine der Reformation. Von den 95 Thesen zum Augsburger Religionsfrieden". In *Aus Politik und Zeitgeschichte 52/2016.* BPB. pp. 8–14.

The original can be found here:
http://www.bpb.de/shop/zeitschriften/apuz/239253/reformation (accessed 10/02/2019).

Five steps towards understanding a text

1. Scan through the whole text quickly
   - What do you understand? Can you make any assumptions about the topic and content of the text?
   - Look for vocabulary and for parts that you understand or can deduce. Do not focus on what you do not understand; rather, look for things you do understand. By looking for these "islands of knowledge" you can build bridges between the parts you do not yet understand.
   - Most likely you will have to look up some vocabulary in a dictionary. As you work your way through the layers of the text, try to limit your search to those words that you require at the moment for the comprehension of the text.

2. Locate the subject and the verb of each clause in order to construct a framework (p. 35) for your translation
   - Identify the verb forms and their conjugations.
   - Identify the subject of each clause.
   - These two components will form the framework of your understanding. All other words have to fit into this framework, not the other way around.

3. Locate adverbials and conjunctions that are part of the framework
   - These words govern the logical relationships between clauses and are therefore more important to your framework than, for example, adjectives or prepositions. They are most often found at the beginning of a clause.

4. When translating a sentence, focus on the important parts first
   It is best to begin with the chunks that are central to the comprehension of complex sentences. Isolate prepositional objects and adjectives – leave them for later. Break down long sentences into individual clauses and work on these separately. Work on main clauses first, then on subordinate clauses. Remember, the framework is key to a successful translation, so if you are struggling, you might have to go back to steps 2 or 3.

5 Review your comprehension of the text throughout the process outlined here

   Ask yourself the following questions:
   - Do you have all the information you need from the text?
   - Does everything make sense to you?
   - Does your comprehension support or contradict your previous assumptions about the text?

1 Deductive reasoning; German alphabet and pronunciation; cognates

1.1 Using deductive reasoning to understand written texts

Whenever we are presented with a written text, whether we recognise the language or even the script, we will try to make sense of what is presented. This is part of our nature: our brain is hardwired to try to make meaning of patterns it sees.

Have a look at the following text:

> 7H15 3X4MPL3 5HOW5 YOU HOW YOU C4N M4K3 53N53 OF 73X75 WH3R3 5OM3 1NFORM471ON 15 317H3R M1551NG OR OB5CUR3D.

> 1N 7H3 B3G1NN1NG YOU M4Y H4V3 FOUND 17 H4RD 7O F1GUR3 OU7 7H15 P4773RN BU7 45 YOU CON71NU3 7O R34D 17 YOU F1ND 7H47 17 B3COM35 34513R

Did you manage to figure out the pattern? Some words can only be decoded once you know that 7 stands for T and 3 stands for E, etc., but some other words like C4N, 1NFORM471ON or M1551NG were much easier to figure out due to two factors: first, there were still enough recognisable letters in the word to know what the complete word is. Second, the numbers used resemble the actual letters of the word. If for example an 8 would have been used instead of 5 to represent the letter S, the text would have been more difficult to decode and it would have taken longer.

This example shows us that we can identify words even if a part of them is obscured or unknown to us. In this chapter we will later look at cognates, an approach which works on the same principle, i.e. that you look for parts in the word that you recognise from an English, French or Latin word, in order to guess the meaning of the word.

Have a look at the next example.

○ I'm _____ to the cinema tonight.

Most readers will be able to guess that the missing word here is "going." The main clue is the familiarity of the phrase. Not many other words would be used with this sort of statement. Words like "driving," "wandering" or even "hitchhiking" might be possible, but are less likely. The choice is reinforced by grammatical constraint. First, we are expecting a verb in this position. A noun like "movie" would violate this grammatical constraint. Second, the choice of verb is limited to only such verbs that can be followed by the preposition "to." A verb like "sitting" would not work, because it would require a different preposition ("in").

Here is the next example.

O   I saw Rigoletto in the _____ yesterday.

Many readers, who are unfamiliar with the name Rigoletto, assume it must be some kind of play or movie (especially because our previous example was about going to the cinema). The word "saw" hints at this and Rigoletto is capitalised, so according to English grammar rules it must be a name. Consequently their guess will be some sort of building where one can view these, for example "theatre" or "cinema." It is a guess based on what is most likely to be the correct answer. If, however, you know that Rigoletto is, in fact, an opera, you will opt for the reply "opera house." Your background knowledge means that in this case you can make an educated guess based on the specific knowledge you have of Rigoletto.

Finally, let's have a look at this example.

O   Tim _____ Nina have two _____, a _____, aged 12, and a daughter, _____ 9.

You probably had no problems guessing that the full sentence is "Tim and Nina have two children, a son, aged 12, and a daughter, aged 9." The question here is really how did you manage to guess this so easily? It is again because we are hardwired to decode language (spoken or written) even when it is incomplete. Language production usually has some degree of redundancy in it, which means that not everything is needed for it to still be understood. Take for example a conversation on a noisy train. You might not understand every word clearly in the conversation, but unless the noise is so loud that substantial parts of the conversation cannot be made out, you will usually still be able to understand it. In the previous example, there is still enough information for you to easily understand it. You can figure out "Tim and Nina," because it is highly unlikely that any other word would go between two names. "Children" is the natural guess for the second gap, due to the word "daughter" later on. There are other hints as well. First of all we can expect a noun after "two," and also the context – two names hint at a couple, or the word "aged" – reinforces our guess. A "son" can be guessed because it would not make sense to list the word "daughter" twice.[1] Finally, the word in front of 9 is "aged," due to the parallel structure.

To summarise, you can deduce meaning in language based on:

- likelihood (especially in typical phrases);
- grammatical rules (what type of word would fit the grammatical rules?);
- context (do other parts of the sentence or text suggest any meaning?);
- background knowledge;
- logic (has something already been said or would only certain words make sense?);
- any combination of the above.

The more you understand in a text, the easier it will be to make good guesses for the parts that you do not understand or are unsure about. What this means for reading German texts is that you should not be afraid to try to deduce meaning from the text where you feel you have enough information to make a guess. It can often save time and help with the rest of the text. You should still try and verify your guesses when you can, for example after reading a passage.

1.2 German alphabet

Europäische Union
European Union
Straße
Street

German features a few more letters (or graphemes) than English,

- the umlauts (Ää, Üü, Öö); and
- the ß, which is usually called *Eszett* or *scharfes S*.

> "Diphthongs? Verbs? Subjects? Determiners?"
>
> If these terms are all new to you, check out the section **Grammar terminology explained** in the back of the book (p. 202).

German also uses a number of diphthongs, which are a combination of two vowels to create a new sound. The most notable diphthongs are ie and ei, because they can easily be confused. Although the difference seems small, it affects meaning.

Exercise

Look up the following words in an online dictionary (you will not find all forms in a printed dictionary). You can find some suggestions for useful online dictionaries in the glossary (p. 211).

Bruder – Brüder; fallen – fällen; heilt – hielt; Kuchen – Küchen; Leid – Lied; Meise – mies; Reise – Riese; Tochter – Töchter; Vater – Väter; weise – Wiese; zahlen – zählen

Especially the forms *heilt* and *hielt* are noteworthy here, as one of them *(hielt)* is a past tense form of the verb *halten*. As you will learn later, some irregular verbs use a vowel change to indicate the past tense, i.e. they change the vowel sound in their middle.

Also interesting is that some words use an umlaut to form the plural of that word. This demonstrates that umlauts definitely make a difference in meaning, as for example in *Mutter*, mother, and *Mütter*, mothers.

1.3 German pronunciation

As this book focuses solely on the comprehension of written material in German, you might wonder why there is a section on German pronunciation here. There are a few reasons why it is helpful to have a rough idea of how to pronounce a German word. First, if you want to ask a German speaker for some help with a word or sentence, being able to pronounce German will be helpful. Second, sometimes saying the word out loud will allow you to find a cognate in English. For example, if you pronounce the word *nächste* you will notice it sounds very similar to its English cognate "next." Finally, when reading a text, we pronounce the words in our mind, and understanding how German words are pronounced makes it easier for you to do this; it also facilitates other tasks such as looking up a word in a dictionary, identifying prefixes and suffixes, etc.

German words use syllables, as most other languages do, and syllables typically consist of one vowel-like sound together with some consonants. "Some" is key here, as the syllables in German words can differ greatly in length. Take for example the word *Ruhe* ("silence"). It consists of two syllables, and four graphemes (letters). The combination of two vowels and two consonants makes it easy to identify these syllables. If you compare this to the word *schweigen* ("to be silent"), you will see that this word also has two syllables; however, it consists of nine graphemes – more than double the number of the previous word.

Letters that have been omitted have the same or a very similar sound in both languages (b, c, d, f, h, k, m, n, p, q, t, x, y).

Letter	German example	Pronunciation guide
a	Vater	father
ai	Hai	hi
au	laut	sound
ä	Käse	late
äu	Fräulein	oil
ch	Light vowels: ich, nicht	fish (approximation)
	Dark vowels: Nacht, acht	Loch Ness
chs	sechs, nächste	six, next
e	Tee, Geld	meh!, met
ei	mein, klein	mine
eu	Deutsch	oil
g -ig	Gold	gold
	vierzig	lush
i	ich, wir	see
ie	Bier	beer
j	Januar	yet
o	offen	pot
ö	schön	her, oeuvre
r	hart	heart (approximation)
-er	Ratte	right (approximation)
	immer	father
s	See	Zoo
	ist	see
ß	Straße	pass
sch	Fisch	sheep
sp (at the beginning of a word)	Sport	cash
st (at the beginning of a word)	Staat	rushed
tz	Platz	fits
u	gut	June
ü	über	–
v	vier Vase	fine vain
w	Wer?	vain
z	Zeit	fits

1.4 Cognates

German and English are both Germanic languages and share some similarity in terms of grammar, vocabulary and pronunciation. As you would expect, this means that some words are similar in both languages; words that share a linguistic derivation with a word in another language are known as cognates and there are many of these in German and English. Many cognates are of Latin or French origin, but there are also cognates that have more Germanic roots, and of course words that are borrowed directly from the other language.

In order to identify a cognate, you need to pay attention to the consonants rather than the vowels. Take for example the cognate

allein – alone

The consonants in this cognate are very similar – l and n – but there is a clear vowel change in the word. In general, vowel changes in words are more fluid and more random in contrast to consonant changes. If you look at another cognate,

Weg – way

you see no relation between these two words at first. However, if you know that a g in German is often a y in the English cognate, you have a pattern you can follow.

→ *Weg* – "Wey" – way

These consonant patterns are much more reliable when it comes to guessing the cognate of a German word. For example, take

Auge

and replace the g with a y:

"Auye"

and you are closer to the English word "eye."

When it comes to cognates, guessing their meaning isn't such a bad thing, as we already discussed in 1.1. If you see a German word and you think you might know its English sibling, it is usually best to trust your gut feeling. Of course, you can always use a dictionary, but when you are trying to read a longer text, you might not have the time (or need) to look up every single word.

Follow these steps to make your guesses more accurate:

- Stick with the consonants. Consonant changes between the English and the German word tend to follow clearer patterns and rules, whereas vowel changes can be more random.
- German verbs and infinitives have endings that are often not present in the English word, for example the -en on infinitives. You will have to "remove" these in your mind.
- Say the word out loud. Sometimes it is much easier to guess the English word by hearing the German word than by seeing it written. For example, *nächste* looks very different from "next," but sounds very similar when pronounced.

Exercise

A. What could the following words mean? Pay more attention to consonants than to vowels – vowels tend to change more often than consonants.

braun sechs hart Land Markt lang warm oft jung roh mehr Ende

B. Try to figure out the following sentences.
1. Deutschland liegt in Europa. Es hat neun Nachbarländer. Die Hauptstadt ist Berlin.
2. An der Universität Ulm studieren Studenten Naturwissenschaften, Politik, Geschichte, Philosophie, Musik, Kunst, Religion, Anglistik und Germanistik. Was studierst du?
C. This table lists examples of typical consonant changes between English and German cognates.

For example, if you exchange the b in *geben* for a v, you can guess that the cognate in English is "give."

Try to work out the English cognates of these words.

German b → English v/f			
geben	to give	über	
haben		halb	
German v → English f			
voll		bevor	
der Vater		vier	
German ff/f/pf → English p			
helfen		scharf	
offen		der Pfeffer	
German d → English th			
denken		die Erde	
das Ding		der Tanz	
German t/tt → English d/th			
alt		die Mutter	
selten		tot	
German s/ss/ß (=sz) → English t			
das Wasser		besser	
vergessen		groß	
German z/tz → English t			
zehn		sitzen	
das Herz		zu	
German zw → English tw			
zwölf		zwei	
zwanzig			
German ch/cht → English gh/ght			
das Licht		hoch	
die Sicht		das Recht	
German ch → English k			
machen		sprechen	
das Buch		suchen	
German k → English c/ch			
kalt		der Kanzler	
kommen		klar	
German ig/g → English i/y			
windig		der Tag	
German j → English y			
jung		das Jahr	

D. What could the following words mean? Some of these cognates differ in more than one element to their English counterpart.

der Freund		die Zunge	
die Nacht		hassen	
die Straßenlaterne		der Ellenbogen	
durch		fliegen	
der Fiebertraum		die Dornenkrone	
die Leiter		die Katze	
beide		die Erdnuss	

False Friends

There are unfortunately a couple of words that may look like a cognate, but have a different meaning. For example, *das Gift* is German for "poison" and has no relation with the English word "gift," or the German word *aktuell* means "current" in English, and not "actual." These "false cognates" are usually referred to as False Friends. Do not worry too much about these; in time you will become familiar with them.

Note

1 This can be further explained with Grice's conversational maxim of quantity, which states that a contribution should provide as much information as necessary for its understanding, but also not more information than is necessary. In the example, a second mentioning of "daughter" would be unnecessary information.
  Grice, Paul (1975). "Logic and conversation." In Cole, P.; Morgan, J. *Syntax and semantics*. 3: Speech acts. Academic Press. pp. 41–58.

2　Fundamental German and English grammar concepts; German sentence structure

2.1 Fundamental German and English grammar concepts

When you look at a German word, there are four aspects that are of interest to us:

1. Meaning
2. Type (or "parts of speech")
3. Function
4. Form

Meaning – Often the first thing we want to know when we look at a word is its meaning. For example, *Freund* means "friend" in English. As we build up a German vocabulary, there are more words we recognise and remember. There are also words where we can guess the meaning (cognates), and some, where we can deduce it from the context (for example, most prepositions). The meaning is crucial to our understanding of a German text, but should not be seen as the most important aspect of a word.

Type – There are eight major categories of words in English and German (sometimes referred to as "parts of speech"): These are:

1. Nouns
2. Pronouns
3. Verbs
4. Adjectives
5. Articles (or determiners)
6. Adverbs (or adverbials)
7. Prepositions
8. Conjunctions

In addition there is a group called "particles" which does not fit in with any of the main parts of speech described previously; it contains words such as the English "to" in "to fly." These words do not change and their exact purpose is often difficult to define.

Knowing the type of word is key for identifying its function.

Function – The role the word has in a sentence is its function. Typical functions are:

1. Subject
2. Direct object
3. Indirect object
4. Prepositional object

5. Finite verb
6. Verb component such as participle or infinitive

In some way, the function of a word is as important as its meaning. If we have a sentence where we know that one word is a direct object, but we do not know its meaning, we can still make sense of everything else up to that point.

Functions are limited to certain types of words. For example, only verbs can be a finite verb or a verb component, and only nouns can be a subject or object. However, German allows you to change the type of a word and, consequently, its meaning in a similar fashion as English does. For example, "to drive" is a verb, but we can form the word "driver" from it, a noun, which has a related but different meaning.

Form – Words inflect (or change their forms/endings) according to their function in a sentence. In German this often has spelling changes that you can see easily, in English this happens less frequently. For example, if you compare the words *Auto* and *Autos* you will see that an "s" has been added to show the plural. While the same happens in English – "car" and "cars" – German has many more of these plural inflections, e.g. *das Buch*, *die Bücher*. *Der Mann, den Mann, dem Mann, des Mannes* all have a different form (reflecting a different function in a sentence), whereas English only has two such inflections: "the man" and "the man's."

There is also often an agreement between words. For example, the subject and verb of a sentence agree in number and person: "I am" as opposed to "many people are."

In German, the article of a noun is usually the best indicator of its form. In the case of verbs and adjectives, the front part of the verb usually stays the same and only the ending is changed.

2.2 Introductory text: Sprachen in der Europäischen Union

Skim through the introductory text and underline the words you think you recognise from English or which you can deduce.

Sprachen in der Europäischen Union (Januar 2019)

Die Europäische Union hat 28 Mitgliedsstaaten und benutzt 24 verschiedene Sprachen als offizielle Amts- und Arbeitssprachen. Alle EU-Bürger haben nach §24 AEUV das Recht, europäische Institutionen in einer der 24 Sprachen zu kontaktieren. Die Antwort ist in dieser Sprache.

Europäische Institutionen übersetzen alle wichtigen Dokumente in alle 24 Amtssprachen. Intern verwendet die Europäische Union aber vor allem Englisch, Deutsch und Französisch.

Die Europäische Union fördert Sprachenvielfalt. Jeder Europäer soll nicht nur seine Muttersprache und Englisch, sondern auch eine „Adoptivsprache" lernen. Minderheitensprachen unterstützt die Europäische Union auch, das sind Sprachen wie zum Beispiel Luxemburgisch, Jiddisch, Romani oder Irisch, die nur wenige Menschen in der Europäischen Union sprechen. Man kann an die Europäische Union in den „halbamtlichen" Sprachen Katalanisch, Baskisch, Galizisch, Schottisch-Gälisch oder Walisisch schreiben, aber sie sind keine offiziellen Amtssprachen. Dazu kommen spezielle Situationen, wie z.B. Russisch in den Baltischen Staaten oder Türkisch in Zypern. In diesen Ländern gibt es viele Menschen, die diese Sprachen als Muttersprache oder häufig im Alltag sprechen.

Die häufigste Muttersprache in der Europäischen Union ist Deutsch mit 18% der Bürger. An zweiter Stelle steht Französisch mit 14% und an dritter Stelle Englisch und Italienisch mit jeweils 13%. Weil aber 51% aller EU-Bürger Englisch sprechen, ist Englisch die populärste Sprache in der Europäischen Union.

Vocabulary

aber – however, but
amtlich – official
Amtssprache, die (-, -n) – official language
auch – as well, also
benutzen – to use
etwas fördern – to support something

2.3 German sentence structure (subjects, objects, verbs, sentences and clauses explained)

In a statement, a typical sentence will usually contain information about who does what. The agent of the sentence is the subject, or the "who," and the action, the "what," is the verb. If we want

> *"Subject? Verb? Clause? Preposition?"*
>
> If these terms are all new to you, check out the section **Grammar terminology explained** in the back of the book (p. 202).

to know who (or what) is affected by the action, an object is added to the sentence.

WHO (Subject) → WHAT (Verb) → TO WHOM OR WHAT (Object)

Die Europäische Union fördert Sprachenvielfalt.
The European Union (subject) supports (verb) language diversity (object).

Die Kommission verwendet im internen Gebrauch drei Arbeitssprachen.
The commission (subject) uses (verb) for its internal practice (prep. object) three working languages (object).
(Prepositional objects provide additional information.)

Position of the subject

English follows a very simple syntax (the rules of how we construct sentences) that always requires these components to be in the exact order Subject → Verb → Object. German is more flexible and can put something other than the subject at the beginning of a sentence, but the verb will always be in the second position of main clauses.

Die Europäische Union (**subject**)	fördert	Sprachenvielfalt.
Minderheitensprachen	unterstützt	die Europäische Union (**subject**) auch.
Position 1	**Position 2 (verb)**	

In the second sentence the subject moved behind the verb. This is quite common in German and is usually called Subject-Verb-Inversion. This is often done either because of emphasis or to avoid starting two sentences with the same words.

You will always find the subject towards the beginning of a clause, but it will often be behind the verb, not in front.

Verb position and clauses

A sentence is made up of at least one clause, and makes sense overall. Sentences typically end with a full stop. Clauses are smaller units and can end with a comma. There are different types of clauses: main clauses and a range of subordinate clauses. Main clauses make sense on their own, subordinate clauses only make sense with the main clause they are referring to.

Let's have a look at a rather complex sentence here as an example:

Minderheitensprachen unterstützt die Europäische Union auch, das sind Sprachen wie zum Beispiel Luxemburgisch, Jiddisch, Romani oder Irisch, die nur wenige Menschen in der Europäischen Union sprechen.

The example sentence begins with a main clause. The end of the main clause is marked with a comma.

Minderheitensprachen (object)	unterstützt (verb)	die Europäische Union (subject) auch	,
Minority languages	supports	the European Union as well	
Position 1	**Position 2**	**Position 3**	**Position 4**

As mentioned before, the verb is in the second position and the subject and object have "swapped" places. If we want to translate the sentence into English, we need to reverse this change in our translation, e.g. "The European Union supports minority languages as well."

The second clause is quite similar:

das	sind (verb)	Sprachen (subject) wie zum Beispiel, Luxemburgisch, Jiddisch, Romani oder Irisch	,
these	are	languages such as for example Luxembourgish, Yiddish, Romany or Irish	
Position 1	**Position 2**	**Position 3**	**Position 4**

This is a main clause as well. The verb is in the second position. We again have the subject after the verb.

In this case the *das* in the first position is actually also a subject, but we will look into the so-called predicate nouns in a later chapter. For now, remember that a main clause can follow a main clause. A comma separated these clauses, but they could also be connected with an *und* ("and") or an *oder* ("or").

Let's have a look at the final clause:

die (relative pronoun – a connector)	nur wenige Menschen (subject)		in der Europäischen Union	sprechen (verb).
which/that	only few people		in the European Union	speak.
Position 0* between the clauses	**Position 1**	**Position 2**	**Position 3**	**Position 4**

Here it gets a little bit tricky. As you can see, the verb is not in the second position but in fourth position. This is the case for most subordinate clauses.

Die can have different functions. It can be a determiner ("the"), but here it is a relative pronoun and is translated as "who, which" or "that."

It introduces a relative clause, which, as the name implies, is dependent on the main clause in front of it in order to make sense.

Were someone to enter a room full of people and only say "which only a few people in the European Union speak," the people in the room would not understand the speaker and ask what he or she is referring to. Hence we need a main clause for a relative or subordinate clause to make sense.

In this type of clause the verb is located at the very end of the sentence, here marked as position 4. The subject is still located towards the front of the sentence.

When trying to understand a German sentence, you should therefore start by locating the verb of each clause first. Always check for it towards the beginning of the clause ("position 2") and the end of the clause ("position 4"). The subject will usually be towards the beginning of the clause.

2.4 *Man, zu* and *es gibt*

Man

> *Man kann an die Europäische Union in den „halbamtlichen"*
> *Sprachen (..) schreiben.*
> One/You can write to the European Union in the semi-official
> languages.

The word *man* is used as a general subject form in German and it is often translated as "you," "one" or "people" in English. "You" is usually the better translation ("you should learn"), but if you are only trying to understand the clause, the slightly untypical "one" ("one should learn") can be helpful, as it helps avoid mistakes.

One helpful thing about *man* is that it will always be the subject of a clause. Do not confuse it with *Der Mann* (the man) though; the two of them have nothing to do with each other!

Zu

Let's have a look at a very frequent German word: *zu*

> *Alle EU-Bürger haben (..) das Recht, europäische Institutionen (..) zu*
> *kontaktieren.*

The word *zu* can have different functions (there are different types of the word *zu*), but the translation is usually "to." Simple infinitive constructions can be formed with the infinitive of a word and the particle *zu*, and sometimes a comma separates these clauses.

Exercise

Translate these sentences.

1. Viel Alkohol zu trinken ist nicht gesund.
2. Ich habe die Erlaubnis, den Artikel zu veröffentlichen.

Vocabulary

Erlaubnis, die (-, -se) – permission
gesund – healthy
veröffentlichen – to publish

Es gibt

Finally, let's have a look at another expression here:

> *In diesen Ländern* **gibt es** *viele Menschen, die...*
> In these countries **there are** many people, who...

Es gibt is a very common idiomatic construction that always translates as "there is/are" and it is always singular in German, even if it is talking about plural concepts.

2.5 Capitalisation of nouns

All nouns are capitalised in German. *Mitgliedsstaaten, Europäische Union* and *Sprachen* are all nouns.

German is very consistent with only capitalising nouns; there are only very few names where an adjective is capitalised as part of it. Compare the following:

> *der amerikanische Tourist*   the American tourist

Tourist is a noun in German, so it is capitalised. Because *amerikanische* is an adjective, it is not capitalised. You might argue that *amerikanische* should be considered a proper name, but it only functions as an adjective here to qualify the noun *Tourist,* and that is not enough for Germans to capitalise it. There are a few exceptions, such as *der Erste Weltkrieg* (First World War), which is capitalised because the whole unit is the name of a specific war.

Verbs are not capitalised and this can be very useful to identify the type of word you are dealing with, in order to understand the structure of the sentence.

Exercise

Which of the following are nouns and which are not? Look them up in your dictionary to see how different the meaning can be.

spinnen – Spinnen; Fahrer – fahren; licht – Licht; los – Los; das Dritte Reich

2.6 Compound nouns

Example of a compound noun:

Donaudampfschifffahrtsgesellschaftskapitän

German is famous for its long words. The truth is, however, somewhat disappointing: German likes to "cheat" and simply "glue" words to other words to create those impressively long words. The grammatical term for this is compound nouns.

Take the verb *braten*, to fry, and *die Wurst*, the famous sausage. If you put these together you have *die Bratwurst*, a fried sausage. Or take the word *der Zahn*, the tooth, and the word *der Arzt*, the surgeon/doctor. If you put these together you have *der Zahnarzt*, the German word for a dentist. And the dentist's assistant, *der Helfer* (or his female counterpart *die Helferin*) is simply *der Zahnarzthelfer* or *die Zahnarzthelferin*. The most common combinations are combining nouns, but as you saw with *die Bratwurst*, Germans can also combine other types of words with nouns in this way. The results can be some seriously long words.

You should approach these compound nouns without fear. Simply break them down into their original parts and you can often see what they mean. The final word of the compound is the most important one, as it determines the main meaning and the gender (which we'll look at in the next chapter).

So a "something-"*helfer* is always some sort of assistant, and the example at the beginning of this section translates to some sort of captain.

Exercise

Here are some compound nouns. Try to figure out what they could mean.

der Autofahrer   die Studentenermäßigung
der Schreibtisch   der Hörsaal
der Zeigefinger   der Abfalleimer

die Bohrmaschine das Motorboot
der Werbespruch der Deutschlehrer
der Buchladen der Verkehrsunfall
die Glühbirne das Milchgesicht
die Nagelfeile die Gesichtsmilch
die Kirschmarmelade
das Rindfleischetikettierungsüberwachungsaufgabenübertragungsgesetz
(At one point this was the longest word in German; it even has its own
Wikipedia page!)

Vocabulary

Abfall, der (-s, Abfälle) – rubbish
Aufgabe, die (-, -n) – task
Auto, das (-s, -s) – car
Birne, die (-, -n) – pear
bohren – to drill
Buch, das (-(e)s, Bücher) – book
Deutsch, das (-s, no plural) – German
Eimer, der (-s, -) – bucket
Ermäßigung, die (-, -en) – discount
Etikett, das (-s, -e/-en) – label
fahren – to drive
Feile, die (-, -n) – file, rasp
Fleisch, das (-(e)s, no plural) – meat
Gesetz, das (-es, -e) – law
Gesicht, das (-s, Gesichter) – face
glühen - to glow
hören - to listen

Kirsche, die (-, -n) – cherry
Laden, der (-s, Läden) – shop
Lehrer, der (-s, -) – teacher
schreiben – to write
Rind, das (-(e)s, Rinder) – cattle (ox/cow)
Saal, der (-(e)s, Säle) – hall
Spruch, der (-(e)s, Sprüche) – saying, phrase
Tisch, der (-(e)s, -e) – table
übertragen – to delegate (a task)
überwachen – to surveil/monitor
Unfall, der (-s, Unfälle) – accident
Verkehr, der (-s, -e) – traffic
werben – to advertise
zeigen – to point at, to show

2.7 The present tense

In the following tables you will find the conjugation patterns of the German
present tense *(das Präsens)*, divided into regular verbs (also called "weak
verbs") and irregular verbs (called "strong verbs"). Infinitive forms are also
given and you can see that these usually end in -en, for example *haben, sagen,
arbeiten* and in a few cases just -n, for example *sein, tun, hungern, regeln*.

How to conjugate a verb

In order to conjugate a verb, you take the infinitive of the verb (step 1). Then
the infinitive ending is cut off, leaving the word stem (step 2).

Next the appropriate conjugation ending is added on to the word stem
(step 3), which is the one that depends on the subject. The verb will agree
with the subject in the person aspect and the number (singular or plural).

Step 1: Peter <sagen> Hallo.
Step 2: Peter <sag-> Hallo.
Step 3: Peter <sag-t> Hallo. (The subject Peter is third person singular)
The final sentence is: Peter sagt Hallo.

Regular/weak verbs

Infinitive: **sagen** (to say)
Word stem: sag-

	Singular		Plural			Singular		Plural	
1. Person	ich	sage	wir	sagen	1. Person	I	say	we	say
2. Person	du	sagst	ihr	sagt	2. Person	you	say	you	say
3. Person	er/sie/es	sagt	sie/Sie	sagen	3. Person	he/she/it	says	they/you	say

Third person forms have more than one entry as a possible subject. The singular form is used for "he/she/it," singular nouns and *man*. The plural form is used for "they" and plural nouns as well as the formal form. The formal form is both singular (i.e. addressing only one person) and plural (i.e. addressing more than one person), but it always uses the third person plural verb form, and the pronoun is usually capitalised.

Some regular verbs whose word stem ends in d or t will add an additional e in the word to make the ending pronounceable.

Here is an example with the verb *finden*:

Step 1: Peter <finden> eine Münze.
Step 2: Peter <find-> eine Münze. (The word stem ends in d.)
Step 3: Peter <find - e - t> eine Münze. (We add an extra e before the ending -t.)
The final sentence is: Peter findet eine Münze. (Peter finds a coin.)

Infinitive: **arbeiten** (to work)
Word stem: arbeit-

	Singular		Plural			Singular		Plural	
1. Person	ich	arbeite	wir	arbeiten	1. Person	I	work	we	work
2. Person	du	arbeitest	ihr	arbeitet	2. Person	you	work	you	work
3. Person	er/sie/es	arbeitet	sie/Sie	arbeiten	3. Person	he/she/it	works	they/you	work

Irregular/strong verbs

The following strong verbs are very common in German and you should memorise them the best you can. They will pop up again and again in German sentences.

They are also considered to be auxiliary verbs, which means that they can be used together with other verbs in certain tenses and constructions. As you will learn later, *werden*, for example is also used to form the German future or the passive.

Infinitive: **sein** (to be)
Word stem: NA

	Singular		Plural			Singular		Plural	
1. Person	ich	bin	wir	sind	1. Person	I	am	we	are
2. Person	du	bist	ihr	seid	2. Person	you	are	you	are
3. Person	er/sie/es	ist	sie/Sie	sind	3. Person	he/she/it	is	they/you	are

Infinitive: **haben** (to have)
Word stem: hab-

	Singular		Plural			Singular		Plural	
1. Person	ich	habe	wir	haben	1. Person	I	have	we	have
2. Person	du	hast	ihr	habt	2. Person	you	have	you	have
3. Person	er/sie/es	hat	sie/Sie	haben	3. Person	he/she/it	has	they/you	have

Infinitive: **werden** (to become)
Word stem: werd-

	Singular		Plural			Singular		Plural	
1. Person	ich	werde	wir	werden	1. Person	I	become	we	become
2. Person	du	wirst	ihr	werdet	2. Person	you	become	you	become
3. Person	er/sie/es	wird	sie/Sie	werden	3. Person	he/she/it	becomes	they/you	become

Note: the 3rd person singular form *wird* is pronounced as if it ended in a t, not a d.

Exercise

Here is a range of exercises aimed at helping you get familiar with the German present tense forms.

A. Regular/weak verbs

Practise the German present tense by completing the following chart. All these verbs are examples of regular/weak verbs.

Person	kommen	wohnen	machen	schreiben	trinken
ich			mache		
du		wohnst			
er, sie, es					trinkt
wir	kommen				
ihr				schreibt	
sie, Sie			machen		

B. Irregular/strong verbs: *haben, sein, werden*

These verbs are very central in German and often occur as auxiliary verbs. They are also irregular.

Person	haben	sein	werden
ich	habe		
du			
er, sie, es			
wir		sind	
ihr			
sie, Sie			werden

C. Irregular verbs: vowel change in the second and third person singular

Many irregular verbs have a vowel change in the second and third person singular. These are typically a → ä, e → i (short sound) or ie (long sound), and occasionally au → äu or o → ö. Try to guess what the correct forms could be, then check your answers.

e-sounds

Person	sprechen	vergessen	sehen	essen	nehmen
ich					
du	sprichst			isst	
er, sie, es			sieht		nimmt
wir		vergessen			
ihr					
sie, Sie					

a-, au- and o-sounds

Person	fallen	laufen	schlafen	stoßen	gefallen
ich			schlafe		
du		läufst			
er, sie, es	fällt				
wir					gefallen
ihr					
sie, Sie				stoßen	

Which ones surprised you and why? What do you notice about the plural forms?

D. Look at the following forms and try to identify what person and number they could go with:

   rate   verstehen   kündigt   lügst

E. Verbs with the stem ending in -d or -t
Remember: some verbs such as *arbeiten* or *finden* have a word stem that ends in -d or -t. In these cases, an extra e is inserted into the word to make the ending pronounceable.
Example: ~~du findst~~ → du findest.

Try to conjugate the following verbs:

Person	gründen	töten	arbeiten	binden
ich	gründe			
du		tötest		
er, sie, es				
wir			arbeiten	
ihr				
sie, Sie				binden

2.8 Summary of chapter

Here are nine things that we have learned in this chapter:

1. Clauses are individual parts of longer sentence structures. There are main clauses and subordinate clauses. Main clauses can stand completely on their own, but subordinate and relative clauses rely on a main clause to make sense. In German, clauses can start with objects.
2. Clauses are divided by commas or *und/oder*.

3. Words such as *der, die, das* can have several meanings, types and functions. They do not always mean "the."
4. In German, verbs are always in the second position of a clause or at the end of the clause (the fourth position). Often, German verbs end in -t or -en, but they can have other endings as well.
5. Subjects are usually in the front of a clause, but they can be either in front or behind the verb.
6. *Man* is always the subject of a clause. It is a general subject that can be translated as "one" or "you."
7. The word *zu* can have different functions in a clause, but it is almost always translated as "to."
8. *Es gibt* is a very common idiomatic expression that means "there is/are."
9. Nouns in German are always capitalised. Compound nouns are words that consist of several parts "glued together," but the last part is the most important part as it tells us all the grammatical information we need to know.

Exercise

Translate the introductory text with the help of a dictionary to the best of your ability.

3   German genders; plurals in German; separable verbs; how to identify verbs

3.1 Introductory text: Kartoffelsalat

Rezept: Kartoffelsalat mit Majonäse

Zutaten:

800 g Kartoffeln
100 g Gurken
2 Zwiebeln
3 hartgekochte Eier
6 EL Majonäse (alternativ: saure Sahne)
3 EL Gurkenwasser vom Glas
1 EL Senf
Salz
Schwarzer Pfeffer
1 Büschel Petersilie

1. Die Kartoffeln waschen und 20 Minuten in Salzwasser kochen. Dann abgießen und abkühlen lassen. Die warmen Kartoffeln schälen und kleinschneiden.
2. Die Zwiebeln schälen und kleinhacken. Die Eier und Gurken kleinschneiden. Alles in eine Schüssel mit den Kartoffeln geben.
3. Die Majonäse mit dem Gurkenwasser und dem Senf mischen. Die Petersilie kleinhacken und alles in die Schüssel geben und mischen. Mit Salz und Pfeffer abschmecken.

Das passt dazu: Bratwurst oder Wienerwürste

Vocabulary

abgießen (sep.v.) – to drain
etwas abschmecken (sep.v.) – to season sth. by taste
alles – everything
Büschel, das (-(e)s, -) – bunch
Gurke, die (-, -n) – gherkin, pickle
klein – small
Sahne, die (-e, -n) – cream
schälen – to peel
Schüssel, die (-, -n) – bowl
Senf, der (-(e)s, -e) – mustard
Zwiebel, die (-, -n) – onion

Abreviations

EL – Esslöffel (table spoon)
g – Gramm (gram)

3.2 Genders in German

> *Der Hund, die Katze, das Pferd.*
> The dog, the cat, the horse.

In English, the gender of words is assigned in a natural way: a female person/animal is considered feminine (she), a male is considered masculine (he) and most other things are considered neuter (it). The determiners are identical for all of these nouns: "the" or "a."

German uses three different genders and these are assigned on a grammatical basis; this is sometimes referred to as a grammatical gender or grammatical sex. People have a natural gender or natural sex, like English, but all other German nouns have a grammatical gender. Animals are a mixed bag; most follow a grammatical gender.

At first, most of these genders seem randomly selected, but there are at least a few hints to knowing the gender of some words. Other than that, German genders are one of the more difficult bits to master. Do not let this discourage you though.

English		Gender	German		Gender
the	police man	masculine	der	Polizist	masculine
the	bus driver	can be masculine or feminine	der die	Busfahrer Busfahrerin	masculine feminine
the	nurse	can be masculine or feminine	der die	Krankenpfleger Krankenschwester/ die Krankenpflegerin	masculine feminine
the	girl	feminine	das	Mädchen	neuter, because of the ending "-chen"
the	mustard	neuter	der	Senf	masculine
the	onion	neuter	die	Zwiebel	feminine
the	egg	neuter	das	Ei	neuter

With all words that relate to a person, the real gender you see will be the grammatical gender. A female bus driver will have a feminine grammatical gender assigned. A male bus driver will have masculine grammatical gender assigned. The only exceptions are diminutive forms, which typically change the gender to neuter, or people where the gender is not always clear (for example, *das Kind* – the child).

Der, die, das and *ein, eine, ein* are the nominative singular forms (the "basic" form of determiners). Here is an overview of the definite and indefinite determiners in German with the plural and translations. Please look at it carefully.

	Masculine	Feminine	Neuter	Plural
Definite article	**der** Hund the dog	**die** Katze the cat	**das** Pferd the horse	**die** Kühe cows
Indefinite article	**ein** Hund a dog	**eine** Katze a cat	**ein** Pferd a horse	Kühe cows

Plural forms are always *die*, i.e. all nouns in German use the same determiners for plural, regardless of their gender; you could say that all plural nouns look feminine. There is no plural for *ein* – you could use a number then (*zwei Kühe*) or another indefinite determiner such as "many" (*viele Kühe*).

Note: articles indicate gender in the nominative case only. If you see a word with *der* in front of it, do not automatically assume it has to be masculine, it could be that the article has been inflected for a different case (we will look at this in chapter 5). If you are unsure about the gender of a word, the best way to check is to use a dictionary.

Using the dictionary

The way in which dictionaries indicate the gender of German words can differ depending on the publisher. The letters "m, f, n" indicate masculine, feminine or neuter. Another common way to indicate the gender is by giving the definite determiner *der, die, das.*

Plural forms will be indicated in most dictionaries (very compact dictionaries sometimes omit these due to space restrictions). In many dictionaries, typical entries will read, for example:

Parallele (-, -n), f parallel

This entry tells us that the word is feminine *(die Parallele)*. The first entry in the

> **"What dictionary do you recommend I use/buy?"**
>
> This is a question students have often posed to me over the years. My thoughts and views on this, as well as some more general points on the different types of dictionaries, are on p. 211. Ultimately, the choice depends on personal circumstances and preference.

bracket is the genitive form (the genitive case will be discussed in chapter 5). In this case it is identical to the basic form, which is why there is only a dash in the bracket. The second entry is the plural form. In this case the entry tells us it is *die Parallelen*, with an -n added at the end.

Ritter, der (-s, -) – knight

This entry tells us that the word for knight in German is masculine by using the article of the basic form of the word *(der Ritter)*. The genitive form is *des Ritters,* indicated by the -s. The plural form is *die Ritter*; the second dash tells us there is no change to form for the plural, it does not mean that there is no plural. (Chapter 5 will explain why the article changes to *des* and *die*). If a word has no plural, this is commonly indicated in the bracket:

Deutsch, das (-s, no plural) – German

There can be several variations on these types of entries, for example here is one taken from an older Cassell's German Dictionary:

Arzt m. (-es, pl. ⸚e) doctor, physician

The strange symbol after the first entry in the bracket, which looks like a hyphen with two dots above it, tells us that the plural is formed with an umlaut.

A verb entry will not include information about the gender of the word or its forms, but it will tell us other information, such as whether a verb is reflexive, transitive or intransitive, irregular, separable, etc.

Exercise

Look up the following words in a dictionary. What is their gender, what is the plural form?

Mann; Terminus; Detail; Publikation; Messer

3.3 Gender by endings

The genders of the following words can be guessed easily. Why do you think that is the case?

Vater	Mutter	Sohn	Bär	Bärin
Polizist	Krankenschwester		Ärztin	

The answer is that natural persons and some animals have a so-called natural gender.

The best way of identifying a gender, other than learning it off by heart, is by looking at the ending of a noun.

Feminine endings (in alphabetical order):

- a *(die Villa, but not -ma)*
-anz/-enz *(die Präsenz)*
-most words ending in -e (exceptions are *der Tee, der Kaffee, der Name, das Café*)
-ei *(die Bücherei)*
-heit *(die Menschheit)*
-ie *(die Chemie)*
-ik *(die Botanik, but: der Atlantik, der Pazifik)*
-in *(die Ärztin, Polizistin, Freundin)*
-keit *(die Heiterkeit)*
-schaft *(die Bürgschaft)*
-sion *(die Explosion)*
-tät *(die Identität)*

-tion/-ion *(die Nation)*
-ung *(die Regierung)*
-ur *(die Natur,* but: *das Abitur, Futur)*
-sis *(die Katharsis)*

Masculine endings are:

-ant *(der Konsonant)*
-ast *(der Ballast)*
-er (if referring to a person, i.e. *der Wissenschaftler, Fahrer*; often these are
    nouns derived from a verb)
-ich *(der Teppich)*
-ig *(der Honig)*
-ismus *(der Kommunismus)*
-ling *(der Däumling)*
-mus/-us *(der Rhythmus)*
-or *(der Motor)*
-pf *(der Kopf)*
-tz *(der Blitz)*

Neuter endings are:

-chen *(das Mädchen*; note that this is a diminutive form and can be attached
    to most nouns, making them all neuter in the process: *die Wurst → das
    Würstchen*; a vowel change to an umlaut is common in these words)
-ell *(das Bordell)*
-ett *(das Ballett)*
-il *(das Ventil)*
-in *(das Benzin)*
-it *(das Dynamit,* but: *der Profit, Granit)*
-lein *(das Fräulein*; this is also a diminutive form that is no longer used by
    most German-speaking people)
-ma *(das Schema,* but: *die Firma)*
-ment *(das Firmament,* but: *der Zement)*
-o/-eau *(das Büro)*
-tel *(das Hotel)*
-tum/um *(das Eigentum,* but: *der Irrtum, der Reichtum)*

Exercise

Guess the genders based on the information you have just read. Enter *der, die* or *das* in the box "article."

A.

Article		Article	
	Weisheit		Terminator
	Illusion		Frucht
	Physik		Futternapf
	Dokument		Lieferant
	Hänselei		Atrophie
	Baustelle		Gebirge

B.

Article		Article	
	Gerede		Hypothek
	Eigentum		Kommunismus
	Krankheit		Schmetterling
	Garage		Geographie
	Distanz		Teppich
	Politik		Parlament
	Rarität		Honig
	Klima		Topf
	Rotor		Nachbarschaft

3.4 A brief introduction to the German case system

We will have a much closer look at the German case system in chapter 5, but here are some early pointers so that you do not feel too confused about these forms. German uses cases to express who is doing what in a sentence. In English, this is determined by word order (whatever comes before the verb is usually the subject). The German word order is more flexible and the nominative case indicates where the subject is.

	Masculine	Feminine	Neuter	Plural
Nominative	der Mann	die Frau	das Kind	die Leute
Accusative	den Mann	die Frau	das Kind	die Leute
Dative	dem Mann	der Frau	dem Kind	den Leuten
Genitive	des Mannes	der Frau	des Kindes	der Leute

The nominative case is the **subject** of a sentence.
Dieser Mann ist der Präsident von Amerika.
<u>This man</u> is <u>the president of America</u>.
(*Dieser* is a variation of *der* and means "this" rather than "the.")

The accusative case is the **direct** object of a sentence.
Ich sehe den Film Titanic.
I am watching <u>the movie Titanic</u>.

The dative case is the **indirect** object of a sentence.
Sie gibt ihrem Mann einen Kuss.
She gives <u>her husband</u> a kiss.

The genitive case shows **possession**.
Die Jacke der Frau ist rot.
The jacket <u>of the woman</u> is red.

3.5 Plurals in German

German plural forms can have several endings and can be difficult to distinguish from singular forms.

Usually the safest way of knowing a plural form is by looking at the determiner (discussed in chapter 5) or in the dictionary, as we just explained in 3.1. There are a few pointers though that can make things easier:

1. Foreign words often use an -s for their plural endings. The -s ending is also common in words that end on a vowel other than -e.

    das Büro – die Büros
    das Portemonnaie – die Portemonnaies

2. Masculine words ending in -l and all words ending in -er usually have no additional ending added. The determiner will indicate whether it is plural or singular.

    der Titel – die Titel (however: *die Fabel – die Fabeln*)
    der Fahrer – die Fahrer

3. Many words use either -e or -(e)n as a plural ending. If the singular form already ends in -en, it is unlikely to have a different ending in plural.

    das Mädchen – die Mädchen
    die Vase – die Vasen

4. Some authors prefer to keep the original Latin words in their German texts and these will then use the Latin endings of course (-i, -ae, -a); some Latin words have also been entered in the German lexicon with their Latin ending; finally, many Latin-based words ending in -um in their singular form use a more "German-sounding" -en or -ien ending for plural.

> *der Terminus – die Termini*
> *das Forum – die Foren*
> *das Studium – die Studien*

Exercise

Have a look through the introductory text on p. 24 and underline all the plural forms you can find.

3.6 Feminine forms for people

Nouns referring to a profession can have an -in added if they refer to a female person.

In plural, -innen is added if all members of the group are female.

If a group of people are of mixed gender, the masculine ending is used.

> *der Polizist* (police officer, male) – *die Polizistin* (police officer, female)
> *der Arzt* (male doctor) – *die Ärztin* (female doctor)
> *der Forscher/Wissenschaftler* (male scientist/scholar) – *die Forscherin/ Wissenschaftlerin* (female scientist/scholar)

Exercise

Tick all applicable boxes in the following chart. Which forms are unclear without more information?

	Masculine	Feminine	Singular	Plural
Fahrer				
Fußballspielerinnen				
Ritter				
Krankenschwester				
Krankenpflegerin				
Physikerin				
Deutsche				
Poet				

3.7 Prepositional phrases

A preposition is a type of word that combines with a noun to form a prepositional phrase. They typically express notions of place, direction or time. We will take a closer look at prepositions in chapter 11, but due to the frequency with which they occur, a short introduction here is sensible.

Here is a sentence from the introductory text:

*Die Petersilie (subject) kleinhacken (verb) und alles (subject) **in die Schüssel** geben und mischen (verb).*

> **Typical German prepositions:**
>
> Ab, an, auf, aus, bei, für, in, neben, mit, unter, über, von, zu, zwischen

In die Schüssel is a prepositional phrase. As such it is neither subject nor object. This is very important to remember for German Reading Skills, as it means you can handle prepositional phrases very flexibly.

All of the following translations are correct approximations of the sentence's meaning, even if they are stylistically questionable:

1. Chop the parsley small and put and mix everything in the bowl.
2. Chop the parsley small and put everything into the bowl and mix it.
3. Chop the parsley and, in the bowl, combine everything and mix it.

It is not important to place *in die Schüssel* at the front or end of the sentence. As long as you get the general meaning, the placement is correct. In addition, *in* does not need to be translated as "in" necessarily (even if in this example it fits quite well).

Be flexible with the translation of prepositions. In general, they do not translate terribly well and rarely match up with the target language. Rather follow the idiomatic use of the phrase in the target language to find a good way to render it.

Prepositional phrases are not key to the understanding of the action that is taking place. This means you can flexibly place them in your translation where you deem fit. If you think of a puzzle analogy, prepositional phrases are a special puzzle piece that can be connected to several different other pieces. In complex sentences, it is often helpful to leave the translation of prepositional phrases to the end.

Exercise

Which translations are correct in regard to content (even if they are stylistically questionable)?

Am Samstag geht Peter mit seinem Bruder Max ins Kino.

   a. Peter is going to the cinema with his brother Max on Saturday.
   b. On Saturday, Max is going to the cinema with his brother, Peter.
   c. On Saturday, Peter is going to the cinema with his brother, Max.
   d. On Saturday, Peter is going with his brother Max to the cinema.

Fan rennt auf Spielfeld beim Superbowl.

   a. Fan runs on to the playing field during the Superbowl.
   b. During the Superbowl, a fan runs onto the playing field.
   c. A fan runs around the playing field with the Superbowl.

Deutschland lässt Brasilien beim Endspiel keine Chance.

   a. Germany leaves the final match in Brazil without chance.
   b. During the final match, Germany leaves Brazil no chance.
   c. Brazil leaves Germany no chance at the final match.
   d. Germany leaves Brazil without chance at the final match.

3.8 Finite and non-finite verb forms

Verbs are inflected to agree with the subject in number. They are also inflected to agree with other aspects of language, such as tense, mood or voice. This process is called conjugation, and a conjugated verb is referred to as a finite verb. Many clauses will also use non-finite verb forms that are not conjugated, for example infinitives or participles (chapter 6).

   In the chart, note in particular how the finite verb agrees with the subject (all subjects are located in the first column). The non-finite verb forms are always placed at the end of a clause.

	Finite verb		Non-finite verb
Die Mutter	küsst	das Kind.	
Wir	müssen	etwas	essen.
Du	hast	ein Auto	gekauft.

Knowing the difference between finite and non-finite verbs is helpful, as the finite verb can help you locate the subject more easily. However, when looking for the verb of a clause, you should consider finite and non-finite verbs to be a unit, as they both are needed to construct the meaning in the sentence. For example, in the last sentence you should consider *hast gekauft* to be the verb of the sentence and not just *hast*.

 When trying to understand a German clause, start by identifying the verb first, and then the subject, rather than the other way around. The verb and subject will agree in number, i.e. a singular verb will have a singular noun as subject and a plural verb will have a plural noun. These two grammatical units, verb and subject, form the **framework** of your sentence. Everything else has to fit around this frame, not the other way around.

Framework

This is not a grammatical term, but rather a term I use to describe subject–verb agreement.

Look at the following nonsense sentence:

Ghgjhghgj **verrät der Spion** *hgjghgh jhghghg ghgghjgh ghg ghgjhgjghjgjhgj.*

Let's pretend that at this stage we have no idea what the other words mean (they are nonsense anyway). However, we have spotted the subject and the verb in the sentence, and we can now build a framework into which everything else has to fit. In this case it is *der Spion verrät* (the spy betrays). Once this set is in place, we have a wooden frame around which we can start to build the rest of the house (metaphorically). If something does not make sense, we go back to the framework: Is it correct? If yes, then the mistake lies somewhere else. The subject–verb framework therefore acts as your failsafe, your point to go back to if things go wrong. You should try to approach every complex clause in this way and always build the subject–verb framework first.

Exercise

Try to locate all the verbs in the following sentences.

1. Ich verstehe Spanisch und Italienisch.
2. Die Schweiz hat vier offizielle Sprachen.
3. Viele Menschen in England fahren im Sommer nach Spanien.
4. Sie begrüßt die Flüchtlinge aus Syrien.

5. In den USA leben 266 000 Navajo und ca. 170 000 sprechen die Sprache als Muttersprache.
6. Den Text muss ich ins Deutsche übersetzen.
7. Er schreibt einen Text auf Französisch.
8. Wo wohnst du im Moment?
9. Der Forscher kann Französisch sprechen.
10. Das Model hat die Nagelfeile vergessen.

3.9 Separable verbs

Der Vater **macht** *der Tochter die Tür* **auf.**
The father **opens** the door for the daughter.

If you look up *machen* in the dictionary, you will find "to make" or "to do" as the translation. However, in the above sentence, the verb is not actually *machen*, but rather *aufmachen* ("to open"). The prefix *auf-* has been separated from the verb and is found at the end. We call this a separable verb *(trennbares Verb)*.

A separable verb is a verb whose infinitive has a prefix attached to it. This is the form you typically find in a dictionary. When conjugated, this prefix is separated and placed at the end of the clause. The prefix indicates that the verb has a different meaning.

When used as a finite verb, the separable verb behaves as follows:

• In a main clause, the conjugated verb form is placed in second position and the cut-off prefix is moved to the end of the clause (fourth position).
• In a question or command, the conjugated verb starts the sentence and the cut-off prefix is at the end of the clause (fourth position).
• In a subordinate clause, the prefix stays on and the finite verb is at the end of the clause (fourth position).

(einen Termin) **absagen** – to cancel (an appointment)

		Position 2		Position 4
Main clause	Ich	**sage**	den Termin	**ab.**
	I cancel the appointment.			
Question/command		**Sagst**	du den Termin	**ab?**
	Are you cancelling the appointment?			
Subordinate clause	Ich weiß nicht,	ob	er den Termin	**absagt.**
	I do not know if he is cancelling the appointment.			

This may seem straightforward, but it is a common problem when translating complex texts. The prefixes can look identical to German prepositions and that can be very confusing. If the split-off prefix is not recognised as part of the verb, people often look up the wrong verb in the dictionary (in this example, just "sagen" would mean "to say," whereas "absagen" means "to cancel") and end up with a meaningless preposition and a wrong verb.

 To avoid this pitfall, remember: if there is a word that looks like a preposition (but without a noun following it) at the end of a clause, consider that it might be part of a separable verb. To look up the word in the dictionary, reattach the prefix to find the correct meaning.

*Er **schaute** zu dem Turm **auf**.*   Infinitive: *auf|schauen* (to look up to)
He looked up to the tower.

What if I overlook this?

So what if you go wrong? Well, you shouldn't, because you would still be left with a preposition at the end of your sentence that does not make a lot of sense, as it is not followed by a noun, therefore that should raise some alarm bells in your head. If you happen to come across a separable verb that does not have a prefix that looks like a typical preposition, you could miss this, but fortunately these separable verbs tend to be so logical that in most of these cases you would actually get the translation right.

Wir gehen nach Hause zurück.   Infinitive: *zurück|gehen*
We go back home.

Ich gebe meine Jacke weg.   Infinitive: *weg|geben*
I give my jacket away.

If a separable verb is used in an infinitive construction that requires the particle *zu* (to), the particle will be placed between the prefix and the verb stem.

Ich versuche, das Wort korrekt auszusprechen.   Infinitive: *aus|sprechen*
I try to pronounce the word correctly.

Exercise

A. Which verb would you look up in the dictionary? Can you translate these sentences with the help of a dictionary?

1. Ich schalte den Fernseher ein.
2. Ich schalte auf einen anderen Kanal um.
3. Der Mann zieht eine warme Jacke an.
4. Die Familie zieht in eine neue Wohnung um.
5. Die Katze zieht die Maus aus dem Loch hervor. (*Hervor* is optional here.)
6. Wir hören Musik.
7. Wir hören mit der Musik auf.
8. Ich lade mein Handy auf.
9. Ich lade Peter zu der Party ein.
10. Ich lade meine Pistole.
11. Mit dem Brief lädt das Gericht den Zeugen vor.
12. Bevor wir heiraten, leben wir fünf Jahre lang zusammen.
13. Ich gehe heute Abend noch einmal weg.
14. Er kommt vor Mitternacht zurück.
15. Verschiedene Laute kommen in der Natur in großer Fülle vor.
16. Man geht von der Hypothese aus, dass die Tiger fast ausgestorben sind.
17. Man geht von der Hypothese, dass die Tiger fast ausgestorben sind, aus.
18. Vergiss nicht, das Licht auszumachen und die Tür zuzumachen!

Vocabulary

Abend, der (-s, -e) – evening
ausgestorben sind – have become extinct
fast – almost, nearly
in großer Fülle – in a large extent/amount
Loch, das (-(e)s, Löcher) – hole
verschieden – different
Wohnung, die (-, -en) – apartment
Zeuge, der (-n, -n) – witness

B. Look at the following sentences. Find the verbs and pinpoint the main clause. If you can, try to translate them with the help of a dictionary.

1. Er sieht die Katze im Garten, obwohl es Nacht ist.
2. Weil er schon seit Tagen nichts gegessen hat, sieht er dünn aus.
3. Während er nach Hause geht, fängt es an zu regnen.
4. Er parkt sein Auto in der Wiesenstraße, obwohl es verboten ist und er kein Geld für eine Strafe hat.

5. Niemand weiß, dass Herr Steiner der Dieb ist.
6. Warum rufen wir nicht an und fahren dann hin?
7. Die deutsche Sprache korrekt auszusprechen, finden viele Ausländer schwer. (The comma in this sentence is optional, but it helps you see the two clauses.)
8. Wie meine Mutter das gemacht hat, ist ein Rätsel.

Vocabulary

Ausländer, der (-e, -) – foreigner
Dieb, der (-(e)s, -e) – thief
dünn – thin
Rätsel, das (-s, -) – mystery, puzzle
seit – since, for
Strafe, die (-, -n) – punishment, here: ticket

3.10 Summary of chapter

Before we continue to the practice text, let us recap seven things that we have learned in this chapter:

1. German has three different genders: masculine, feminine and neuter. Except for natural persons and a few animals, these genders are assigned along grammatical rules or randomly, unlike for example English.
2. The endings of nouns will often point you towards the gender of the noun.
3. Dictionaries are not only good for finding the meaning of a word, they also tell you the type of word, its genitive singular form, its plural form and other essential information.
4. Prepositional phrases can be dealt with on a flexible basis after the rest of the sentence has been "decoded," because they have no core function (subject, verb, object) in a clause. Prepositional phrases always start with a preposition and are followed up by at least one noun.
5. Every clause only has one finite verb, but can have non-finite verb parts as well. Together with the subject it forms the subject–verb framework, the core structure of a clause.
6. Separable verbs such as *aufmachen* send their prefix to the end of the sentence when they are conjugated. These words often have different meanings from the word they stem from.
7. Always check the second and the fourth position of a clause that you are working on. The fourth position holds not only important verb components, but also the separated prefixes of separable verbs.

Practice text: Redewendungen und Aphorismen von Friedrich Schiller

Here are some sayings and aphorisms from works by Friedrich Schiller. Not all of these are very famous, but all of them are thought provoking or humorous. Try to translate the introductory passage first before you tackle them. There are quite a few composite words in this exercise, but only two separable verbs. Also, pay attention to the capitalisation of nouns in this exercise.

Friedrich Schiller ist ein weltbekannter deutscher Autor. Viele seiner *(of his)* Werke sind international bekannt. Es ist nicht überraschend, dass er auch Einfluss auf die deutsche Sprache hat. Auch heute noch gibt es im Deutschen viele Redensarten und Lebensweisheiten aus seinen Werken.

Aus „Wilhelm Tell":
Jede Straße führt ans *(to the)* Ende der *(of)* Welt.
Gott hilft nur dann, wenn Menschen nicht mehr helfen.
Durch diese hohle Gasse muß er kommen. *(One of the most famous sayings.)*
Es lächelt der See, er lädt zum Bade ein.

Das Alte stürzt, es ändert sich die Zeit,
Und neues Leben blüht aus den Ruinen.

Aus „Wallenstein":
Lange Rede, kurzer Sinn. *(The actual quote is longer, but many Germans only know the shortened version.)*
Die Sterne lügen nicht.

Aus „Maria Stuart":
Was man nicht aufgibt, hat man nicht verloren.
Ich bin besser als mein Ruf.
Ein tiefer Sinn wohnt in den alten Bräuchen.

Aus „Die Räuber":
Schlaf und Tod sind nur Zwillinge

Aus „Das Lied von der Glocke":
Das Auge des *(of)* Gesetzes wacht.
Wo rohe Kräfte sinnlos walten.

Aus „Kabale und Liebe":
Sünder und böse Geister scheuen das Licht der *(of)* Welt.

Aus „Der Parasit":
Der Schein regiert die Welt und die Gerechtigkeit ist nur auf der Bühne.

Vocabulary

sich ändern – to change, modify (ignore the *sich* in your translation)
aus – from, out of
bekannt – famous, familiar, known
Brauch, der (-(e)s, Bräuche) – custom, tradition
Bühne, die (-, -n) – stage
dann – then
durch – through
Gasse, die (-, -n) – alley, lane, narrow street
Gerechtigkeit, die (-, -en) – justice, fairness
helfen – to help, support
hohl – hollow, here: narrow or round
das Maß (-es, -e) – measure
etwas scheuen – to shy away from sth., to be afraid of sth.
regieren – govern, rule
Schein, der (-(e)s, -e) – shine, light, appearance
Sinn, der (-(e)s, -e) – sense, meaning, message
stürzen – to rush, fall, overturn
Sünder, der (-s, -) – sinner
verloren – lost; participle from "verlieren"
walten – to rule, preside, are at work
was – what
wenn – when, if

4 Modal verbs; imperative forms; idiomatic expressions with *es*

4.1 German modal verbs

Modal verbs are a category of verbs that usually indicate the attitude of a speaker in regard to an action. They are typically followed up with the infinitive of another verb to make sense and can therefore be classified as auxiliary verbs. When paired with an infinitive, these modal verb constructions do not use the infinitive particle *zu*.

The following sentence translates as "I must go home." The way we have split it up lets you see each individual part for itself. As a general guideline, infinitives are placed at the end of a clause (they are non-finite verb forms).

Ich	**muss**	nach Hause	**gehen.**
Subject	Conjugated modal verb	Prepositional object	Infinitive (part of the verbal construction)
I	must	towards home	go.

All modal verbs are irregular, so it is recommended that you learn their present tense forms off by heart, especially the third person singular and plural forms. For some of the modal verbs, more than one translation is listed. The translations in bold should be considered the "failsafe translations"; in many situations (especially negations) they provide a more accurate translation.

Chart: modal verbs

Person	müssen	können	dürfen	sollen	wollen
Translation	**have to, must**	can, be able to	**be allowed to,** may	supposed to, should, ought to*	to want
ich	muss	kann	darf	soll	will
du	musst	kannst	darfst	sollst	willst
er, sie, es, man	**muss**	**kann**	**darf**	**soll**	**will**
wir	müssen	können	dürfen	sollen	wollen
ihr	müsst	könnt	dürft	sollt	wollt
sie, Sie	müssen	können	dürfen	sollen	wollen

* The indicative form (the one shown here) is usually translated as "supposed to," whereas the subjunctive II form (chapter 13) is usually translated as "should" or "ought to."

False Friends

There are two False Friends hidden among the modal verbs. These are:

will & will

Ich will. = I want   I will. = *Ich werde.*
Er will. = He wants.   He will. = *Er wird.*

nicht müssen & must not

Ich muss nicht. = I need not.   I must not. = *Ich darf nicht.*

(I need not. = *Ich brauche nicht.*)

You can avoid this confusion by going for the failsafe translation of "I do not have to" in the first place.

Ich muss nicht. = I do not have to.

Exercise

A. Try to memorise the words from the modal verb chart. Then cover the chart with a piece of paper and try to complete the exercises below.
B. Circle or clearly mark the correct form! Only one form is correct.
   a. Peter darf/darfst keine Nüsse essen.
   b. Maria müssen/muss in die Schule gehen.
   c. Morgen sollen/soll es regnen.
   d. Wir wollen/will ins Theater gehen.
   e. Ich kann/können Französisch sprechen.

C. Translate the following sentences with the help of a dictionary.
   f. Das Mädchen kann nicht ins Theater gehen.
   g. Ich soll die Hausaufgaben machen.
   h. Christina muss nicht ins Theater gehen.
   i. Christina darf nicht ins Theater gehen.
   j. Ein gutes Ding will Weile haben.[1]

4.2 *Mögen* and *möchten*

There is a sixth modal verb, *mögen*, which means "to like" or, depending on the context, "may" or "might," to express a possibility. Its subjunctive form *möchten* ("would like") is used widely in spoken German and is more common than *mögen*.

    Möchten follows the same rules as modal verbs when it comes to pairing them with infinitives, i.e. it relies on them to create sense and the infinitive particle *zu* is not used. *Mögen*, unlike other modal verbs, can stand without an infinitive when it means simply "to like something."

Person	mögen	möchten
Translation	to like, may	would like
ich	mag	möchte
du	magst	möchtest
er, sie, es, man	**mag**	**möchte**
wir	mögen	möchten
ihr	mögt	möchtet
sie, Sie	mögen	möchten

Exercise

A. Translate and compare the following sentences with the help of a dictionary.
   a. Ich mag klassische Musik.
   b. Ich möchte klassische Musik hören.
   c. Das mag die Realität sein.

Implied meaning

As auxiliary verbs, modal verbs usually require an infinitive to make sense. There are a few exceptions, where a very typical action is implied or the context provides the meaning. These situations are more common in spoken

German than in written German. In the following examples the verb in brackets is often omitted, because it is implied.

Ich muss nach Hause [gehen].
Ich kann Französisch [sprechen].
Ich möchte die Rechnung [haben].

Exercise

B. Which translation is correct?

1. Er darf nicht mit uns auf Klassenfahrt.
   a. He is not allowed to come on the school trip with us.
   b. He doesn't want to come on the school trip with us.
   c. He is not able to come on the school trip with us.

2. Meine Mutter kann gut kochen, aber meine Schwester mag ihr Essen trotzdem nicht.
   a. My mother is not a good cook, but my sister likes her food anyway.
   b. My mother is allowed to cook, but my sister doesn't like her food.
   c. My mother is able to cook well, but my sister doesn't like her food anyway.
   d. My mother wants to cook well, but my sister likes it when her food turns out bad.

3. Er soll zu uns kommen, wenn er sich ein wenig Geld leihen will.
   a. He has to come to us if he would like to borrow a bit of money.
   b. He has to come to us if he wants to borrow a bit of money.
   c. He should come to us if he wants to borrow a bit of money.
   d. He should come to us if he is allowed to borrow a bit of money.

4. Peter muss Spanisch sprechen, sonst kann er auf Ibiza keinen Job finden.
   a. Peter should speak Spanish, otherwise he won't be able to find a job in Ibiza.
   b. Peter has to speak Spanish, otherwise he won't be allowed to find a job in Ibiza.
   c. Peter wants to speak Spanish, otherwise he won't be able to find a job in Ibiza.
   d. Peter has to speak Spanish, otherwise he won't be able to find a job in Ibiza.

5. Anne will nicht nach Russland, denn sie möchte nirgendwo leben, wo es kalt ist.
   a. Anne doesn't want to move to Russia, as she wouldn't like to live anywhere where it is cold.

   b. Anne doesn't need to live in Russia, as she cannot live anywhere where it is cold.

   c. Anne cannot fly to Russia, as she should not go anywhere where it is cold.

6. Ich möchte bitte ein Bier.
   - a. I would like to sell a beer.
   - b. I would like to order/drink a beer.
   - c. I would like to see/smell a beer.

7. Möge er in Frieden ruhen!
   - a. I would like to rest in peace.
   - b. He likes to rest peacefully
   - c. May he rest in peace.

4.3 The imperative

In an instruction or command, the verb is placed at the beginning of the sentence (position I). We call this type of construction the imperative. In its informal singular form, the word stem of the verb in question is used (sometimes an optional -e is added). For the informal plural form, a -(e)t is added to the stem. The formal version for addressing someone in a formal situation uses the third person plural with a capitalised *Sie* for both singular and plural addresses.

Imperative sentences also finish with an exclamation mark (!).

To switch off – ab|schalten   (separable verb. stem: schalt-)

- Informal

Schalt(e) das Handy ab!	Switch the mobile phone off! (directed towards one person)
Schaltet die Handys ab!	Switch the mobile phones off! (directed towards several people)

- Formal

Schalten Sie die Handys ab!	Switch the mobile phones off! (can be directed at either one or several people)

Exception

Strong verbs, whose stem vowel of e changes to i or ie in the second and third person singular, take the same change in the informal imperative singular.

Infinitive	Second person singular present	Imperative singular	Imperative plural
lesen	du liest	Lies!	Lest!
helfen	du hilfst	Hilf!	Helft!
nehmen	du nimmst	Nimm!	Nehmt!

Exercise

A. Tick the box: do the following commands address one person or a group of people?

	Addresses one person	Addresses a group of people
Frag nicht so viel!		
Tragt bitte die Tüten ins Haus!		
Können Sie bitte die Fenster aufmachen?		
Gehen Sie bitte in den Hörsaal!		
Finde deine Schwester!		
Glaubt nicht alles, was ihr hört!		
Öffnen Sie bitte das Gesangbuch auf Seite 41!		
Geht nicht allein aus dem Haus!		
Mach niemandem die Tür auf!		

B. Which is the infinitive form of the following imperatives?
   1. Gib mir das Brot!
       a. giben
       b. geben
       c. gibben
   2. Fragt eure Mütter!
       a. fragen
       b. frugen
       c. fragten
   3. Machen Sie die Tür auf!
       a. machen
       b. machten
       c. aufmachen
       d. machen auf
   4. Betet den neuen Gott an!
       a. anbeten
       b. anbitten
       c. bieten
       d. beten

C. Imperative and separable verbs
This is a different version of the introductory text from chapter 3. This version uses imperative forms. Underline all separable verbs and their separable prefixes.

---

1. Waschen Sie die Kartoffeln und kochen Sie sie (them) 20 Minuten in Salzwasser. Gießen Sie die Kartoffeln dann ab und lassen Sie sie abkühlen. Schälen Sie die warmen Kartoffeln und schneiden Sie sie klein.
2. Schälen Sie die Zwiebeln und hacken Sie sie klein. Schneiden Sie die Eier und Gurken klein. Geben Sie alles in eine Schüssel zusammen mit den Kartoffeln.
3. Mischen Sie die Majonäse mit dem Gurkenwasser und dem Senf. Hacken Sie die Petersilie klein und geben Sie alles in die Schüssel. Mischen Sie alles gut. Schmecken Sie den Kartoffelsalat mit Salz und Pfeffer ab.

4.4 Idiomatic expressions with *es*

There are a small number of idiomatic expressions with "es" in German, which you need to know by heart, as they will come up again and again. Be aware when you translate them that they do not necessarily occur in this order, might have been conjugated in tense or mood, or that they might be split up in a sentence, for example:

Es gibt nichts mehr zu essen.	There is nothing more to eat (no more food).
Warum **gibt** es nichts mehr zu essen?	Why is there nothing more to eat?
Er sagt, dass **es** nichts mehr zu essen **gibt**.	He says that there is nothing more to eat.

Look at the following list and learn the expressions. Cover up the translations – how many can you remember?

Es gibt...	There is/are...	Es gibt im Sommer viele Grillpartys.
Es handelt sich um...	This is/these are... (used to specify a formerly mentioned object or person)	Die Polizei nimmt drei Männer fest. Es handelt sich dabei um Terroristen.
Es geht um..	It is about...	In diesem Buch geht es um die Liebe.
Es geht.../ Das geht...	It is possible/that is possible	Am Montag geht es.
Es ist/sind...	There is/are...	Es ist nur noch eine Tasse im Schrank.

4.5 Summary of chapter

Here are four things that we learned in chapter 4:

1. Modal verbs are a special group of strong verbs. Being familiar with their present tense conjugation – especially the 3rd person singular form is very helpful. Modal verbs indicate the attitude of a speaker towards an action and they are always followed up by an infinitive, unless the action is implied,
2. Most modal verbs have more than one translation. Knowing these can help avoid comprehension mistakes, especially with *mögen, müssen* and *sollen*.
3. In a command, the verb will be in the first position and an exclamation mark will be used.
4. Idiomatic expressions with *es* such as *es gibt* need to be known by heart. Fortunately there aren't many of these and they are common as well in German.

Practice text: Da steh' ich nun, ich armer Tor

The following is a short introduction to Goethe's most famous play *Faust*, followed by two versions of an excerpt from the most famous soliloquy in Goethe's *Faust*, where the protagonist laments his unhappiness at night. The first version is a simplified version; the second is the original. Work on the simplified version and compare it with the second version. You will see that Goethe has omitted a few words and letters that are not necessary for the understanding of the verse.

Die Tragödie „Faust" ist das bekannteste Werk von Johann Wolfgang von Goethe. In dem Schauspiel geht es um Doktor Faust, einen Wissenschaftler. Er ist bereits sehr gebildet und er weiß sehr viel, aber es ist nicht genug. Er will alle Geheimnisse der (of) Welt kennen. Nur dann kann er glücklich sein. Er schließt daher einen Pakt mit dem Teufel. Der Teufel heißt in Goethes Faust „Mephisto". Wenn der Teufel den Doktor Faust glücklich machen kann, soll er Fausts Seele bekommen.

Einfache Version	Original
Ich habe nun Philosophie, Juristerei und Medizin und leider auch Theologie durchaus studiert, mit heißem Bemühen. Da stehe ich nun, ich armer Tor, und bin so klug als wie zuvor. Ich heiße Magister und Doktor sogar und ich ziehe schon seit zehn Jahren meine Schüler an der Nase herum – herauf, herab und quer und krumm. Und ich sehe, dass wir nichts wissen können! Das will mir schier das Herz verbrennen.	Habe nun, ach! Philosophie, Juristerei und Medizin, Und leider auch Theologie Durchaus studiert, mit heißem Bemühn. Da steh' ich nun, ich armer Tor! Und bin so klug als wie zuvor; Heiße Magister, heiße Doktor gar, Und ziehe schon die zehen Jahr Herauf, herab und quer und krumm Meine Schüler an der Nase herum – Und sehe, daß wir nichts wissen können! Das will mir schier das Herz verbrennen

(Faust I, Beginn der Tragödie erster Teil, Nacht, Vers 354–365)

Vocabulary

als wie zuvor – as before
bekannteste – We had a similar word in the practice text of chapter 3. Can
    you guess what this one means?
bekommen – to get (false friend to "become")
Bemühen, das (-s, no plural) – effort
bereits – already
durchaus – indeed
gebildet – educated
genug – enough
heißen – to be called
herab – downwards
herauf – upwards
jemanden an der Nase herumziehen – to trick someone
Juristerei, die (-, no plural) – law (another word for "Jura")
kennen – to know
mir – This is a pronoun that is often translated as "me" or "my."
quer und krumm – literally "across and crooked," here: criss-cross
schier – almost, just about
sogar – even
stehen – to stand
Tor, der (-en, -en) – fool (do not confuse this with *das Tor* – the gate)
weiß – the infinitive of this irregular verb is "wissen"
wenn – when, if

Note

1 The actual saying in German is "Gut Ding will Weile haben."

5 The German case system; negation

In this chapter we will look at the four noun cases that are used in German. They underpin a lot of deictic relationships in German (how words relate/ refer to other words) and you will need to pay close attention to this chapter to make sense of many texts, especially complex academic and literary texts. This chapter builds up progressively. First, the logic behind the case system and each case is looked at. The exercises in each section build on the previous section and will include those cases as well. It is therefore recommended that you work through this chapter in a linear way and only proceed to the next section once you have completed all exercises for each section.

In the final section we look at negation in German. A couple of additional exercises and a text complete this chapter.

5.1 Understanding the logic behind the case system

Der Mann gibt dem Hund des Nachbarn den Knochen.
The man gives the neighbour's dog the bone.

All nouns in the example are singular and masculine. You will have noticed right away that each one of these uses a different-looking determiner. If you look up one of these words in a dictionary, the gender of these nouns will all be marked either as *masculine* or simply with the masculine determiner *der*, the basic nominative form of the masculine gender. The determiners in the example have been inflected (i.e. modified) to reflect the different roles of the nouns in the sentence.

German uses a case system that is similar to languages such as Latin or Greek to indicate the function of nouns or pronouns. This gives the language greater flexibility with the order of words and the position of nouns and pronouns in sentences than for example English, where a very strict subject–verb–object order has to be applied. In German, you instead need to look out for the case of the noun or pronoun in order to determine whether it is a subject or an object. Nouns, pronouns and their determiners and adjectives are inflected according to four different cases.

	Case name in English	Case name in German	Function
1	Nominative	Der Nominativ	Subject
2	Genitive	Der Genitiv	Possession
3	Dative	Der Dativ	Indirect object of an action Sometimes used for possession (often colloquial)
4	Accusative	Der Akkusativ	Direct object of an action

Many grammar books order cases differently, usually nominative – accusative – dative – genitive. This is a more modern order that is based on the typical progress of language learners in class and we go through the cases in the same sequence, as it makes learning easier.

Occasionally, however, you might see references in grammar books or discussions to the first, second, third or fourth case. This refers to the order mentioned previously, e.g. genitive being the second case, dative the third, etc.

Inflection usually involves changing the determiner and in some cases there is also a change at the end of the noun.

Did you know?

English has only one such inflection left over from its Germanic roots – the genitive s, as for example: *This is my father's car.*

5.2 Nominative

The nominative case is used for the subject of a sentence. Typically, every sentence must have a subject in order to be a proper sentence, and this rigidity is helpful when building the verb–subject framework of a sentence: locating the nominative form will be one of your first steps to understanding a sentence. Exceptions are infinitive clauses (where the verb is not conjugated) and some passive constructions that omit *es* as the subject (chapter 9).

> *Die Mutter wäscht das Kind.*
> *Der Vater ist Polizist.*
> *Am Morgen geht der Wissenschaftler in das Labor.*

The determiner (article) will reflect case, gender and number of a word; you could, for example, find *ein* in front of a noun and will then deduce that it could be either masculine singular or neuter singular.

Nominative case	Masculine	Feminine	Neuter	Plural
Definite articles	der	die	das	die
Indefinite articles	ein	eine	ein	-

There's not a lot of mystery to the nominative case; many dictionaries use the determiners *der, die, das* to indicate the gender of a word, as it is the most basic case. As a help, remember that whenever you see a masculine word with the determiner *der* or *ein* it will be the subject of the sentence.

While usually there is only one nominative noun in a sentence (since a sentence can only have one subject), there are a few cases where more than one nominative form could be found in the sentence:

1. *Der Vater und die Mutter gehen ins Theater.*
   (The) father and (the) mother go to the theatre.

Because the two nouns *Vater* and *Mutter* are combined with a conjunction *(und)* there are two nominative forms in this sentence. They are, however, considered to be one subject.

2. *Franz ist (ein) Sprachwissenschaftler.*
   Franz is (a) linguist.
   <u>*Herbert* wird *(ein) Professor.*</u>
   Hebert becomes (a) professor.
   <u>*Christine* bleibt *(eine) Studentin.*</u>
   Christine remains a student.

   Note: the *ein/eine* is usually omitted in these constructions.

A predicative noun with a verb such as *sein, werden, passieren, heißen* or *bleiben* restates the subject or describes it more closely, and, as a result, has two nominative forms in one clause. These are usually very simple statements, basically stating "X is Y," or "X becomes Y," or "X stays Y." These constructions are only possible with a very small number of verbs and because they usually omit the determiner, they are overlooked most of the time.

Other determiners

Other determiners mirror the end sound of the definite article. *Der Mann, dieser Mann, jener Mann, mancher Mann*, etc. are all nominative, masculine singular and all have the characteristic r-sound at the end. The translation will be different, but the case and number will be the same. The last letter of a determiner essentially holds all the grammatical information.

Exercise

What do you think are the subjects (= nominative) of the following sentences?

1. Der Unterhändler der Regierung präsentiert der Öffentlichkeit den Vertrag.

(This one is easy if you remember the rules about typical endings and gender from chapter 3.)

2. Die Akte schließt die Sekretärin noch heute.
3. „Wie heißt du?" fragt Herrn Keuner die Tochter der Gastwirtin.

(This one is quite complicated for this early in the book, but give it a go. Which noun can be eliminated? Where does the ambiguity stem from?)

5.3 Accusative

The accusative case is used for direct objects. Usually these are the nouns that are logically connected to the action implied by the verb. The majority of German verbs have an accusative object.

Ich kaufe die Handtasche.
I buy the handbag.

Wir sprechen Französisch.
We speak French.

Accusative case	Masculine	Feminine	Neuter	Plural
Definite articles	den	die	das	die
Indefinite articles	einen	eine	ein	-

The accusative is the most common object case and most verbs describing an activity use this case. However, as you progress to more advanced texts, the frequency with which dative and genitive cases occur will increase, due to the "higher register" that is often used in these texts.

The n of the masculine singular form can be considered a "signature" sound of the accusative, but be careful: it is also used for the (less common) dative plural.

The accusative case is also used with many prepositions.

Exercise

A. Nominative or accusative? Tick the correct box.

	Nominative	Accusative	Both cases possible
die Frau			
diesen Tisch			
der Hut			
die Sprachen			
das Buch			

den Raben			
das Mädchen			
die Studenten			
die Hunde			

B. Translate these sentences and give the gender and case of each noun.
   1. Safran macht den Kuchen gelb.
   2. Kinder und Betrunkene sprechen die Wahrheit.
   3. Die Forscher veröffentlichen die Ergebnisse.
   4. Der Hund frisst den Vogel.
   5. Den Vogel frisst der Hund.
   6. Den Hund frisst der Vogel.
   7. Den gregorianischen Kalender führte man im 16. Jahrhundert im Heiligen Römischen Reich ein.
   8. Schlafende Hunde soll man nicht wecken.
   9. Was Hänschen nicht lernt, lernt Hans nimmermehr. (*Hänschen*, a diminutive form, refers to little/younger Hans, *Hans* to grown-up Hans; you can almost translate this literally word by word).
   10. Alles hat ein Ende, nur die Wurst hat zwei. (This is a rather silly saying.)

5.4 Dative

The dative is used for the indirect object of an action. A German sentence with the subject in the first position will usually place an indirect object before a direct object.

> *Ich kaufe <u>der Frau</u> die Tasche.*
> I buy the bag for the woman.
> *<u>Dem Hund</u> gehört der Knochen.*
> The bone belongs to the dog.

Dative case	Masculine	Feminine	Neuter	Plural
Definite articles	dem	der	dem	den
Indefinite articles	einem	einer	einem	-

The m of the masculine and neuter singular nouns is the "signature sound" of the dative and is very easy to spot. It is not used for any other case in German.

Beware of the r used in *der* and other determiners! It is used for the nominative, dative and genitive case and the only way you will know which case you are dealing with, is by knowing the gender and number of the noun.

Like the accusative case, the dative case is often used with prepositions.

There are several verbs that go with only a dative object and no accusative object. These verbs are usually intransitive and cannot be put in the passive voice.

Translation of the dative

To make the translation of the dative easier in English, it is often necessary to add a "to" or "for" into the translation.

> *Ich kaufe meiner Tochter das Ticket.*
> I buy the ticket **for** my daughter.

Exercise

Identify the dative forms in the following sentences and translate them.

1. Man soll den Tag nicht vor dem Abend loben.
2. Ich gebe dem Hund einen Knochen.
3. Der Professor beantwortet den Studenten die Fragen.
   (If you find this sentence awkward, remember the advice about adding a "to" or "for" into the translation.)
4. Die Untersuchung hilft dem Forschungsfeld.
5. Der Politikerin sollte der Wähler besser nicht vertrauen.
6. Senden wir dem Verlag das Manuskript zu!
7. Der Mann kauft der Frau die Tasche.
8. Wer schenkt dem Lügner noch Vertrauen?
9. Dem Gesunden fehlt viel, dem Kranken nur eins. (*Gesunden* is a nominalisation of the adjective *gesund* and means "the healthy person"; note that *fehlen* has more than one meaning.)
10. Alter schützt vor der Liebe nicht, aber Liebe vor dem Altern. (Coco Chanel; *Alter* and *Altern* do not have the same translation!)

5.5 Genitive

The genitive is used for the possessive in German.

> *Ich fahre das Auto <u>des Vaters</u>./Ich fahre <u>Vaters</u> Auto.*
> I drive father's car.

> *Ich kenne den Namen <u>der Person</u> nicht.*
> I do not know the name of the person.

When dealing with a person or somebody's name, the genitive form will usually precede the noun it refers to. In all other cases (i.e. when not dealing with a person or name) the genitive form follows the noun it refers to.

Wo ist Peters Rechnung?
Where is Peter's bill?
Wo ist die Rechnung der Firma?
Where is the company's bill/the bill from the company?

Genitive case	Masculine	Feminine	Neuter	Plural
Definite articles	des	der	des	der
Indefinite articles	eines	einer	eines	-

The s is the signature sound of the genitive and is used by both the masculine and neuter singular forms. While s occurs in the determiner *das*, the determiner *des* is easily distinguishable due to the different vowel.

Unfortunately, the r of the feminine and plural forms is tricky and can be confused with nominative or dative forms.

Nouns in the genitive case tend to follow the nouns that they relate to. Therefore, if you cannot make sense of a sentence because of the nouns, check if perhaps one noun is referring to a noun just in front of it. The order can often be a strong hint as to which form is genitive.

A small number of verbs and prepositions are followed by genitive forms instead of the usual accusative or dative. The verbs relate to remembering *(gedenken, erinnern)* and the prepositions have no sense of location *(trotz, wegen, während)*.

Translation of the genitive

The typical way to translate a genitive form is by adding an "of" in front of it.

Exercise

Identify the genitive forms in the following sentences and translate them, unless you're dealing with somebody's name.

1. Ich gebe dem Hund des Nachbarn einen Knochen.
2. Wir gedenken der Opfer des Zweiten Weltkriegs.
3. Der Sohn des Pfarrers ist nicht in der Kirche.
4. Peters Frau klopft an die Tür.
5. Wir warten auf den Brief des Verlegers.
6. Ich suche die Tasche meiner Frau.
7. Die Kinder der Revolution wollen immer noch die Bestätigung der Eltern.

8. Im Schweiße deines Angesichtes sollst du dein Brot essen, denn du bist Erde und sollst zu Erde werden.
   (This is in reference to Genesis 3:19.)
9. Wer den Pfennig nicht ehrt, ist des Talers nicht wert.
10. Dieses Buch ist definitiv nicht der Weisheit letzter Schluss.
   (This last sentence combines a genitive case with a predicate noun. Pay attention to the genders of the nouns to get it right.)

5.6 Overview of the four German cases

	Determiner	Masculine	Feminine	Neuter	Plural
Nominative	definite article	der Mann	die Frau	das Auto	die Kinder
	indefinite article	ein	eine	ein	
	possessive	mein	meine	mein	meine
	demonstrative	dieser	diese	dieses	diese
Accusative	definite article	den Mann	die Frau	das Auto	die Kinder
	indefinite article	einen	eine	ein	
	possessive	meinen	meine	mein	meine Kinder
	demonstrative	diesen	diese	das	diese Kinder
Dative	definite article	dem Mann	der Frau	dem Auto	den Kindern
	indefinite article	einem	einer	einem	
	possessive	meinem	meiner	meinem	meinen
	demonstrative	diesem	dieser	diesem	diesen
Genitive	definite article	des Mannes/ Manns	der Frau	des Autos	der Kinder
	indefinite article	eines	einer	eines	
	possessive	meines	meiner	meines	meiner
	demonstrative	dieses	dieses	dieses	dieser

RESE–NESE

A popular method of remembering the declination of German cases is the RESE–NESE pattern.

First, we take the definite articles of all cases in German and capitalise the last letter of the articles.

	M	F	N	Plural
Nom	deR	diE	daS	diE
Acc	deN	diE	daS	diE
Dat	deM	deR	deM	deN
Gen	deS	deR	deS	deR

Now we reduce the chart to only the capital letters.

R	E	S	E
N	E	S	E
M	R	M	N
S	R	S	R

The new chart is much simpler, and the similar sounding RESE–NESE is easy to remember.

There are two caveats with this memory aid. First, you still need to remember the role of each case and what it does in a sentence, i.e. what the role of accusative is and where it would be used over nominative, or what the difference between dative and genitive is.

The second is that the pattern shows the endings of definite articles and not of the indefinite articles and as such, the masculine and neuter endings reflect that.

There is one very helpful aspect of this pattern. As a visual aid, you can see right away that the m occurs only in one case. You can also see how "n" has two occurrences only (and both are object functions). Finally, you can see why "r" is the trickiest of the endings: it occurs across three cases and can be both singular and plural. Finally, while "s" also occurs across three cases, the genitive forms are usually easier to distinguish from the nominative and accusative forms of neuter words.

5.7 Negation

Hast du eine Karte?
  – *Nein, ich habe keine Karte.*
Do you have a map? – No, I do not have a map. (lit. No, I have no map.)

Hast du meine Karte gesehen?
  – *Nein, ich habe deine Karte nicht gesehen.*
Have you seen my map? – No, I have not seen your map.

There are two ways to express negation in German. With nouns, usually a form of *kein* is used, which follows the same declension as the indefinite determiner *ein*, just with a k added (*kein* also has plural forms). With verbs and activities, *nicht* is used. Usually both of these are translated as "not" in English.

Hast du schon einmal Frankreich besucht?
  – *Nein, ich war noch nie in Frankreich.*
Und Belgien?
  – *Nein, ich war weder in Frankreich noch in Belgien.*
Have you ever visited France? – No, I have never been in France.
And Belgium? – No, I have neither been to France nor to Belgium.

Other ways of expressing negation

There are a few more ways of expressing negation in German. One is by using *nie* or *niemals* with a verb to express "never." The other is to use *weder... noch...* to express "neither... nor...."

Finally, while it is technically not a form of negation, many adjectives can be reversed by adding the prefix un- in front of them, which can have the same effect.

*Das Lösen der Aufgabe in der Zeit ist **möglich**.*	Solving the question in the time is possible.
*Das Lösen der Aufgabe in der Zeit ist **nicht möglich**.*	Solving the question in the time is not possible.
*Das Lösen der Aufgabe in der Zeit ist **unmöglich**.*	Solving the question in the time is impossible.

Exercise

A. The following sentences contain all four cases and negation. Determine the cases and translate them.

1. Bei Neumond steht der Mond im Schatten der Erde.
2. Das Krokodil beißt dem Kasper das Bein ab.
3. Weder mein Lehrer noch mein Kursbuch kennen die Antwort auf die Frage.
4. Die Musterlösung für diese Aufgabe ist unklar.
5. Die Indianer jagen keine Büffel mehr.
6. Der Professor will den Studenten das Problem nicht erklären.
7. Man wächst mit den Aufgaben.
8. Der Freund der Verlobten sendet der Mutter der Braut eine E-Mail.
9. Wir sind die Kinder Gottes.
10. Keine Antwort ist auch eine Antwort.
11. Der Dativ ist dem Genitiv sein Tod. (This is the title of a book about modern German.)
12. Ich spreche weder Französisch noch Spanisch, dafür aber Russisch.
13. Den Vorbereiteten überrascht nichts.
14. Sag niemals nie!

Vocabulary

erklären – to explain
die Braut – bride

B. Identify the subject and the main verb of each clause.
   Hint: the commas tell you where one clause ends and another starts.

1. Solche Fehler korrigiert die Lehrerin so oft, dass sie die Fehler manchmal schon übersieht.
2. Obwohl Universitäten in Europa meistens keine Privatinstitutionen sind, verbreiten sich marktwirtschaftliche Ideen auch dort, wo man es nicht erwartet.

Practice text: Oropos und die Graer

The following text is an adapted extract from an essay by the German classicist Ulrich von Wilamowitz-Möllendorff (1886); it summarises the content of an ancient Greek text, which describes the rules by which a priest of the god Amphiaraus had to live.

Have a quick look through the text and find parts you already understand. Read through the questions after the text. Then start to translate the text with the help of a dictionary and answer the questions as you come across answers. When translating, always find the finite and non-finite verbs first, and then work from there.

Oropos und die Graer

Der Priester des Amphiaraos soll zum Ende des Winters das Heiligtum beziehen und bis Anfang des nächsten Winters dort aushalten, so dass er mindestens 10 Tage in jedem Monat zur Stelle ist. Das Heiligtum liegt von der Stadt Oropos entfernt im Gebirge; im Winter waren nicht viele Besucher des Traumorakels zu erwarten: so bestimmten die Priester, wie bei einem Badeort, Anfang und Ende der Saison im Voraus und machten sie ein für alle Mal dem Publikum bekannt. Der Priester hat neben seinem Ehrenamt eine bürgerliche Beschäftigung und wohnt natürlich in der Stadt. So ist es unmöglich für ihn, die ganze Saison im Tempel zu sein. Die folgenden Bestimmungen geben frommen Besuchern die Möglichkeit auch in Abwesenheit des Priesters zu opfern, aber zum Orakel musste er ohne Zweifel anwesend sein. Daher soll er wenigstens jeden dritten Tag durchschnittlich seines Amtes walten.

Adapted excerpt from: von Wilamowitz-Möllendorff, Ulrich. (1886). "Oropos und die Graer." In *Hermes*, 21. Bd., H. 1. Franz Steiner Verlag. pp. 91–115.

Vocabulary

Abwesenheit, die (-, -en) – absence
Anfang, der (-s, Anfänge) – beginning
bestimmen – to decide
die folgenden Bestimmungen – the following orders/instructions
ein für alle Mal – once and for all
entfernt – distant
daher – because of this, due to this
durchschnittlich – on average
fromm – pious
Heiligtum, das (-s, Heiligtümer) – holy site
konnten – past tense of *können*
mindestens – at least
musste – past tense of müssen
zur Stelle sein – to be present
im Voraus – in advance
wenigstens – at least

Comprehension questions – Which statements are correct?

1. Is the job at the sacred site the priest's only job?
   a. Yes, priests can only be priests.
   b. No, the priest has to fulfil several roles at the sacred site.
   c. No, the priest can also have a civil job in the city.
2. Where is this sacred site located?
   a. In the city of Oropos, which is a kind of ancient seaside resort.
   b. On a mountain, far away from the city of Oropos.
   c. In a valley next to a stream called Oropos.
3. What services does the sacred site offer?
   a. The priest will interpret people's dreams and people can make sacrifices there.
   b. People can sacrifice animals and buy little keepsakes.
   c. People can stay at the resort for long periods of time to relax.
4. Which of these sentences are true (more than one!)?
   a. The priest has to be present at least 10 days a month.
   b. The priest can leave the sacred site for a week at a time.
   c. Many priests lived in the city and only came to the sacred site when they had to.
   d. The seasons at the sacred site were not fixed and could be different each year.
   e. It was not clear to the public when the site would be open.
   f. Only a priest can carry out an oracle.
   g. People could not sacrifice on their own – there had to be a priest to supervise.
   h. There was a huge swimming pool at the sacred site.

6 The past tense forms

6.1 Introductory text: Jesus und die Ehebrecherin

Jesus und die Ehebrecherin

Frühmorgens aber kam Jesus wieder in den Tempel und alles Volk kam zu ihm und er setzte sich und lehrte sie. Da brachten die Gelehrten und die Pharisäer eine Frau, beim Ehebruch ergriffen, und stellten sie in die Mitte und sprachen zu Jesus: "Meister, man hat diese Frau beim Ehebruch auf frischer Tat ertappt. Mose hat uns im Gesetz befohlen, solche Frauen zu steinigen. Was sagst du?" Das sagten sie aber, um ihn zu versuchen. Jesus (..) richtete sich auf und sprach zu ihnen: „Wer* unter euch ohne Sünde <u>ist</u>, der <u>werfe**</u> den ersten Stein auf sie." (..) Als sie das hörten, gingen sie hinaus, einer nach dem anderen. (..) Und Jesus blieb allein mit der Frau (..) und sprach zu ihr: „Wo sind sie, Frau? Hat dich niemand verdammt?" Sie aber sprach: „Niemand, Herr." Jesus aber sprach: „So verdamme ich dich auch nicht. Geh hin und sündige hinfort nicht mehr."

Johannes Evangelium, 8: 2–11; revised 2017 Luther Bible; this passage is not found in the earliest version of the New Testament, which has cast doubt on its authenticity.
There have been very minor changes to the original text: it has been shortened where indicated.

Vocabulary

Ehebruch, der (-(e)s, Ehebrüche) – adultery
ergreifen – to seize
jmdn. auf frischer Tat ertappen – to catch so. in the act or red-handed
hinfort – hereinafter, henceforth

jmdn. steinigen – to stone so. to death

verdammen – to condemn (more commonly: to damn, doom)

jmdn. versuchen – to tempt so. (note that this is different from the normal
    versuchen – to try, attempt)

* Wer... ist – who; here it is best translated as "He, who is..." or "Anyone
    who... is"

** werfe – this is a subjunctive I form and is best translated as "shall throw"
    or "may throw"

6.2 Extended infinitive constructions with *um*

If an infinitive clause is introduced with *um*, it is best translated as "in order
to." This type of clause is called an extended infinitive clause or construction; a comma always separates it from other clauses. The *um* will be immediately after the comma.

Exercise

Translate these sentences.

1. Ich rufe an, um einen Tisch im Restaurant zu reservieren.
2. Das sagten sie aber, um ihn zu versuchen. (From the introductory text,
   see the vocabulary notes.)
3. Um eine Beförderung zu bekommen, muss der Forscher viele Artikel
   veröffentlichen.
4. Er ruft an, um seinen Freund zu einer Party einzuladen.

6.3 Past tense forms in German

> Und Jesus **blieb** allein mit der Frau und **sprach** zu ihr.
> And Jesus stayed alone with the woman and spoke to her.

In this chapter, we will be looking at past tense forms in German. As the
previous chapter, it is rather long and complex, but central in identifying
and translating verb forms.

German tenses are divided into two groups. The first group of non-compound past tenses has only two tenses – the present tense and the preterite
tense (simple past). This means that these tenses only need one verb form
to be complete. All other tenses in German fall into the second group of
compound tenses, where an auxiliary verb is used together with another
verb form. The past tense forms here are the perfect and the pluperfect (or
past perfect, in some books). The German future tenses are also compound
tenses and will be looked at later in this book (chapter 9).

A couple of different names exist for the tenses, in the following chart you can see which of them denominate the same tense. Note: languages other than German or English might have different definitions of some of these terms.

The name used in this book	Alternative name(s)		Example
Present tense *Präsens*	Simple present	*Gegenwartsform*	*Ich mache.* I make.
Preterite *Präteritum*	Simple past *Vergangenheitsform* Imperfect *Imperfekt*	*Unvollendete Vergangenheit Erste Vergangenheit*	*Ich machte.* I made.
Present perfect *Perfekt*	Perfect	*Vollendete Vergangenheit Zweite Vergangenheit*	*Ich habe gemacht.* I have made.
Pluperfect *Plusquamperfekt*	Past perfect	*Vorvergangenheit Vollendete Vergangenheit Dritte Vergangenheit*	*Ich hatte gemacht.* I had made.

How do these tenses relate to each other? Here is a visual depiction of the timeline German tenses form:

Actions already completed in the past	Past tense	Present (here and now)	Future
•Pluperfect	•Preterite •Present perfect	•Present tense	•Future I & II •The present tense can be used for plans

Regarding the use of different past tenses

Germans in general are a bit more liberal in their use of different past tenses and will often mix preterite and present perfect forms, especially in spoken language. While the present perfect forms are common in informal language, German will often opt for the shorter preterite forms of *sein* and *haben* in the same breath. In written and formal language, the preterite is more common and less "mixing" occurs, but you should be prepared for the same thing to happen, especially since some preterite forms can sound old-fashioned and stilted.

When translating a German sentence into English, you can change the preterite to the present perfect and vice versa, according to what works better in English. There are sentences where keeping the same tense in the translation would clash with English grammar rules; there is no loss of meaning – as shown in the timeline – both tenses depict the past.

For example, the German sentence *Ich habe am Montag Pasta gegessen* would literally be "I **have eaten** pasta on Monday," which would better be rendered as "I **ate** pasta on Monday" in English, due to the exact time reference. Likewise, in German it is perfectly normal to say something such as *Der Professor **war** in Italien und **hat** die Bibliothek von Florenz **besucht*** (preterite in the first part of the sentence/present perfect in the second), but you would stick to one tense in English. Hence, the literal translation "The professor was in Italy and has visited the library" would not be appropriate.

The pluperfect is different in this regard. It signals that an action was already complete in the past, e.g. finished or "over." Since this form is only used when it is necessary to make such a relationship clear, it will not be mixed in randomly, even though German is slightly more forgiving on bending this rule than English is.

We will now have a look at the first of these forms, the preterite.

6.4 The preterite

Preterite forms tend to be used more in writing, for narratives, reports or accounts. There are three conjugation patterns, a regular one, a mixed one and a strong one.

> *Ich kam, sah und siegte.*
> I came, saw and won. (From the Latin "Veni, vidi, vici": I came, I saw, I conquered.)

The present tense and the preterite are the only two tenses in German that do not require any other verb form to complete the verbal function (they are non-compound tenses). What this means is that a verb like *(sie) trinkt* and the preterite version of it *(sie) trank* are complete just by themselves. All other tenses in German require usually two verb forms to complete the verbal function (they are compound tenses), e.g. the present perfect uses an auxiliary verb and a participle, i.e. *(sie) hat getrunken,* or the future tense, which uses a form or *werden* and an infinitive, e.g. *(sie) wird trinken.*

I. Regular/weak verbs form their preterite by adding the following endings to the verb stem:

Infinitive: machen (to make)
Word stem: mach-

	Singular		Plural			Singular		Plural	
1. Person	ich	machte	wir	machten	1. Person	I	made	we	made
2. Person	du	machtest	ihr	machtet	2. Person	you	made	you	made
3. Person	er/sie/es	machte	sie/Sie	machten	3. Person	he/she/it	made	they/you	made

As with the present tense, some regular verbs whose word stem ends in d or t need to add an additional e in the word to make the ending pronounceable. These can sound a bit awkward in German.

Infinitive: arbeiten
Word stem: arbeit-

	Singular		Plural			Singular		Plural	
1. Person	ich	arbeitete	wir	arbeiteten	1. Person	I	worked	we	worked
2. Person	du	arbeitetest	ihr	arbeitetet	2. Person	you	worked	you	worked
3. Person	er/sie/es	arbeitete	sie/Sie	arbeiteten	3. Person	he/she/it	worked	they/you	worked

II. Mixed pattern verbs

The mixed pattern verbs change their stem just as strong verbs do, but use the same endings as weak verbs.

Examples include:
bringen – ich brachte   *denken – ich dachte*
nennen – ich nannte   *wissen – ich wusste*

Infinitive: bringen
Word stem: bring-

	Singular		Plural			Singular		Plural	
1. Person	ich	brachte	wir	brachten	1. Person	I	brought	we	brought
2. Person	du	brachtest	ihr	brachtet	2. Person	you	brought	you	brought
3. Person	er/sie/es	brachte	sie/Sie	brachten	3. Person	he/she/it	brought	they/you	brought

III. Irregular/strong verbs

The third group is characterised by a stem change and does <u>not</u> use the endings from the other two groups. This makes the common third person form look somewhat strange, almost as if its ending had been forgotten (e.g. *er kam nach Hause, sie trank den Tee, es gab viel zu tun*).

Examples include:
gehen – ich ging
trinken – ich trank
singen – ich sang
lesen – ich las
essen – ich aß

Infinitive: gehen
Word stem: geh-

	Singular		Plural			Singular		Plural	
1. Person	ich	ging	wir	gingen	1. Person	I	went	we	went
2. Person	du	gingst	ihr	gingt	2. Person	you	went	you	went
3. Person	er/sie/es	ging	sie/Sie	gingen	3. Person	he/she/it	went	they/you	went

Here's a useful tip if your head is beginning to smoke from all the different endings: you do not really need to learn the preterite endings/forms if you know the present tense forms very well and can differentiate between them and the preterite forms. They are the only non-compound tenses.

Exercise

Two versions of an introduction to the Nibelungenlied are presented next. The first is an adapted version using the preterite for most of the text, though not exclusively. The second version is the original text written by Sonja Glauch in July 2002 for the website Mediaevum.de, using the present tense. Underline the verb forms in the texts and compare them. Then work on a translation of the first text. After this, consider how the second text would differ. Vocabulary is at the end of the second version.

Version 1 – Preterite

Das Nibelungenlied erzählt in zwei Teilen von der Ermordung Siegfrieds durch die burgundischen Könige (1.–19. âventiure[1]) und von der Rache seiner Witwe Kriemhild an den Mördern (20.–39. âventiure).

Siegfried verfügte über mythische Fähigkeiten (Tarnmantel, Unverwundbarkeit) und einen mythischen Goldschatz (Nibelungenhort). Er bekam die burgundische Königsschwester Kriemhild nur unter der Bedingung zur Frau, dass er seinen zukünftigen Schwager Gunther bei der Werbung um die – ebenfalls mit mythischer, übernatürlicher Kraft ausgestattete – isländische Königin Brünhild unterstützte. Gunther und Siegfried tauschten heimlich die Rollen in einem Wettbewerb. Gunther gewann durch diese List den Wettbewerb und er konnte Brünhild heiraten. Dies führte Jahre später zum Streit zwischen Kriemhild und Brünhild und zur Beleidigung der Königin. Diesen Konflikt löste Hagen, Ratgeber des Königs Gunther, durch die heimtückische Ermordung Siegfrieds. Die Witwe, Kriemhild, heiratete später den Hunnenkönig Etzel. Durch die Heirat erhielt Kriemhild die Möglichkeit, ihre Rache zu planen: sie lud ihre Brüder und Hagen ins Hunnenland ein. Da Hagen die Gefahr erkannte, erschien er mit einer großen Armee. Kriemhild provozierte einen Angriff und benutzte sogar ihren und Etzels kleinen Sohn als Köder. Innerhalb von zwei Tagen und drei Nächten starben Tausende von Hunnen und Burgunden in den Kämpfen. Am Ende tötete Kriemhild den Mörder Hagen eigenhändig mit Siegfrieds Schwert. Das durfte sie aber nicht ohne die Erlaubnis des Königs. Für diese Tat wurde Kriemhild dann selbst erschlagen.

Version 2 – Present tense

Das Nibelungenlied erzählt in zwei Teilen von der Ermordung Siegfrieds durch die burgundischen Könige (1.–19. âventiure) und von der Rache seiner Witwe Kriemhild an den Mördern (20.–39. âventiure).

Siegfried verfügt über mythische Fähigkeiten (Tarnmantel, Unverwundbarkeit) und einen mythischen Goldschatz (Nibelungenhort). Er bekommt die burgundische Königsschwester Kriemhild nur unter der Bedingung zur Frau, dass er seinen zukünftigen Schwager Gunther bei der Werbung um die – ebenfalls mit mythischer, übernatürlicher Kraft ausgestattete – isländische Königin Brünhild unterstützt. Gunther und Siegfried tauschen heimlich die Rollen in einem Wettbewerb. Gunther gewinnt durch diese List den Wettbewerb und er kann Brünhild heiraten. Dies führt Jahre später zum Streit zwischen Kriemhild und Brünhild und zur Beleidigung der Königin. Diesen Konflikt löst Hagen, Ratgeber des Königs Gunther, durch die heimtückische Ermordung Siegfrieds. Die Witwe, Kriemhild, heiratet später den Hunnenkönig Etzel. Durch die Heirat erhält Kriemhild die Möglichkeit, ihre Rache zu planen: sie lädt ihre Brüder und Hagen ins Hunnenland ein. Da Hagen die Gefahr erkennt, erscheint er mit einer großen Armee. Kriemhild provoziert einen Angriff und benutzt sogar ihren und Etzels kleinen Sohn als Köder. Innerhalb von zwei Tagen und drei Nächten sterben Tausende von Hunnen und Burgunden in den Kämpfen. Am Ende tötet Kriemhild den Mörder Hagen eigenhändig mit Siegfrieds Schwert. Das darf sie aber nicht ohne die Erlaubnis des Königs. Für diese Tat wird Kriemhild dann selbst erschlagen.

Stylistic note

The two different versions of the text here are for comparative purposes only. Please be aware that a text discussing a work of art or the plot from a play or a story (such as the Nibelungenlied would use the present tense, not the preterite. A historical account, on the other hand, would use the preterite, not the present tense.

Vocabulary

zur Frau bekommen – to be given her hand in marriage
die Werbung um Brünhild – here: the courting of Brünhild
die heimtückische Ermordung – sneaky murder
wurde erschlagen – was killed

ausgestattet (participle) – equipped
Beleidigung, die (-, -en) – insult
eigenhändig – herself, with her own hands
Fähigkeit, die (-, -en) – ability
heimlich – secretly
Köder, der (-s, -) – bait
Kraft, die (-, Kräfte) – strength
List, die (-, -en) – trick, deception
Tarnmantel, der (-s, Tarnmäntel) – invisibility cape
Tat, die (-, -en) – action, deed
jmdn. bei etwas unterstützen – to support someone with (doing) sth.
Unverwundbarkeit, die (-, -en) – invulnerability
über etwas verfügen – to have sth. at one's disposal, to possess sth.
Wettbewerb, der (-es, -e) – competition

6.5 The present perfect

Hat dich niemand verdammt?
Has nobody condemned you?

The present perfect is a so-called compound tense, put together from an auxiliary verb and a past participle. It is translated as either preterite or present perfect in English, i.e. "I did something" or "I have done something."

The present perfect is formed by using a conjugated form of the auxiliary verbs *haben* or *sein* in position 2 of a main clause and a participle in the fourth position (at the end of the sentence).

Here is an example of the German sentence *Peter hat ein Haus gebaut* (Peter has built a house).

Peter	hat		ein Haus	gebaut.
	Auxiliary verb in second position (finite verb)			Participle in fourth position (non-finite verb)

Perfect with *haben (+bauen)*

	Singular		Plural			Singular		Plural	
1. Person	ich	habe gebaut	wir	haben gebaut	1. Person	I	have built	we	have built
2. Person	du	hast gebaut	ihr	habt gebaut	2. Person	you	have built	you	have built
3. Person	er/sie/es	hat gebaut	sie/Sie	haben gebaut	3. Person	he/she/it	has built	they/you	have built

Perfect with *sein (+gehen)*

	Singular		Plural			Singular		Plural	
1. Person	ich	bin gegangen	wir	sind gegangen	1. Person	I	have gone	we	have gone
2. Person	du	bist gegangen	ihr	seid gegangen	2. Person	you	have gone	you	have gone
3. Person	er/sie/es	ist gegangen	sie/Sie	sind gegangen	3. Person	he/she/it	has gone	they/you	have gone

The difference between haben and sein

Most present perfect forms are constructed using *haben* and a participle, but when describing movement or relating to a change in some (bodily) state, the auxiliary verb *sein* must be used.

Ich bin krank gewesen.
I have been sick.

Ich bin nach Hause gefahren.
I have driven home.

The list of verbs that use *sein* is fairly short, it includes – besides <u>all</u> verbs of movement – the following verbs: *werden* (its participle *geworden* means "become"), *passieren, sein* (its participle *gewesen* is "been" in English), *aufstehen*. Bear in mind that you do not necessarily need to know all of these, as long as you recognise them to be a present perfect form and translate them as a past tense. Identifying the participle is usually the best way to be right on track, which is what we are going to look at next.

Use of the present perfect in German as opposed to the preterite

The present perfect is used in German to express things in the past, similar to the preterite. Unlike in English, there are fewer rules which should be used in German. In general, the present perfect is more common in spoken German than in written German and often interspersed with short forms of the preterite, especially *war* and *hatten*, simply because these are shorter. The preterite has traditionally been more common in written German, but you should expect to encounter the present perfect just as much. In general, there is no relevant difference when translating the present perfect or preterite into English, as long as the meaning is the same.

*Die Bürger **haben** in den Wahlen vom März 1990 **gewählt**.*

The citizens have voted in the elections from March 1990.
or
The citizens voted in the elections from March 1990.

In the example sentence, we have given two different translations in English, one using the English simple past and one using the English present perfect. In this case, most English speakers would choose to use the simple past, due to the date in the past. As long as the meaning does not differ, you do not need to be worried about choosing either for a translation into English. German is in fact more flexible with its tenses than English, so there can be cases where an English tense must be used to make it grammatically correct.

Ich habe 2014 in Birmingham gewohnt.
~~I have lived in Birmingham in 2014.~~
I lived in Birmingham in 2014.

Ich wohne seit Mai in Durham.
~~I live in Durham since May.~~
I have been living in Durham since May.

Dates, time, numbers?
Dates, time and numbers are explained on p. 208.

Use your own judgement for these cases. If you are only trying to understand the texts, it is not a thing you need to worry about unnecessarily as
long as you are aware that tenses sometimes do not match up exactly and
that German is a bit more liberal in this sense.

Exercise

Go back and work on the introductory text (Jesus und die Ehebrecherin).
Underline all verb forms in the text, whether they are conjugated forms,
infinitives, participles, preterite or perfect. Then try to translate the text; you
should be able to figure out the meaning of the text even without us having
looked at participles yet.

What can you notice in regard to the use of the preterite and present
perfect in the text passage?

6.6 Past participles

> *Moses hat uns **befohlen**.*
> Moses has **ordered** us.

In the previous section, you learned that the present perfect is formed by a
conjugated form of an auxiliary verb (*haben, sein*) and a past participle. In
this section we will have a closer look at these participles.

A few things to remember

- In German, there are two different participles, the past participle (participle II), and the present participle (participle I), which will be covered
  in chapter 8. The past participle is the more common one and, as far as
  its uses are concerned, the more important one. If a text refers only to
  "participle," you should therefore assume that it is referring to the past
  participle form.
- Past participles always only have one fixed translation. *Gebaut* is always
  translated as "built." This makes things easier, as you do not have to
  change the translation whether it is present perfect, pluperfect, a passive
  construction or a participle used as an adjective.
- Participles are often key words, when trying to understand/translate a
  text. Once you have located a participle, you will need to assess its
  relation to the structure and framework of the sentence. Missing a participle can indeed make it very difficult to get the correct meaning of a
  sentence.

When working on texts, always try to spot participles early on since they can be an integral part of the verb. Even if they are not part of the verb, they can still be part of a longer extended participial phrase (chapter 14), which can be quite tricky.

A <u>regular past participle</u> is formed by taking the infinitive of a verb, cutting off the -en and adding the prefix ge- and suffix -t. Separable verbs will put the prefix ge- between the separable part and the verb stem.

Examples: *bauen, kochen, machen, einkaufen, wohnen*

Infinitive	Step 1 Remove the -en from the infinitive	Step 2 Add ge- and -t	Participle
bauen to build	*bau-*	*ge-bau-t*	*gebaut* built
machen to make, do	*mach-*	*ge-mach-t*	*gemacht* made
aufmachen to open	*auf-mach-*	*auf-ge-mach-t*	*aufgemacht* opened

There are many irregular participles in German. The most common irregularity is the use of -en instead of -t at the end of the participle (see the following examples). Note that in the participle of *essen*, an additional g is added to make the pronunciation of the word easier. This is not a rule, it is simply part of this particular irregular verb.

Examples: *fahren, lesen, essen*; with ablaut (vowel change) in the preterite: *sprechen, schreiben, helfen*

Infinitive	Step 1	Step 2	Participle
fahren to drive	*fahr-*	*ge-fahr-en*	*gefahren* driven
essen to eat	*ess-*	*ge-g-ess-en*	*gegessen* eaten
anrufen to call (on the phone)	*an-ruf-*	*an-ge-ruf-en*	*angerufen* called

Verbs whose infinitive ends on -ieren do not add the prefix ge-.
Examples: *passieren, probieren, positionieren, stationieren, regieren*

Infinitive	Step 1	Step 2	Participle
passieren to happen	*passier-*	*passier-t*	*passiert* happened
ausprobieren to try out	*aus-probier-*	*aus-probier-t*	*ausprobiert* tried out

Some verbs have non-removable prefixes such as ent-, be-, ver-, unter-, etc.
These verbs keep their prefix in their participle form and will not use the
prefix ge-. This can make it rather tricky to spot some of these participles.
Some can look exactly the same as the infinitive; some others look like the
3rd person singular of the present tense.
Examples: *entfernen, entnehmen, zerstören, zerfallen, bearbeiten, betonen,
vergessen, verlassen, untergehen, hinterfragen*

Infinitive	Step 1	Step 2	Participle
entfernen to remove	*ent-fern-*	*ent-fern-t*	*entfernt* removed
bearbeiten to process	*be-arbeit-*	*be-arbeit-e-t*	*bearbeitet* processed
vergessen to forget	*ver-gess-en*	*ver-gess-en*	*vergessen* forgotten
untergehen to sink	*unter-geh-en*	*unter-ge-gangen*	*untergegangen* sunk

Finally, some irregular participles follow no particular rule and look very
different from the infinitive form.

Infinitive	Step 1	Step 2	Participle
sein to be		*ge-*	*gewesen* been
gehen to go	*geh-*	*ge-*	*gegangen* gone
sitzen to sit	*sitz-*	*ge-*	*gesessen* sat
werden to become	*werd-*	*ge-word-en*	*geworden* become

wissen to know	*wiss-*	*ge-wuss-t*	*gewusst* known
befehlen to order	*befehl-*	*befohl-en*	*befohlen* ordered
brechen to break	*brech-*	*ge-broch-en*	*gebrochen* broken
nehmen to take	*nehm-*	*ge-nomm-en*	*genommen* taken
aufschließen to open, unlock	*auf-schließ-*	*auf-ge-schlossen*	*aufgeschlossen* opened, unlocked

Advice on how to find a participle

 Fortunately, you do not need to remember every single irregular form. Most of the time, there are "telltale signs," i.e. obvious indicators that will let you spot a participle much more quickly and without looking it up in a dictionary.

- Location, location, location! If a participle is part of the verb form, it will always be at the end of the clause. This is in many ways the easiest way for you to locate participles. If it is used as an adjective, it will be in front of the word it modifies (and have an adjective ending attached).
- Look for signature elements of participles, the prefix ge- and the suffixes -en or -t.
- Auxiliary verbs can be a hint as well. Look out for forms of *haben*, *sein* and *werden*, including their past tense and subjunctive forms.

If you think you have found a participle, but are unsure of its infinitive form, this is probably because it is irregular and has gone through some vowel or even consonant changes. There is a bit of a system behind these changes and we will explain these in the next section.

6.7 Strong verb vowel changes (ablauts)

As you probably have noticed by now, some irregular verbs change their main vowel sound for their preterite form or for their past participle, for example *er geht* becomes *er ging* in the preterite and the participle is *gegangen*; the sound has changed from e to i in the preterite and then to a for the participle. This type of change is referred to as an ablaut and is common in Germanic languages. The verb "to sing, sang, sung" is an example of this in English. When reading German texts, this can cause problems when you come across an irregular form and are not sure what its infinitive form is.

For example, you might have come across the verb *lag* in a text and cannot find an infinitive form *lagen* in your dictionary. Being aware of these patterns will help you to look up verbs with a different vowel sound and with a bit of trial and error you will eventually find *liegen* to be the infinitive of the word you were looking for. Many online dictionaries will also be able to identify these irregular forms and show you the correct infinitive.

There are several patterns of ablaut changes, but fortunately a lot of verbs have similar changes, typically a light vowel (i, e) to a dark vowel (a, u, o) or a diphthong (a "double sound" like ei, au) to a monophthong (i, ie, o). For the purpose of reading German, you need to be aware that these changes exist, but you do not need to learn the patterns by heart – there are too many and it would not be of great benefit. Rather you should be aware that they exist and be able to deduce typical changes.

The following is a list of the most common changes. A few unique changes (*) that only occur with one irregular verb have also been listed, as these verbs are fairly common.

 When you encounter a verb or participle in a text and you find it difficult to identify its correct infinitive form, try looking up a version with a different vowel sound, such as ei, i/ie, a, e and au, o.

The order in the table below is always the same: infinitive sound, preterite sound and participle sound.

Infinitive	Pattern	Example
ei	ei – i – i ei – ie – ie	reiten – ritt – geritten bleiben – blieb – geblieben
i/ie	i – a – o i – a – u ie – o – o	beginnen – begann – begonnen finden – fand – gefunden fliegen – flog – geflogen
au	au – o – o	saugen – sog – gesogen
a	a – ie – a a – u – a	lassen – ließ – gelassen waschen – wusch – gewaschen
e	e – a – o e – a – e	sprechen – sprach – gesprochen vergessen – vergaß – vergessen
o	o – a – o	kommen – kam – gekommen
*	i – a – e e – u – o i – u – u e – a – a o – ie – o ü – o – o ö – o – o	sitzen – saß – gesessen werden – wurde – geworden wissen – wusste – gewusst denken – dachte – gedacht stoßen – stieß – gestoßen lügen – log – gelogen schwören – schwor – geschworen

Exercise

After having studied the previous chart, try to complete the following table while focusing on the vowel changes. The verbs are always grouped in similar pairs of three.

The focus of this exercise is to get the vowel changes right; you can check the answer key afterwards to correct any consonant changes.

Infinitive	Preterite	Participle
beißen	*biss*	*gebissen*
		geschnitten
	ritt	
binden		
	sang	
		getrunken
fallen		
	ließ	
		geblasen
	trug	
schaffen		
		gewaschen
lesen		
	sah	
		vergessen
		genommen
sterben		
	sprach	
		geschrieben
entscheiden		
	stieg	
		geflohen
verlieren		
	schoss	
*schwimmen		
*		gewusst
*	kannte	

* These verbs do not follow the same pattern, but you still should be able to complete these with the chart from 6.6.

6.8 The verbal bracket

When a main clause has more than one verb component, as is the case of compound tenses like the perfect tense (*ich habe gemacht*) or in modal verb constructions (*ich will machen*), the two components form a verbal bracket. The auxiliary verb will be in the first or second position and the participle or infinitive will always be at the end of the sentence. This construction is called a verbal bracket, because the two parts form a bracket around the centre of the clause. For visualisation, a box has been added in the following examples to show you where the bracket is located.

- In a main clause, the finite verb is in the second position. The non-finite verb is at the end of the clause.

  Ich | *habe gestern ein Hähnchen* **gekocht**|.
  I (have) cooked a chicken yesterday.

- In all commands and questions, the finite verb is placed in the first position. The non-finite verb is at the end of the clause.

  |**Willst** *du in die Stadt* **gehen**|?
  Do you want to go to town?

- In all subordinate clauses, both parts will be at the end of the clause. The finite verb will be the very last word; essentially, there is no verbal bracket in these clauses that could hold any other words.

  Ich denke, dass ich in die Stadt **gehen will**.
  I think that I want to go to town.

  Ich weiß, dass ich gestern ein Hähnchen **gekocht habe**.
  I know that I cooked a chicken yesterday.

What is the relevance of the verbal bracket?

For the purpose of reading German, there is no direct relevance of knowing what a verbal bracket is other than understanding what the term means; the term "verbal bracket" occurs regularly in grammar explanations, as it is vital for language production. We have already covered finite and non-finite verb forms as well as German sentence structure (position 1, 2 and 4), and this essentially covers all that you need to know in order to decode a German sentence.

Exercise

Find and underline all participle forms in the following sentences. After you have had a look at these, try and translate them with the help of a dictionary.

1. Die Polizei hat angerufen.
2. Die Soldaten sind in der Kaserne stationiert.
3. Viele Menschen müssen sich im Alter an neue Umstände anpassen.
4. Ich lerne in meiner Freizeit Schwimmen. Als Kind habe ich nie die Gelegenheit gehabt.
5. Ein Erdbeben hat das 1960 gebaute Haus zerstört.
6. Warum hast du die Frage nicht beantwortet? Karl hat sofort auf meine Fragen geantwortet.
7. "Verliebt, verlobt, verheiratet" ist ein Popsong von Peter Alexander.
8. Hat jemand einen Schraubenzieher mitgebracht?
9. Am Samstagabend sind viele Menschen in der Innenstadt ausgegangen.
10. Wir dürfen die Einladung nicht vergessen!

6.9 The pluperfect

The pluperfect is used to indicate that an action was already completed at a point in the past. Review the time line diagram (p. 65) and then return here.

   The pluperfect is a composite tense and is formed in a similar fashion as the present perfect, by combining an auxiliary verb with a participle. In the case of the pluperfect, the past tense forms of *sein* or *haben* (i.e. *waren* and *hatten*) are used.

Present perfect:	*Er ist gegangen.*	Pluperfect tense:	*Er war gegangen.*
	He has gone.		He had gone.
	Sie haben gegessen.		*Sie hatten gegessen.*
	They have eaten.		They had eaten.

When the verb *waren* is used, there can occasionally be some confusion whether a sentence is preterite or pluperfect, usually because of a participle. In those cases, it is best to approach the sentence logically and to ask whether the participle is describing something or someone, for example a state, in which case it will likely be preterite. If this is not the case, ask whether the construction is describing movement, in which case it will be pluperfect.

Sie war verheiratet.	*Sie war um sieben Uhr aufgestanden.*
She was married.	She had gotten up at 7 o'clock.
	(Yes, *aufstehen* is considered a verb of movement in German!)

Here is the complete pluperfect conjugation pattern for both *waren* and *hatten*.

	Singular		Plural			Singular		Plural	
1. Person	ich	hatte gebaut	wir	hatten gebaut	1. Person	I	had built	we	had built
2. Person	du	hattest gebaut	ihr	hattet gebaut	2. Person	you	had built	you	had built
3. Person	er/sie/es	hatte gebaut	sie/Sie	hatten gebaut	3. Person	he/she/it	had built	they/ you	had built

	Singular		Plural			Singular		Plural	
1. Person	ich	war gegangen	wir	waren gegangen	1. Person	I	had gone	we	had gone
2. Person	du	warst gegangen	ihr	wart gegangen	2. Person	you	had gone	you	had gone
3. Person	er/sie/es	war gegangen	sie/Sie	waren gegangen	3. Person	he/she/it	had gone	they/ you	had gone

Exercise

1. Which tenses are pluperfect and which are not? Then translate the sentences.
2. Viele Menschen hatten bereits ihren Urlaub gebucht.
3. Als Kind hatte ich ein Buch mit antiken Sagen.
4. Die Müllers waren in Urlaub gefahren.
5. Die Rechnung war bereits bezahlt.
6. An dem Abend hatte die Scheune noch nicht gebrannt.
7. Später war die Scheune dann komplett abgebrannt.
8. Identify the tenses of the sentences below and then translate the sentences.
9. Ich bin im September im Urlaub in Italien gewesen.
10. Dort war es sehr schön und warm.
11. Ich war davor in Frankreich gewesen und hatte einen Freund von mir besucht.
12. Ich hatte eine tolle Zeit mit meinem Freund in Frankreich gehabt.
13. In Florenz wollte ich ein Museum besuchen.
14. Das Museum war aber geschlossen.
15. Das Museum war aber geschlossen gewesen.
16. Es hatte in der Nacht zuvor einen kleinen Brand gegeben und das Haus war beschädigt.
17. Ich habe dann einen Park besucht und eine Pizza gegessen.
18. Nächstes Jahr werde ich nach Spanien fahren.

6.10 Chart: modal verbs in the present and the past tense

Preterite forms of modal verbs are irregular, but have a certain simplicity in their irregularity: they lose the umlaut.

	müssen (to have to/must)	können (to be able/ allowed to/ can)	dürfen (to be allowed to/may)	sollen (should/ supposed to)	wollen (to want)	mögen (to like)	möchten (would like to)
Present tense							
ich	muss	kann	darf	soll	will	mag	möchte
du	musst	kannst	darfst	sollst	willst	magst	möchtest
er/sie/es	muss	kann	darf	soll	will	mag	möchte
wir	müssen	können	dürfen	sollen	wollen	mögen	möchten
ihr	müsst	könnt	dürft	sollt	wollt	mögt	möchtet
sie/Sie	müssen	können	dürfen	sollen	wollen	mögen	möchten
Preterite							
ich	musste	konnte	durfte	sollte	wollte	mochte	*
du	musstest	konntest	durftest	solltest	wolltest	mochtest	*
er/sie/es	musste	konnte	durfte	sollte	wollte	mochte	*
wir	mussten	konnten	durften	sollten	wollten	mochten	*
ihr	musstet	konntet	durftet	solltet	wolltet	mochtet	*
sie/Sie	mussten	konnten	durften	sollten	wollten	mochten	*

* There is no corresponding past tense form of *möchte*. The past tense of *wollen* is the closest form in meaning.

Present perfect for modal verbs

Modal verbs can be used in the present perfect, but an infinitive is used instead of a participle. The participle of modal verbs is, however, occasionally found in colloquial language use.

> *Die Regierung hat die Steuern erhöhen müssen.*
> The government had to raise the taxes.

> *Du hast die Polizei anrufen sollen.*
> You were supposed to call the police.

> *Ich habe das einfach nicht gekonnt.* (colloquial)
> I just wasn't able to do that.

Note

1 Âventiure – a kind of unit used for chapters in medieval tales.

7 Adjectives and adverbs; comparative and superlative; *als* and *wie*

7.1 Adjectives

Adjectives further describe or qualify nouns, verbs, actions (i.e. verbs) or other adjectives. Note that grammar terminology differs sometimes significantly when it comes to adjectives (and their uses), adverbs and adverbials.

- If an adjective describes a noun, it will be in front of the noun it agrees with and it will have an adjective ending. This is the most common use of an adjective. This is called attributive use.

*Der **gute** Wein.*	The **good** wine.
*Ein **guter** Wein.*	A **good** wine.
***Guter** Wein.*	**Good** wine.

- If an adjective describes an action, it is being used similarly to an adverb. It will then typically be close to the verb and not in front of a noun. It will also not have an adjective ending. In English, depending on the verb of the sentences, these forms can have a -ly added on to them. You can say that the adjective is in adverbial use in this case.

*Der Wein ist **gut**.*	The wine is **good**.
*Die Kinder spielen **fröhlich**.*	The children play **happily**.

- Although it is less common than the other two cases, adjectives can also qualify other adjectives. In this case they precede the adjective they are qualifying and do not have an adjective ending. In English, -ly is usually attached to these adjectives. This can be also called an adverbial use.

Dieser Wein ist **wirklich** gut.	This wine is **really** good.

There are two important things to look out for when dealing with adjectives: placement and ending. If the adjective has an adjective ending attached to it and/or is in front of a noun, it will be used to describe a noun. If it does not have an adjective ending and/or is close to a verb or adjective, it is used adverbially.

Adjective endings

Your dictionary will give you the basic form of an adjective. You will find for example *gut*, *fröhlich* and *wirklich* as the basic forms in your dictionary. Note that adjectives whose basic forms end in el or er, for example *edel*, *dunkel*, *teuer*, *bitter* omit an "e" when declined, so the basic form in the dictionary might look slightly different to the one in a text (*edel* as opposed to *der edle Wein* – "the classy/refined wine").

Adjectives used with nouns have an additional ending added on. This ending agrees in number, gender and case with the noun. The most common endings are -e or -en, but the endings -er, -es and even -em also exist. There are three essential declension patterns, and the complete patterns are listed in the following chart. Due to the complexity of these patterns it is recommended that you focus on being able to identify an adjective and whether it is used with a noun or a verb. Learning the endings by heart is not recommended.

The three patterns are:

1. With a definite article, i.e. *der, dieser, jener, mancher…*
   → The endings used are either -e or -en. This is considered a weak declension.
2. With an indefinite article, i.e. *ein, zwei, drei, viele, einige…*
   → The endings are -e or -en, except where a definite article would have been *der/das/des*; in those cases an -er or -es is used to mirror the ending of the missing definite article:

   der neue Hut → ein neuer Hut

   This is considered a strong declension.
   The combination of plural forms with an indefinite article is rare, which is why they are marked with an asterisk.
3. Without any determiner,
   → The same strong declension as for indefinite articles is used; this occurs most often with plural nouns.

	Masculine nouns	Feminine nouns	Neuter nouns	Plural nouns
Nominative	der alte Artikel (the old article) ein alter Artikel alter Artikel	die strenge Regel (the strict rule) eine strenge Regel strenge Regel	das neue Buch (the new book) ein neues Buch neues Buch	die aktuellen Nachrichten (the current news items) * aktuelle Nachrichten
Accusative	den alten Artikel einen alten Artikel alten Artikel	die strenge Regel eine strenge Regel strenge Regel	das neue Buch ein neues Buch neues Buch	die aktuellen Nachrichten * aktuelle Nachrichten
Dative	dem alten Artikel einem alten Artikel altem Artikel	der strengen Regel einer strengen Regel strenger Regel	dem neuen Buch einem neuen Buch neuem Buch	den aktuellen Nachrichten * aktuellen Nachrichten
Genitive	des alten Artikels eines alten Artikels alten Artikels	der strengen Regel einer strengen Regel strenger Regel	des neuen Buchs eines neuen Buchs neuen Buchs	der aktuellen Nachrichten * aktueller Nachrichten

Participles used as adjectives

Participles can also be used as adjectives. If they qualify a noun, an adjective ending is added on. Like other adjectives, they can also qualify verbs or adjectives (second example).

> *Ich suche ein **gebrauchtes** Auto.*
> I'm looking for a used car.

> *Die Situation ist **verwirrend**.*
> The situation is confusing.

7.2 Possessive adjectives

> *Unsere Abteilung hat mehr Finanzmittel als deine.*
> Our department has more financial means than yours.

Words like *mein, dein, sein, ihr, unser...* describe ownership and are called possessive adjectives; other names include possessive articles or possessive pronouns. This "fuzziness" stems from the fact that they blur the lines between articles and adjectives.

They can be seen as having two parts – a meaning part and a grammatical part. The meaning part is the front of the word and what you translate (which is always the same). The ending inflects according to number and case of the following noun(s) as adjectives would do. This is the second part, the grammatical information, which is not translated. Hence, in sentences such as *Das ist mein Auto* and *Das ist meine Tasche*, the possessive adjectives *mein/meine* are translated the same way as "my," regardless of the adjective ending on it.

	Singular		Plural	
1. Person	mein	my	unser	our
2. Person	dein	your	euer	your
3. Person	sein/ihr/sein	his/her/its	ihr	their
Formal			Ihr	your

As you can see in the chart, *ihr* occurs quite a lot. Its meaning is determined by its function in the sentence or the noun that follows it. There is also the personal pronoun *ihr*, which is used for the second person plural ("you"); this is a different word type, so do not confuse them.

When addressing someone directly, all possessive adjectives referring to that person are capitalised.

Exercise

Translate these sentences.

1. Der junge Mann ist mein Sohn.
2. Er hat die Haare seiner Mutter, aber die Augen meines Großvaters.
3. Leider haben unsere Kinder auch die Sturheit ihrer Eltern geerbt.
4. „Herr Professor, Ihre Frau hat angerufen. Sie bittet Sie, Ihre Tochter vom Kindergarten abzuholen."

7.3 *Zu* and adjectives

When *zu* is placed in front of an adjective, it means "too." Note that while this is identical in sound to the other major translation of *zu* (to), it has a different meaning.

Exercise

A. Translate these sentences with the help of a dictionary.

1. Die Suppe ist zu scharf.

2. „Zu schnell und zu gefährlich" beschreibt die Achterbahn sehr gut.

    Vocabulary
    Achterbahn, die (-, -en) - roller coaster

B. There are quite a few adjectives in the following sentences. Write them on the blank line and decide whether they qualify (i.e. relate to) a noun, verb or other adjective. The lines underneath each sentence give you a hint of how many adjectives there are in each sentence.

1. Er hat ihren unveröffentlichten Artikel schnell gelesen.
_____ ☐ qualifies a noun ☐ qualifies a verb ☐ qualifies another adjective
_____ ☐ qualifies a noun ☐ qualifies a verb ☐ qualifies another adjective
_____ ☐ qualifies a noun ☐ qualifies a verb ☐ qualifies another adjective

2. Der Inhalt deines Artikels ist so komplex, dass ich ihn einfach nicht verstanden habe.
_____ ☐ qualifies a noun ☐ qualifies a verb ☐ qualifies another adjective
_____ ☐ qualifies a noun ☐ qualifies a verb ☐ qualifies another adjective
_____ ☐ qualifies a noun ☐ qualifies a verb ☐ qualifies another adjective

3. Mein Hut ist neu.
_____ ☐ qualifies a noun ☐ qualifies a verb ☐ qualifies another adjective
_____ ☐ qualifies a noun ☐ qualifies a verb ☐ qualifies another adjective

4. Der Hut ist ein neuer. (Why is this sentence so different from the previous one? What is missing?)
_____ ☐ qualifies a noun ☐ qualifies a verb ☐ qualifies another adjective

5. Ich suche den grünen und roten Stift. (Why is there only one line in this example?)
_____ ☐ qualifies a noun ☐ qualifies a verb ☐ qualifies another adjective

6. Ich lese oft aktuelle Artikel, um auf dem Laufenden (up to date) zu bleiben. (Note that *oft* is simply an adverbial.)
_____ ☐ qualifies a noun ☐ qualifies a verb ☐ qualifies another adjective

7. Das Resultat ist eindeutig, aber leider unerwünscht. (*Leider* is an adverbial.)
_____ ☐ qualifies a noun ☐ qualifies a verb ☐ qualifies another adjective
_____ ☐ qualifies a noun ☐ qualifies a verb ☐ qualifies another adjective

8. Neulich haben Experten eine alte Fliegerbombe aus dem Zweiten Weltkrieg in unserer Nachbarschaft entschärft. (Why is *Zweiten* capitalised?)

_____ ☐ qualifies a noun ☐ qualifies a verb ☐ qualifies another adjective
_____ ☐ qualifies a noun ☐ qualifies a verb ☐ qualifies another adjective
_____ ☐ qualifies a noun ☐ qualifies a verb ☐ qualifies another adjective

9. Suchen Sie Ihre Brille? Sie liegt auf dem kleinen Tisch.

_____ ☐ qualifies a noun ☐ qualifies a verb ☐ qualifies another adjective
_____ ☐ qualifies a noun ☐ qualifies a verb ☐ qualifies another adjective

10. Spätrömische Dekadenz ist ein negativ konnotierter Begriff.

_____ ☐ qualifies a noun ☐ qualifies a verb ☐ qualifies another adjective
_____ ☐ qualifies a noun ☐ qualifies a verb ☐ qualifies another adjective
_____ ☐ qualifies a noun ☐ qualifies a verb ☐ qualifies another adjective

7.4 Comparative

> *Je höher der Flug, desto tiefer der Fall.*
> The higher the flight, the deeper the fall.

Comparatives are a special form of adjectives that show the relation of one state to another. As the name implies, they are used for comparison. If, for example, you are comparing the height of two of the famous seven dwarfs in the fairy tale of Snow White, you could say that dwarf A is taller than dwarf B. However, because this is relative and you are comparing dwarfs in the first place (and not, for example, giants), you have to remember that it does not make any statement about whether dwarf A is actually tall or not. Therefore, comparatives are all about comparing an attribute, but not making overall statements.

The German comparative is very similar to the English comparative in that it is formed by adding the suffix -er-/-r to the adjective (plus a potential adjective ending). This makes them look and feel very similar. The two main differences are that comparative forms in German can quite often have a spelling change (usually the vowel in a monosyllabic adjective becomes an umlaut). The other difference is that German does not use words such as "more" or "most" with long adjectives. In German, comparatives are always formed by adding -er, no matter the length of the word (fourth example).

Der kleine Junge.	→	*Der kleinere Junge.*
The small boy.	→	The smaller boy.
Der alte Mann.	→	*Der ältere Mann.*
The old man.	→	The older man.

| *Die hohe Wand.* | → | *Die höhere Wand.* |
| The high wall. | → | The higher wall. |

| *Das unbequeme Bett.* | → | *Das unbequemere Bett.* |
| The uncomfortable bed. | → | The more uncomfortable bed. |

7.5 *Als, wie*

Als and *wie* occur quite often with comparative forms. In comparisons, *als* is usually translated as "than." It is used when two aspects are compared that differ in some way or another. *Wie* is also used for comparisons, but only if things are similar in the aspect. It is sometimes combined with *genauso*, which means exactly.

Peter ist größer als Max. **compare with:** *Peter ist genauso groß wie Tim.*

Peter is taller than Max. Peter is exactly as tall as Tim.

Both *als* and *wie* have more than one meaning.

Als can also be part of phrasal verbs and is usually translated as "as," for example *gelten als* (to be regarded as).

Wie can mean "how" and often occurs as part of a question.

Als can also be used as a temporal conjunction for events that took place once in the past and then means "when."

Wie can also mean "when" or "whenever," but only for events that occur regularly (either in the past or in the present).

Finally, both *als* and *wie* can also be used with the subjunctive mood to mean "as if" (covered in chapter 13).

Possible translations for *als* are:

Er gilt als gefährlich	He is known/regarded **as** dangerous.
Ich arbeite als Deutschlehrer.	I work **as** a German teacher.
...als je zuvor	...**than** ever before
...als ich 8 Jahre alt war...	...**when** I was 8 years old... (only in the past tense)
...immer wenn es regnet...	...**when/whenever** it rains...
Er benimmt sich so, als wäre er erst 7 Jahre alt.	He behaves (in such a way), **as if** he were only 7 years old.
Wir möchten wissen, wie es zu dieser Situation gekommen ist.	We would like to know, **how** this situation came to be.

Exercise

Chose the best translation for *als/wie* in these examples.

	as	how	than	when	as if
Tu nicht so, als könntest du Französisch verstehen! Ich weiß, dass du kein Französisch gelernt hast.					
Ich habe keine Uhr. Ich weiß nicht, wie spät es ist.					
Das neue Parteiprogramm der Partei ist konservativer als das letzte.					
Mein Vater arbeitet als Gesangslehrer, aber er ist als Klempner ausgebildet.					
Als wir in Frankreich waren, habe ich eine tolle Oper besucht.					
Neil Armstrong betrat als erster Mensch den Mond.					
Obwohl Helium nicht so leicht wie Wasserstoff ist, benutzt man es heute in Zeppelinen.					

7.6 Superlative

The superlative denotes the maximum/best/worst item of a given sample. If you have a bunch of bananas and are looking for the ripest one, you will refer to one single banana as "the ripest banana" of the sample. There could of course be even riper bananas out there in the world, but in the sample before you, the superlative denotes one banana with the greatest ripeness.

As with the comparative, superlative forms in German are similar to English forms in that they use a similar suffix, in this case -est/-st (plus a potential adjective ending). If Germans want to say that something "is the highest/best/worst..." they will add the preposition *am* as well, or use the superlative as a noun.

klein	→	*kleiner*	→	*am kleinsten/der Kleinste*
small	→	smaller	→	the smallest/the smallest one
gut	→	*besser*	→	*am besten/der Beste*
good	→	better	→	the best/the best one

hoch	→	*höher*	→	*am höchsten/der Höchste*
high	→	higher	→	the highest/the highest one

teuer		*teurer*		*am teuersten*
expensive	→	more expensive	→	the most expensive

Exercise

Translate these sentences.

1. Guter Rat ist teuer.
2. Möge der Bessere gewinnen!
3. Die Letzten werden die Ersten sein.
4. Teurer Wein ist teuer, aber billiger Wein ist billiger. (Careful with this one! Which adjectives are comparative forms, which ones are not?)
5. Es ist leichter, gute Ratschläge zu geben, als sie zu befolgen.
6. Ehrlich währt am längsten.
7. Man isst die Suppe nicht so heiß, wie man sie kocht.
8. Das Treffen morgen ist zu früh für mich.
9. Seneca der Ältere war der leibliche Vater von Seneca dem Jüngeren. (*Leiblich* comes from *der Leib*, but here you will need to translate it in a different way. Can you guess from the context?)
10. Die Natur kann grausam sein, aber noch grausamer sind die Menschen.
11. Die Kerze leuchtet in der dunklen Nacht am hellsten.
12. Es kann der Frömmste nicht in Frieden leben, wenn es dem bösen Nachbarn nicht gefällt. (from Wilhelm Tell by Friedrich Schiller)
13. Obwohl der K2 nicht so hoch wie der Mount Everest ist, ist er viel gefährlicher für Bergsteiger als der Everest.

Vocabulary

Bergsteiger, der (-s, -) – climber
fromm – pious, godly
grausam (ad.) – cruel
Kerze, die (-, -n) – candle
Rat, der (-(e)s, no plural) – advice
Ratschlag, der (-(e)s, Ratschläge) – advice

Practice text: Rumpelstilzchen

This is a fairy tale by the Brothers Grimm. The story is longer than other texts you have worked on so far and features a lot of preterite and separable verbs. Be sure to read the vocabulary section first before you start translating it. It includes advice/ translations on several old-fashioned or unusual expressions. There are also a number of words in this text – *als*, *so*, *wenn*, *noch* – that are on the list of difficult or tricky words in the appendix; check their entries as well.

Diminutive forms are a special type of noun derivation used to show that something is a smaller version, or affection or belittlement (e.g. *das Männlein, das Häuschen*). If you want to know more about these forms, read the section in the appendix on diminutive forms (p. 207).

Rumpelstilzchen

Es war einmal ein Müller. Er war arm, aber er hatte eine schöne Tochter. Nun passierte es, daß er mit dem König zu sprechen kam, und um sich ein Ansehen zu geben, sagte er zu ihm: „Ich habe eine Tochter, die kann Stroh zu Gold spinnen." Der König sprach zum Müller: „Das ist eine Kunst, wenn deine Tochter so geschickt ist, wie du sagst. Bring sie morgen in mein Schloß, da will ich sie auf die Probe stellen!"

Als nun das Mädchen zu ihm kam, führte der König es in eine Kammer. Die Kammer lag ganz voll mit Stroh. Er gab ihr Rad und Haspel und sprach: „Jetzt mache dich an die Arbeit, und wenn du diese Nacht durch bis morgen früh dieses Stroh nicht zu Gold versponnen hast, so mußt du sterben." Darauf schloß er die Kammer zu, und sie blieb allein darin. Da saß nun die arme Müllerstochter und wußte keinen Rat: sie wußte nicht, wie man Stroh zu Gold spinnen konnte, und ihre Angst ward immer größer, so daß sie zu weinen anfing. Da ging auf einmal die Türe auf, und ein kleines Männchen trat herein und sprach: „Guten Abend, Jungfer Müllerin, warum weint Sie so sehr?"

„Ach," antwortete das Mädchen, „ich soll Stroh zu Gold spinnen und verstehe das nicht." Da sprach das Männchen: „Was gibst du mir, wenn ich dir's spinne?" – „Mein Halsband," sagte das Mädchen. Das Männchen nahm das Halsband, setzte sich vor das Rädchen, und schnurr, schnurr, schnurr, dreimal gezogen, war die Spule voll. Dann steckte es eine andere auf, und schnurr, schnurr, schnurr, dreimal gezogen, war auch die zweite voll: und so ging's fort bis zum Morgen, da war alles Stroh versponnen, und alle Spulen waren voll Gold.

Bei Sonnenaufgang kam der König, und als er das Gold erblickte, erstaunte er und freute sich, aber sein Herz ward nur noch geldgieriger. Er brachte die Müllerstochter in eine andere, viel größere Kammer voll Stroh und befahl ihr, auch in dieser Nacht zu spinnen, wenn ihr das Leben lieb wäre. Das Mädchen wußte sich nicht zu helfen und weinte, da ging abermals die Türe auf, und das kleine Männchen erschien und sprach: „Was gibst du mir, wenn ich dir das Stroh zu Gold spinne?"

„Meinen Ring von dem Finger," antwortete das Mädchen. Das Männchen nahm den Ring, fing wieder an zu spinnen mit dem Rade und hatte bis zum Morgen alles Stroh zu glänzendem Gold gesponnen. Der König freute sich sehr bei dem Anblick, war aber noch immer nicht Goldes satt. Er brachte die Müllerstochter in eine noch größere Kammer voller Stroh und sprach: „Die mußt du noch in dieser Nacht verspinnen: gelingt dir's aber, so sollst du meine Gemahlin werden." Als das Mädchen allein war, kam das Männlein zum dritten Mal wieder und sprach: „Was gibst du mir, wenn ich dir noch einmal das Stroh spinne?" – „Ich habe nichts mehr, das ich geben kann," antwortete das Mädchen. „So versprich mir dein erstes Kind, wenn du Königin wirst." Die Müllerstochter wußte nicht, wie sie sich anders helfen konnte; sie versprach es dem Männchen und das Männchen spann noch einmal das Stroh zu Gold. Und als am Morgen der König kam und das Gold fand, heiratete er sie und die schöne Müllerstochter ward eine Königin.

Über ein Jahr später brachte sie ein schönes Kind zur Welt und dachte gar nicht mehr an das Männchen: da trat es plötzlich in ihre Kammer und sprach: „Nun gib mir, was du versprochen hast." Die Königin erschrak und bot dem Männchen alle Reichtümer des Königreichs an, wenn es ihr das Kind ließ. Aber das Männchen sprach: „Nein, etwas Lebendes ist mir lieber als alle Schätze der Welt." Da fing die Königin an zu jammern und zu weinen und das Männchen hatte Mitleid mit ihr: „Drei Tage gebe ich dir," sprach er, „wenn du bis dahin meinen Namen weißt, so sollst du dein Kind behalten."

Die Königin dachte die ganze Nacht über an alle Namen und schickte einen Boten in das Land, um sich nach weiteren Namen zu erkundigen. Am nächsten Tag kam das Männchen und sie fing mit Kaspar, Melchior, Balzer an und sagte alle Namen, aber bei jedem sprach das Männlein: „So heiß ich nicht." Am zweiten Tag fragte sie in der Nachbarschaft herum, wie die Leute da hießen, und sagte dem Männlein die ungewöhnlichsten und seltsamsten Namen: „Heißt du vielleicht Rippenbiest oder Hammelswade oder Schnürbein?" Aber es antwortete immer: „So heiß ich nicht."

Den dritten Tag kam der Bote wieder zurück und erzählte: „Neue Namen habe ich keine finden können, aber ich kam an einen hohen Berg im Wald, wo Fuchs und Hase sich gute Nacht sagen, da sah ich ein kleines Haus, und vor dem Haus brannte ein Feuer, und um das Feuer sprang ein gar lächerliches Männchen, das hüpfte auf einem Bein und schrie:

„Heute back' ich,
Morgen brau' ich,
Übermorgen hol' ich der Königin ihr Kind;
Ach, wie gut ist, daß niemand weiß,
daß ich Rumpelstilzchen heiß'!"

Ihr könnt euch denken, wie die Königin froh war, als sie den Namen hörte, und als bald hernach das Männlein hereintrat und fragte: „Nun, Frau Königin, wie heiß ich?" fragte sie erst: „Heißt du Kunz?" – „Nein." – „Heißt du Heinz?" – „Nein." – „Heißt du etwa Rumpelstilzchen?"

„Das hat dir der Teufel gesagt, das hat dir der Teufel gesagt," schrie das Männlein und stieß mit dem rechten Fuß vor Zorn so tief in die Erde, daß es bis an den Leib hineinfuhr, dann packte es in seiner Wut den linken Fuß mit beiden Händen und riß sich selbst mitten entzwei.

Vocabulary

wenn ihr das Leben lieb wäre – if her life was dear to her
ungewöhnlichsten und seltsamsten – the most unusual and weirdest
wo Fuchs und Hase sich gute Nacht sagen – where fox and hare bid each other goodnight
etwas Lebendes ist mir lieber – something alive/living is me dearer, I prefer something alive/living

dir's – shortened form of: es dir/dir es
ging's – shortened form of: es ging/ging es

abermals – (once) again, one more time
als – This word is on the list of tricky words; have a look at the entry and then decide what translation fits best.
anders – differently
Ansehen, das (-s, no plural) – reputation, standing, esteem, prestige
brauen – to brew
entzweireißen (sep.v.) – to tear or rip asunder
erschrecken – to scare, frighten, startle; here: to be startled

Lebende, das (-n, -n) – the living (thing or person), something alive

gar – this word can have many different, contextual meanings; here: altogether

geldgieriger – greedier

Gemahlin – female form of *Gemahl*, an uncommon word for spouse, wife

größer – bigger; noch größer – even bigger

hernach – after that

hineinfahren (sep.v.) – to drive into

Jungfer, die (-, -n) – mistress, maiden, damsel, spinster

könnte – could

lächerlich – ridiculous

Leib, der (-(e)s, -er) – body

mitten – in the middle

Rad und Haspel – spinning wheel and reel

reicher – richer

satt sein – to have had enough of something, be full of something

sich selbst – itself

sich zu helfen wissen – to find a way/solution

spinnen – to spin

Spule, die (-, -n) – reel, spool

verspinnen – synonym to *spinnen*

ward – this is an old form of *wurde*

wie – how

8 Subordinate and relative clauses; commas; present participles

8.1 Subordinate clauses introduced by conjunctions

Subordinate clauses have been mentioned several times already (2.2, 3.8 and 6.7). Here we will take a closer look at the conjunctions that introduce most of these constructions.

Most conjunctions such as *weil, da, nachdem, obwohl*, send the verb of the clause to the end of a sentence. There are also a few coordinating conjunctions that introduce a main clause with the verb in the second position; *aber, denn, und, sondern* and *oder* are the most prominent members of this group. A common explanation is that these conjunctions are in position 0 and therefore not really part of the clause.

Here is an example of how the structure of a main clause changes if it becomes a subordinate clause. The conjunction *weil* ("because") sends the finite verb to the very end of the clause (fourth position); the less common conjunction *denn* (a synonym of *weil*) keeps the finite verb in the second position.

Main clause: *Ich **habe** einen Kaffee getrunken.*
I have drunk a coffee.

With *weil*: *Ich fühle mich besser, weil ich einen Kaffee getrunken **habe**.*

With *denn*: *Ich fühle mich besser, denn ich **habe** einen Kaffee getrunken.*

Both are translated the same: I feel better, because I have drunk a coffee.

For reading German it does not make a major difference, as you will always look at the second and fourth position of a clause to build the subject–verb framework. What is more important is to spot and correctly translate the conjunction in the first place, as the logical connection of the subordinate clause to the main clause hinges on your understanding of this word. Here are some examples:

Der Artikel ist veraltet, weil es neue Forschungsergebnisse gibt.
The article is outdated, because there are new research findings.

Der Artikel ist (noch) relevant, obwohl es neue Forschungsergebnisse gibt.
The article is (still) relevant, although there are new research findings.

Der Artikel ist dann veraltet, wenn es neue Forschungsergebnisse gibt.
The article will then be outdated, when there are new research findings.

Der Artikel ist nicht veraltet, aber es gibt neue Forschungsergebnisse.
The article is not outdated, but there are new research findings.

Most subordinate clauses can also be placed in front of a main clause. When this happens, the subject and finite verb in the main clause change place (this is called subject–verb inversion) and the finite verb is placed right after the comma. Here is an example of this:

*Der Artikel **ist** veraltet, weil es neue Forschungsergebnisse gibt.*

→ *Weil es neue Forschungsergebnisse gibt, **ist** der Artikel veraltet.*

Exercise

A. Translate these sentences with the help of a dictionary. Pay attention to the way the conjunctions change the overall meaning of the sentences.

1. Ich gehe nicht ins Kino, weil ich ins Theater gehe.
2. Ich gehe nicht ins Kino, sondern ich gehe ins Theater.
3. Ich gehe nicht ins Kino, nachdem ich im Theater war.
4. Der Prinz und die Prinzessin heiraten, obwohl sie aus verschiedenen Ländern kommen.
5. Der Prinz und die Prinzessin heiraten, da sie aus verschiedenen Ländern kommen.
6. Falls der Artikel veraltet ist, müssen wir einen neuen suchen.
7. Der Prinz stimmt der Hochzeit zu, während die Prinzessin sie ablehnt.
8. Dass das passieren kann, habe ich nicht gewusst.
9. Wir fragen uns oft, ob jemand über uns wacht.
10. Indem er bekannte Quellen neu auswertete, hat der Forscher etwas Neues zum Thema beitragen können.

Vocabulary

etwas auswerten (sep.v.) – to evaluate sth., interpret sth., analyse sth.
etwas beitragen (sep.v.) – to contribute sth., add sth.

Distinguishing conjunctions from other words such as
prepositions or adverbials

Some conjunctions can look a lot like another word type, for example a preposition. In this case, you need to remember that conjunctions introduce a clause and will be at the beginning of the clause. Otherwise you are dealing with an adverbial or a preposition. In the case of a preposition, a noun must follow the preposition.

Finally, adverbials often have the same role in a clause and create a logical connection with the previous clause; however, adverbials are part of the clause and not between clauses (position 0). Sentences with an adverbial will use the main clause structure and do not send the verb to the end of the sentence. Furthermore, adverbials take up space "in the clause," which means that they can occupy position 1 (conjunctions are "between" clauses). Adverbials can also be moved after the verb; they do not have to be at the start of a clause.

Exercise

B. Look at the following sentences and decide if you are dealing with a conjunction, an adverbial or a preposition.

	Conjunction	Adverbial	Preposition
Während der Arbeit klingelt oft mein Handy.			
Nachdem ich gegessen habe, gehe ich nach Hause.			
Ich esse jetzt zu Ende, **danach** gehe ich nach Hause.			
Der Artikel ist fertig, wir müssen **allerdings** die Quellen aktualisieren.			
Der Artikel ist fertig, **aber** wir müssen die Quellen aktualisieren.			
Da drüben steht ein Baum.			
Der Verleger kürzt den Artikel, **damit** er in die Ausgabe passt.			

Nested clauses

A nested clause is a clause that is located within another clause. It is separated by a comma at the beginning and at the end. Here is an example with an extended infinitive clause nested in a main clause. The interrupted main clause is in bold.

> ***Wir müssen den Artikel,*** *um Fehler zu vermeiden,* ***noch einmal***
> ***korrekturlesen.***
> We must, in order to avoid mistakes, proofread the article once more.

It is often advisable not to translate these constructions literally, but to simplify the structure in English.

8.2 Relative clauses

> *Josef, ihr Mann, der gerecht war*
> Josef, her husband, who was just/faithful to the law

> *...denn das Kind, das sie erwartet, ist vom Heiligen Geist.*
> ...because the child, which she is expecting, is from the Holy Spirit.

Relative clauses are a type of subordinate clause that describes a noun or concept in more detail. They are similar to adjectives, only that the description is usually more complex and takes shape in a complete clause with subject and verb. They are introduced by relative pronouns rather than conjunctions, and the relative pronoun is always located towards the front of the relative clause, usually right after a comma.

German has three different sets of relative pronouns. The first, most common set looks like determiners, e.g. *der*, *die*, *das* and inflections of these. While they can look a lot like the definite articles, the dative plural and both genitive forms are different (*denen*, *dessen*, *deren*).

The second set consists of cognates of the English word "which": *welcher*, *welche*, *welches*.

The third set is a bit more complex and can look like question words, *was*, *wo*, or like prepositions with a *wo-/wor-* prefix added to them: *worüber*, *woher*....

In English, the first two sets are translated as "who, which" or "that." The translation of the third group depends on what is suitable for the sentence. All of these relative pronouns follow the sentence structure for subordinate clauses and send the verb to the fourth position of the clause.

Relative pronouns relate in number and gender to the last noun in the previous clause that shares the same attributes; occasionally that is not the last noun of the previous clause.

> **Der Spieler** der gegnerischen Mannschaft, **der** *uns am gefährlichsten ist, ist der linke Stürmer.*
> **The player** of the opposing team, **who** is the most dangerous for us, is the left forward.
> (*Mannschaft* is a feminine word!)

Relative clauses can only follow a main clause; they cannot be in front of it. Note that relative pronouns do <u>not</u> follow the case of the noun they refer to; instead their case inflects according to the needs of the new clause, which can be different.

> *Das ist der Mann, den ich kenne.*
> That is the man, whom I know.

All of the relative pronouns in the following chart can be translated as "which" or "that." I have listed some additional translations in the masculine column.

	Masculine	Feminine	Neuter	Plural
Nominative	der (who)	die	das	die
Accusative	den (whom)	die	das	die
Dative	dem (to whom)	der	dem	denen
Genitive	dessen* (whose, of whom)	deren	dessen	deren
Nominative	welcher	welche	welches	welche
Accusative	welchen	welche	welches	welche
Dative	welchem	welcher	welchem	welchen
Genitive	–	–	–	–

In some cases, *wessen* can be used instead of *dessen*. Do not be confused as *wessen* can also be a question word ("whose?").

Prepositions and relative pronouns

Similar to English, a preposition can be added before a relative pronoun.

> *In dem Wald, **durch den** der Pfad führt, leben viele Räuber.*
> Many bandits live in the forest, **through which** the path leads.

Exercise

Pay attention to which words are relative pronouns and translate the sentences with the help of a dictionary.

1. Der Ring, der der Frau gehört, ist aus Silber.
2. Die Personen, denen ich vertraue, kann man an einer Hand zählen.
3. Die Weihnachtsansprache, auf die wir warten, ist für 20:00 Uhr geplant.
4. Er besiegt einen Boxer, dessen Gewicht eine Klasse über seinem liegt.
5. Den Studenten des Kurses, die die Prüfung geschrieben haben, schreibe ich, dass das Gremium, das die Ergebnisse veröffentlicht, die Prüfung wiederholen will.
6. Er verwendet ein Schreibprogramm, das in der Lage ist, die Fehler, die er macht, zu korrigieren. (*In der Lage* is usually not translated as a noun in English.)

8.3 Use of *wo, was, wer* to introduce subordinate or relative clauses

Wo, was, wer and other interrogative pronouns can be used as conjunctions or relative pronouns to introduce subordinate clauses. They send the finite verb to the fourth position.

Some typical examples are:

> *Wir wissen nicht, wer in diesem Haus wohnt.*
> We do not know who lives in this house.

> *Ich weiß nicht, wo mein Auto ist.*
> I do not know where my car is.

> *Denn sie wissen nicht, was sie tun.*
> For they know not what they do.

Was can be translated as "that" rather than "what" in some cases.

> *Ich vermeide alles, was mich krank machen kann.*
> I avoid everything that can make me sick.

Other interrogative pronouns can work in the same way.

> *Wissen Sie, worauf der Polizist draußen wartet?*
> Do you know what the police officer outside is waiting for?

Exercise

Translate these sentences.

1. Die Regeln im Waisenhaus legen fest, wann man essen und schlafen muss.
2. Es ist schwierig zu verstehen, worauf uns der Autor aufmerksam machen will.
3. Wir werden uns für das, was wir getan haben, vor Gericht verantworten müssen.
4. Es ist unglaublich, in was für eine Schieflage die Bank geraten ist. (This one cannot be translated literally.)

Vocabulary

etwas festlegen (sep.v.) – to define, determine or fix sth.
in etwas geraten – to get into sth.
Schieflage, die (-, -n) – tilt, difficult or ailing position
Waisenhaus, das (-(e)s, Waisenhäuser) – orphanage

8.4 The helpful commas

In German, comma rules are much stricter than in English. Normally, a comma is used in one of the following ways:

- To separate clauses from each other.
  Wir wissen nicht, was wir tun.
  We do not know, what we are doing.
- To separate items on a list or several adjectives.
  Ich packe meine Socken, Hosen, Hemden und Unterhosen für die Reise.
  I pack my socks, trousers, shirts and underpants for the trip.
- To separate an incomplete clause from a complete clause.
  Die Reparationen müssen alle erbracht werden, z. B durch Sachleistungen.
  All the reparations must be made, for example through compensation in kind.

This is extremely helpful for those attempting to read German sentences. Commas in German never separate adverbs or adverbial phrases, or other short introductions. Compare the following examples and how the German sentences do not separate the first part with a comma.

Am Montag müssen wir nach Hause fahren.	On Monday, we must drive home.
Allerdings muss gesagt werden, dass...	However, it must be said that...

Most of the time the comma will tell you where one clause ends and where another starts, or where a clause is interrupted by a nested clause.

Der Regierungsbericht, der jetzt in der Zeitung steht, wurde bereits zwei Monate vorher intern veröffentlicht, aber er wurde wenig von Beamten beachtet.

The government's report, which is now in the newspaper, had already been published internally two months ago, but officials did not pay much attention to it.

In this example, all three clauses have one **finite** verb.

Der Regierungsbericht **wurde** bereits zwei Monate vorher veröffentlicht	Main clause
der jetzt in der Zeitung **steht**	Relative clause (here nested inside the main clause)
aber er **wurde** wenig von Beamten beachtet	Subordinate clause

When trying to understand a complex or very long sentence, look for the commas. This way you can often break down a complex structure into smaller clauses, each with their own finite verb.

In German, unlike in English, there is rarely a comma before *und* ("and") or *oder* ("or"). These conjunctions can connect two separate clauses, but it is sometimes not as obvious as in English, where a comma would tell the reader that a new clause is starting.

Here is a variation of the previous example to illustrate this:

> *Der Regierungsbericht, der jetzt in der Zeitung steht, wurde bereits zwei Monate vorher intern veröffentlicht **und** er wurde wenig von Beamten beachtet.*

> The government's report, which is now in the newspaper, had already been published internally two months ago, **and** officials did not pay much attention to it.

The last part, *wurde wenig von Beamten beachtet*, is a separate clause, but it is less evident without the comma. In addition, both the *er* and/or the *wurde* could be omitted, because they are exactly the same as in the previous clause and therefore could be implied.

These three variants,

- *...und er wurde wenig von Beamten beachtet*
- *...und wurde wenig von Beamten beachtet*
- *...und wenig von Beamten beachtet*

would all be correct. When translating these, you could also choose to simply put a full stop and start a new sentence.

> The government's report, which is now in the newspaper, had already been published internally two months ago. Officials did not pay much attention to it (the report).

Cutting a long and complex German sentence into smaller sentences, even if you have to repeat some words, is a great way of simplifying things. The meaning generally stays the same.

Exercise

There are two tasks for you in the following passage. First, identify finite and non-finite verb forms. Second, identify the type of clause you are dealing with, e.g. a main clause, an infinitive construction, a subordinate or a relative clause, a nested clause, etc.

The text itself is quite hard, you do not need to translate it.

Max Weber: Wissenschaft als Beruf (1919)

Ich soll nach Ihrem Wunsch über „Wissenschaft als Beruf" sprechen. Nun ist es eine gewisse Pedanterie von uns Nationalökonomen, an der ich festhalten möchte: daß wir stets von den äußeren Verhältnissen ausgehen, hier also von der Frage: Wie gestaltet sich Wissenschaft als Beruf im materiellen Sinne des Wortes? Das bedeutet aber praktisch heute im wesentlichen: Wie gestaltet sich die Lage eines absolvierten Studenten, der entschlossen ist, der Wissenschaft innerhalb eines akademischen Lebens sich hinzugeben? Es ist zweckmäßig, vergleichend zu verfahren und sich zu vergegenwärtigen, wie es im Ausland dort aussieht, wo in dieser Hinsicht der schärfste Gegensatz gegen uns besteht: in den Vereinigten Staaten.

Bei uns – das weiß jeder – beginnt normalerweise die Laufbahn eines jungen Mannes als Privatdozent. Er habilitiert sich nach Rücksprache und mit Zustimmung des betreffenden Fachvertreters an einer Universität und hält nun – unbesoldet – Vorlesungen, deren Gegenstand er innerhalb seiner venia legendi selbst bestimmt. In Amerika beginnt die Laufbahn normalerweise ganz anders durch Anstellung als „assistant". In ähnlicher Weise etwa, wie das bei uns an den großen Instituten der naturwissenschaftlichen und medizinischen Fakultäten vor sich geht, wo die förmliche Habilitation als Privatdozent nur von einem Bruchteil der Assistenten und oft erst spät erstrebt wird. Der Gegensatz bedeutet praktisch, daß bei uns die Laufbahn eines Mannes der Wissenschaft im Ganzen auf plutokratischen Voraussetzungen aufgebaut ist.

Weber, Max (1988). "Wissenschaft als Beruf." In *Max Weber. Gesammelte Aufsätze zur Wissenschaftslehre*. Mohr Siebeck.
This essay was first published in 1919.

8.5 Present participles

German has two different participle forms: the past participle, which you already encountered in chapter 6, and the present participle. Here is a contrasting example:

Infinitive	Present participle/participle I	Past participle/participle II
arbeiten (weak verb) to work	*arbeitend* working	*gearbeitet* worked
bringen (strong verb) to bring	*bringend* bringing	*gebracht* brought

The present participle is formed by taking the word stem of a verb and adding -nd or -end. The typical translation of such a participle is by using the "-ing" form in English. There are no "irregular" present participles.

Present participles have one major difference in comparison to past participles: they cannot be part of a verb, such as a compound tense. Present participles have no verb function and can only function as adjectives. They will often have an adjective ending as well, as in the first example here:

- Present participle used as an adjective in front of a noun:
  *Der **weinende** Junge.*   The crying boy.

- Present participle in adverbial use in front of another adjective:
  *Das Wasser ist **kochend** heiß.*   The water is boiling hot.

- Present participle in adverbial use with a verb:
  *Die Supper schmeckt **hervorragend**.*   The soup tastes excellent.

A few words occur often as present participles, for example:

hervorragend – excellent
wütend – mad
bahnbrechend – ground-breaking

Exercise

Translate these sentences.

1. Die Bundeskanzlerin hält eine bewegende Rede.
2. Viele Schutz suchende Menschen sind im Sommer 2015 nach Deutschland gekommen. (*Viele* agrees with *Menschen* in this example, not with *Schutz*.)
3. Wegen strömenden Regens unterbrechen wir das Fußballspiel.

8.6 Summary of chapter

Here is a summary of six things that we learned in this chapter.

1. Subordinate and relative clauses cannot stand on their own. They need a main clause to make sense.
2. In the vast majority of subordinate and relative clauses, the finite verb will be at the very end of the sentence (fourth position). There are a few coordinating conjunctions, such as *aber*, *denn*, *und*, *sondern* and *oder* where the finite verb stays in the second position.
3. Relative pronouns can look like articles or question words. They are always located after the comma of the previous clause. Relative pronouns can also be combined with a preposition, such as *in der* or *unter die*.
4. Commas in modern German have a grammatical and not a stylistic function. They are very helpful for determining where one clause ends and another one begins, especially in very long and complex sentences.
5. In German, commas before *und* or *oder* are not common, even if a new clause begins.
6. Present participles have no verb function in German and can only be used as an adjective. They can easily be spotted due to the characteristic -nd suffix.

Practice text: Hintergründe zum Weltbevölkerungswachstum

The following text is a slightly adapted selection of texts from the website of the charity organisation *Deutsche Stiftung Weltbevölkerung*, found at https://www.dsw.org. Instead of all six negative facts about the growing world population, there are only two listed here.

ZWEI POSITIVE FAKTEN DER WACHSENDEN WELTBEVÖLKERUNG	
1. Menschen werden älter Dank des medizinischen Fortschritts und der besseren Lebensbedingungen leben wir heute länger als je zuvor. Dies gilt sowohl für Industrie- als auch für Entwicklungsländer. Während die durchschnittliche Kinderzahl pro Frau fast überall auf der Welt abnimmt, erreichen die Menschen in vielen Teilen der Erde ein höheres Alter.	**2. Mehr Kinder überleben** Dank der industriellen Revolution und der weltweiten Fortschritte etwa im Gesundheitsbereich und bei der Ernährungssituation sank die Kindersterblichkeit erst in den industriellen Ländern und später auch in den Entwicklungsländern. Aber: Dass mehr Kinder überleben, ist auch ein Grund für viele Eltern, weniger Kinder zu bekommen. Hohe Überlebenschancen von Kindern führen zum Geburtenrückgang, weil Eltern weniger um das Überleben ihrer eigenen Kinder besorgt sein müssen.

SECHS NEGATIVE FAKTEN DER WACHSENDEN WELTBEVÖLKERUNG
...und wie wir sie angehen!

1. Viele Menschen wurden nie sexuell aufgeklärt (were never sexually educated)

Aufklärung ist die Grundlage dafür, dass sich Jugendliche und Erwachsene mit Verhütungsmitteln wie Kondomen vor ungewollten Schwangerschaften und sexuell übertragbaren Krankheiten wie HIV schützen. Doch über Sexualität zu reden, gilt in vielen Gesellschaften immer noch als Tabubruch. Nicht darüber zu sprechen, ist aber sehr gefährlich. Denn so verfestigen sich Mythen rund um das Thema Sexualität und um den eigenen Körper. Das kann gravierende Folgen für Mädchen und Frauen haben, wenn sie – oft ungewollt – schwanger werden.

Nur wer über ausreichend qualifizierte Informationen verfügt, kann sein Leben selbstbewusst und selbstbestimmt angehen.

Was die DSW tut

- Wir haben ein Netzwerk von ca. 400 Jugendklubs in Ostafrika aufgebaut. Dort finden Jugendliche speziell ausgebildete, gleichaltrige Jugendberater, mit denen sie über Sexualität sprechen können.
- In unserer politischen Arbeit setzen wir uns dafür ein, dass Sexualaufklärung weltweit eine größere Bedeutung bekommt.

4. Armut und Perspektivlosigkeit hemmen den Fortschritt

Die Bevölkerung wächst besonders in den ärmsten Ländern der Welt. Viele Kinder bieten eine Möglichkeit der Versorgung im Alter und bei Krankheit. Dabei könnte (could) freiwillige Familienplanung die Entwicklungschancen armer Länder nachhaltig verbessern. In kleineren Familien sind die Kinder im Durchschnitt gesünder, haben bessere Ausbildungschancen und Möglichkeiten am Erwerbsleben teilzunehmen. Das hat damit auch einen positiven Einfluss auf die nächste Generation.

Junge Menschen in Entwicklungsländern verdienen eine bessere Bildung, eine gute Gesundheitsversorgung und vor allem eine Perspektive auf einen erfüllenden Arbeitsplatz.

Was die DSW tut

- Wir bieten in unseren Projekten Aus- und Weiterbildungsmöglichkeiten und damit auch Berufsperspektiven für Jugendliche an.
- Wir schulen Jugendliche im Einmaleins der Wirtschaft.
- Die Jugendlichen setzen ihre eigenen Ideen um, wie sie den Jugendklub finanziell am Laufen halten. Wir unterstützen sie dabei!
- Wir setzen uns für eine Erhöhung der Entwicklungsgelder ein, damit arme Länder bessere Entwicklungsmöglichkeiten erhalten.

Vocabulary

dank – thanks to (preposition with genitive)
Einmaleins, das (-es, no plural) – basics
sich für etwas einsetzen (sep.v.) – to advocate sth., plead for sth.
gelten als – to be known as, regarded as, to be said to be
gleichaltrig – of the same age
etwas hemmen – to hinder or prevent sth.
am Laufen halten – to keep sth. running
selbstbewusst – self-confident
selbstbestimmt – self-determined

9 *Werden* and its different uses; passive voice; future and future perfect

In chapter 2 we looked at the three main auxiliary verbs that German uses: *sein, haben* and *werden*.

In this chapter we will take a closer look at *werden* and its three different uses: as a verb meaning "to become," in the passive voice and in the future tense.

1) *werden = to become*
   werden + adjective or noun

Nach dem Studium wird Max Anwalt.	After studying, Max becomes a lawyer.
Nachts wird es kalt.	At night it gets (becomes) cold.
Ich will Professor werden.	I want to become a professor.

2) *werden in the future tense*
   werden + infinitive

Morgen werden wir spazieren gehen.	Tomorrow we will go for a walk.
Werden wir ins Kino gehen?	Are we going to go to the cinema?
In ein paar Tagen werde ich Vater werden.	In a few days I will become a father.

3) *werden in the passive voice*
   werden + past participle

Der Vogel wird von dem Hund gefressen.	The bird is being eaten by the dog.
Das Problem wird heiß diskutiert.	The problem is (being) hotly debated.
Es wird viel in der Küche gekocht.	A lot is (being) cooked in the kitchen.
In der Disko wird viel getanzt.	In the disco, a lot of dancing is going on.

Note that in English the passive is usually translated with forms of "to be" (more on this later).

If you want to find out the use of *werden* in a sentence, it is best to imagine a simple "tick box" system in your head. Ask yourself: is there a form of *werden* in this clause? Is there a participle in this clause? Is there an infinitive in this clause? You simply tick all appropriate boxes and will automatically have the right use of *werden*.

werden	Infinitive	Past participle	Result
X			"to become"
X	X		Future tense
X		X	Passive
X	X	X	Future tense and passive

Where is the subject?
It might seem as if the example sentence *In der Disko wird viel getanzt* had no subject. Typically, if the subject of a passive voice clause is *es*, this can be omitted. It is then implied and usually not relevant for a translation. This happens especially if a prepositional object is at the beginning of the clause *(in der Disko)*, but the prepositional object is not a requirement for this to happen.

Es wird viel in der Disko getanzt.	=	*In der Disko wird viel getanzt.*
Es wird nachts geschlafen.	=	*Nachts wird geschlafen.*

Exercise
Check the following sentences for *werden* and identify its correct use by using the tick box system. Then try to translate the sentences. If you are struggling with the translation of the sentences in the passive voice, read the next section **9.1 The passive voice** first.

Note: the word *worden* is a special form of *werden* that is always used for the passive voice. You can translate it as "been."

a. Mein Assistent hat das Hotelzimmer für mich gebucht.

☐ werden   ☐ infinitive   ☐ past participle

b. In der Schule werden viele Tests geschrieben.

☐ werden   ☐ infinitive   ☐ past participle

c. Das Vertrauen alter Menschen kann für illegale Aktivitäten missbraucht werden.

☐ werden   ☐ infinitive   ☐ past participle

d. Es wird oft gesagt, dass zu viel Fernsehen schlecht für Kinder ist.

☐ werden ☐ infinitive ☐ past participle

e. Die Winter heutzutage werden immer wärmer.

☐ werden ☐ infinitive ☐ past participle

f. Nächstes Jahr werden wir nach Spanien fahren.

☐ werden ☐ infinitive ☐ past participle

g. Am Dienstag wird mein Vater aus dem Gefängnis entlassen werden.

☐ werden ☐ infinitive ☐ past participle

h. Am Max-Planck-Institut in Heidelberg wird Licht aus kosmischen Quellen untersucht.

☐ werden ☐ infinitive ☐ past participle

i. Alle vertraulichen Daten sind gelöscht worden.

☐ werden ☐ infinitive ☐ past participle

j. Die Politik dieses Präsidenten wird in wenigen Jahren vergessen worden sein.

☐ werden ☐ infinitive ☐ past participle

9.1 The passive voice

An active voice sentence tells us who is carrying out an action and what the action is. Both parts, agent and action, are equally important. A passive voice sentence is different, because it focuses on the action and not on who is carrying it out. In German the passive is often used for neutral, impersonal statements, and as a result it occurs quite often in higher register language publications.

You can simplify the difference between active and passive like this:

- ▪ Active – Who does what?
- ▪ Passive – What is happening?

Active sentence: *Der Hund frisst den Vogel.*
(The dog eats the bird.)

Passive sentence with agent: *Der Vogel wird von dem Hund gefressen.*
(The bird is being eaten by the dog.)

Passive sentence without agent: *Der Vogel wird gefressen.*
(The bird is being eaten).

In the second sentence, the fact that the bird is being eaten is pushed to the foreground as the primary information. The original agent of the action, the dog, is put back into the sentence with a preposition.

However, since passive sentences can do without this information, it will often be omitted, as in the third sentence, where *von dem Hund* is omitted. Here we are no longer interested in who ate the bird, simply that the bird was eaten.

As mentioned earlier, in English, passive sentences are usually formed by adding additional forms of the verb "to be" into the sentence. English does not have a dedicated auxiliary verb like *werden* for the passive voice and this might explain the reluctance of English speakers/writers to use the passive voice frequently. Hence, when translating a German passive sentence, we will need to consider the purpose of the translation. If it is simply for the purpose of understanding the meaning, most passive forms can be expressed by adding a form of "to be" into the English sentence.

> *In Kambodscha werden Spinnen gegessen.*
> In Cambodia spiders are (being) eaten.

However, as the previous example *(In der Disko wird viel getanzt)* showed, sometimes a more idiomatic translation can make sense ("There's a lot of dancing in the disco" as opposed to "In the disco a lot is being danced").

German has two forms of the passive voice

1. *Das Vorgangspassiv*, a passive that expresses a process (that something is being done at the moment). It is formed by using a form of *werden* + participle. This is the one used in the previous examples and is by far the more common form of the passive in German texts. This chapter deals primarily with this type of the passive voice.
2. *Das Zustandspassiv* is a form of the passive that uses *sein* + past participle (instead of *werden*) and describes a static, passive state of a completed action. It is in many ways far subtler and is quite often missed by readers without any negative impact on their understanding of the sentence. This form of passive is sometimes referred to as "statal passive" in grammar books.

Ersatzpassiv with "man"

Finally, German has a number of verbs and constructions that can create so-called "fake passive" constructions, in German *Ersatzpassiv* (literally "replacement passive"). The *Ersatzpassiv* is covered in chapter 15.

The only fake passive form we will look at here are constructions with *man*.

In section 2.4 we learned that *man*, a word that is always a general subject of a sentence, is usually better translated as "you" rather than "one."

However, you can also translate this into English as the passive, which can often sound better. Compare the following correct translations:

In Kambodscha isst man Spinnen.
In Cambodia one eats spiders.
→ In Cambodia you eat spiders.
→ In Cambodia spiders are (being) eaten.

Therefore, the next two sentences have the same meaning and we can see why constructions with *man* can be considered a fake passive.

In Kambodscha werden Spinnen gegessen. = In Kambodscha isst man Spinnen.
In Cambodia, spiders are (being) eaten.

Exercise

Which of these sentences are in the passive voice?

a. Deutsche essen viele Bratwürste.
b. In Deutschland isst man viele Bratwürste.
c. In Deutschland werden viele Bratwürste gegessen.

d. Familie Müller wird ein Haus verkaufen.
e. Familie Müller wird ein Haus verkauft werden. (Careful here!)
f. Familie Müller will ein Haus verkaufen.

g. Die Königin wird den nächsten Premier ernennen.
h. Der nächste Premier wird von der Königin ernannt werden.
i. Wird der nächste Premier ernannt werden?

9.2 The passive voice in different tenses and with modal verbs

The passive voice exists in all tenses and moods (including the subjunctive moods, which will be discussed in chapters 12 and 13). It can also be used with modal verbs. Passive voice sentences follow very strict rules on how they have to be constructed and this is useful for Reading Skills, as the rigidity allows you to identify the correct construction more easily.

Tense	3. Person singular	3. Person plural
Present	Der Artikel wird veröffentlicht. The article is (being) published.	Die Artikel werden veröffentlicht. The articles are (being) published.
	werden + participle II	
Preterite	Der Artikel wurde veröffentlicht. The article was (being) published.	Die Artikel wurden veröffentlicht. The articles were (being) published.
	wurde + participle II	
Present perfect	Der Artikel ist veröffentlicht worden. The article has been published.	Die Artikel sind veröffentlicht worden. The articles have been published.
	sein + participle II + *worden*	
Pluperfect	Der Artikel war veröffentlicht worden. The article had been published.	Die Artikel waren veröffentlicht worden. The articles had been published.
	war + participle II + *worden*	
Future	Der Artikel wird veröffentlicht werden. The article will be published.	Die Artikel werden veröffentlicht werden. The articles will be published.
	werden + participle II + *werden* (infinitive)	
Modal verb, present tense	Der Artikel kann veröffentlicht werden. The article can be published.	Die Artikel können veröffentlicht werden. The articles can be published.
	present tense modal verb + participle II + *werden* (infinitive)	
Modal verb, past tense	Der Artikel konnte veröffentlicht werden. The article could be published./ It was possible for the article to be published.	Die Artikel konnten veröffentlicht werden. The articles could be published./It was possible for the articles to be published.
	preterite tense modal verb + participle II + *werden* (infinitive)	

The difference between worden and geworden

The words *worden* and *geworden* look very similar, but must not be confused.

worden	*geworden*
"been"	"become" or "became"
Always indicates **passive** voice.	Always indicates **active** voice.
Distant relative of *werden*. It is only used in passive voice sentences that feature compound tenses such as the present perfect or the pluperfect.	Past participle of *werden* in its meaning "to become"; because this meaning is intransitive (you cannot "be" become), it can only be used in active voice sentences.

Er war Pfarrer geworden.
He had **become** a priest.

Er ist zum Kardinal ernannt worden.
He has **been** appointed as a cardinal.

9.3 The future and future perfect with *werden*

As mentioned before, the future can be expressed through *werden* + infinitive. This type of future is also known as future I.

Note that Germans will, however, quite often opt to use the present tense instead to express future plans, as it is shorter and can avoid too many forms of *werden* in a sentence. Other words will often make clear that the action is taking place in the future, such as *heute Abend* in the following examples.

Wir werden heute Abend ins Kino gehen.	→	*Wir gehen heute Abend ins Kino.*
We will go to the cinema tonight.	→	We are going to the cinema tonight.
Die Suppe wird heute Abend gegessen werden.	→	*Die Suppe wird heute Abend gegessen.*
The soup will be eaten tonight.	→	The soup is/will be eaten tonight.

For most Germans there is no distinct difference between *Er wird bald Vater*, the example from the beginning of this chapter, and *Er wird bald Vater werden*. In this example the word *bald* ("soon") implies this is still going to happen, which stresses the future aspect, removing the need for a grammatical form of the future.

Future perfect

The future perfect, sometimes referred to as future II, is used to describe activities that will have been completed in the future. It is a rather complex form, using *werden* + past participle + *sein* or *haben* (an infinitive).

*Das Fußballspiel **wird beendet sein**, wenn wir am Stadium ankommen.*
The football match will be finished, when we arrive at the stadium.

*Er **wird** die Karten **verkauft haben**, wenn wir am Stadium ankommen.*
He will have sold the tickets, when we arrive at the stadium.

These ideas can also be expressed in the passive voice by adding *worden*.

*Das Fußballspiel **wird beendet worden sein**, wenn wir am Stadium ankommen.*
The football match will have been finished, when we arrive at the stadium.

> *Die Karten* **werden verkauft worden sein,** *wenn wir am Stadium ankommen.*
> The tickets will have been sold, when we arrive at the stadium.

The future perfect is extremely rare.

Exercise

A. Translate these sentences. Not all of these are passive; which ones are not passive?

1. Albert Einstein wurde am 14. März 1879 in Ulm geboren.
2. Im Bereich der Naturwissenschaften wird sehr viel auf Englisch veröffentlicht.
3. Schulden bei anderen werden oft vergessen.
4. Meine Schulden werden erst in 30 Jahren bezahlt sein.
5. Ich werde deinen Geburtstag bestimmt nicht vergessen.
6. Die Aufklärung des Verbrechens wird von der Familie des Opfers verlangt.
7. Wurde das Haus letztes Jahr gebaut?
8. Verschiedene Vorhersagen wurden von Nostradamus gemacht.
9. Der Dieb ist von der Polizei verhaftet worden.
10. Die Antworten der Klausur waren bereits bekannt gewesen.
11. Die Straße wird im Winter gesalzen werden.
12. In der Klausur sind viele gute Arbeiten geschrieben worden.
13. Die Prüfung war nur von einer Studentin bestanden worden.
14. Professor X hatte die Schule für begabte Kinder gegründet.
15. Alle Hausaufgaben sollen bis Freitag abgegeben werden.
16. Die Klausuren mussten in Rekordzeit korrigiert werden.
17. Einige der Ergebnisse der Studie durften nicht veröffentlicht werden.

B. Which tense is it?
   Determine the tense in each sentence. Not all of these sentences are passive; which ones are? Then translate them into English.

1. Er arbeitete bei Mercedes.
2. Er ist von ihr gefragt worden.
3. Er fragt seine Mutter nach der Frau.
4. Er wurde von ihr gefragt.
5. Es hatte £10 gekostet.
6. Bei Siemens war viel gearbeitet worden.
7. Der Stift gehört ihr.
8. Der Stift gehörte ihr.
9. Der Stift hat ihr gehört.

10. Ich werde gefragt.
11. Ich werde gefragt werden.
12. Ich fragte ihn.
13. Ich habe ihn gefragt.
14. Ich arbeite am Montag.
15. Ich werde am Montag arbeiten.
16. Er sagt, am Montag wird gearbeitet.
17. Er will am Montag arbeiten.
18. Ich musste am Montag arbeiten.
19. Ich habe am Montag arbeiten müssen.
20. Er wird sie fragen müssen.
21. Er soll sie fragen.
22. Er sollte sie fragen.
23. Er musste gefragt werden.
24. Er war nach Deutschland gefahren worden.
25. Er wird nach Deutschland fahren dürfen.

Vocabulary

bei – at (preposition with dative)
Stift, der (-(e)s, -e) – pen
gehören – to belong to

Practice text: Die Zäsur des Mauerbaus 1961

The following text discusses the immediate effect of the construction of the Berlin Wall in 1961 and how it separated the city into East and West.

Pay attention to the use of *werden* in this text and use the tick box system to see if they are all used for the passive voice. The text also features a varied use of adjectives (comparative forms, adverbial use) and relative clauses, so review chapter 7 or 8 if you are unsure about some of these forms.

Die Zäsur des Mauerbaus 1961

In einer Sondersitzung des Politbüros am Freitag, 11. August 1961, wurden die Weichen für den Mauerbau gelegt, der unter der Leitung Erich Honeckers in der Nacht vom 12. zum 13. August 1961 stattfand. Einheiten der Volkspolizei, der Betriebskampfgruppen und der NVA errichteten eine 45km lange Mauer aus Stacheldraht und Beton quer durch Berlin. Der Bau der Mauer zerstörte nicht nur Bindungen zwischen Ost und West, er vernichtete auch die Hoffnungen vieler Bürger der DDR auf eine Liberalisierung und eine freiere Gesellschaft. Politisch bedeutete der Mauerbau, dass die SED die mangelnde

Popularität ihrer Politik und der kommunistischen Ideologie offen zugegeben hatte, auch wenn sie dies nie aussprach. Die Option der Republikflucht war für die meisten Bürger verschwunden, und international wurde die DDR als das Land bekannt, das seine Bürger einsperren musste. Die Mauer wurde ein deutlich sichtbares Symbol für ein System, das nur mit Gewalt aufrechterhalten werden konnte. Die bloße physische Existenz der Mauer war weithin sichtbar aufgrund von Stacheldrahtbarrieren, Grenzbefestigungen, einer permanenten Stationierung sowjetischer Truppen in der Stadt, der ständigen Propaganda des Klassenkampfes. All dies verdeutlichte den Berlinern jeden Tag ihre Situation als „eingemauertes Volk". Vor allem Ärzte und Ingenieure beklagten sich. Aus beruflichen Gründen und zur Weiterbildung hatte die technische und medizinische Intelligenz bislang das Privileg genossen, den Westen besuchen zu können, ein Privileg welches nun mit einem Schlag widerrufen worden war und vielen Mitgliedern dieser Schicht ihre Machtlosigkeit gegenüber dem Staatsapparat verdeutlichte.

Excerpt from: Burdumy, Alexander (2013). *Sozialpolitik und Repression in der DDR. Ost-Berlin 1971–1989.* Klartext Verlag. pp. 81–82.

Vocabulary

all dies – all this, but usually translated as "all of this"
aussprechen (sep.v.) – to pronounce, to proclaim, to announce (Which meaning fits best here?)
Betriebskampfgruppe, die (-, -n) – paramilitary unit made up of company workers
einmauern (sep.v.) – to wall sth. in
Grenzbefestigung, die (-, -en) – border fortification
mangelnd – missing
NVA – this is an abbreviation of "Nationale Volksarmee," the GDR's army
Politbüro, das (-s, -s) – Politbureau, the highest political body in the former German Democratic Republic
mit einem Schlag – at a stroke, with a single blow
Staatsapparat, der (-s, -s) – state machinery
Stacheldraht, der (-s, Stacheldrähte) – barbed wire
die Weiche legen – to select a track for a train, here: to pave the way for something
Weiterbildung, die (-, -en) – further or continuing education

10 Personal pronouns; reflexive pronouns; appositions and phrases

10.1 Personal pronouns

As the name "pronoun" implies, these words stand in for a proper noun. Pronouns inflect in case and number.

*Ich kenne **den Mann.*** → *Ich kenne **ihn.***
Ich know the man. → I know him.

Nominative		Accusative		Dative		Genitive	
ich	I	mich	me	mir	me	meiner	me
du	you	dich	you	dir	you	deiner	you
er	he	ihn	him	ihm	him	seiner	him
sie	she	sie	her	ihr	her	ihrer	her
es	it	es	it	ihm	it	seiner	it
wir	we	uns	us	uns	us	unser	us
ihr	you	euch	you	euch	you	euer	her
sie	they	sie	them	ihnen	them	ihrer	them
Sie	you	Sie	you	Ihnen	you	Ihrer	them

The genitive forms are very rare, as the possessive adjectives (section 7.2) are usually used instead.

Exercise

A. Looking at the chart, what do you find confusing or difficult? What could result in problems?

B. Replace the underlined word with a fitting personal pronoun. Pay attention to the cases; there are two genitive forms in this exercise.

1. Die Geschichte finde ich langweilig.
2. Der Professor erklärt dem Studenten die Gleichung.

3. Das Kind brachte der Patientin einen Blumenstrauß.
4. Die Dozentin gab den Studenten den Test zurück.
5. Der Vater liebt <u>das Kind</u>.
6. Herr im Himmel, erbarme dich <u>der Kinder</u>.
7. <u>Die Frau</u> gibt <u>dem Mann</u> einen Blumenstrauß.
8. <u>Das Mädchen</u> sitzt dort drüben!
9. „<u>Der Tisch</u> ist bereits sehr alt", sagte <u>der Antiquitätenhändler</u> zu <u>der Kundin</u>.
10. <u>Meine Deutschlehrerin</u> bringt heute das schönste Weihnachtslied in <u>den Unterricht</u> mit.
11. Emmanuel Kant: Selbstverschuldet ist <u>Unmündigkeit</u>, wenn die Ursache nicht am Mangel des Verstandes, sondern der Entschließung und des Mutes liegt, sich <u>des Verstandes</u> ohne Leitung eines anderen zu bedienen.

10.2 Reflexive pronouns and reflexive verbs

An action is reflexive when the subject (the agent that is carrying out the action) and the object (the target of the action) are identical. Typically this sort of relationship is marked through the use of a reflexive pronoun.

Accusative:	*Ich sehe **mich** im Spiegel.*
	I see myself in the mirror.
Dative:	*Ich koche **mir** eine Suppe.*
	I cook a soup for myself.

German reflexive pronouns are inflected for accusative or dative, depending on the requirements of the verb. The plural forms are identical and the third person form *sich* is used for both singular and plural, which simplifies things a lot.

	Accusative – singular	Accusative – plural	Dative – singular	Dative – plural
First person (ich/wir)	mich	uns	mir	uns
Second person (du/ihr)	dich	euch	dir	euch
Third person (er/sie/es, sie & formal Sie)	sich	sich	sich	sich

What makes things more difficult (and quite frustrating for learners) is the abundance of reflexive verbs that have a reflexive pronoun as part of their conjugation, but are not translated reflexively.

Wir treffen uns am Bahnhof.
We meet ~~ourselves~~ each other at the train station.

Er freut sich auf das Konzert.
He is looking ~~himself~~ forward to the concert.

In the dictionary, such verbs are usually marked as *ref. V., r.v.* for *reflexives Verb*, or similar. Alternatively, the dictionary might simply add the reflexive pronoun *sich* to the entry.

For the translation, in most cases you can ignore the reflexive pronoun in such a sentence.

Examples of reflexive verbs that are not translated reflexively in English	
sich aufregen	to be upset
sich beeilen	to hurry
sich freuen	to be happy, rejoice
sich an etwas gewöhnen	to become used to something
sich irren	to err
sich um jemanden/etwas kümmern	to care for or look after someone or something
sich schämen	to be ashamed
sich nach etwas sehnen	to long for something
sich auf jemanden oder etwas verlassen	to rely on someone or something
sich weigern	to refuse

However, there are some verbs that change their meaning when they are used with a reflexive pronoun, for example *denken, erinnern, setzen, unterhalten, verlassen, verstehen, vorstellen.*

Er verlässt den Zug.	→	*Er verlässt sich auf den Zug.*
He leaves the train.	→	He is counting on the train.

Verbs that change meaning with a reflexive pronoun			
Without reflexive pronoun	Translation	With reflexive pronoun	Translation
beschweren	to weigh down, to burden	sich beschweren	to complain
denken	to think	sich denken	to imagine
enthalten	to contain	sich enthalten	to abstain

erinnern	to remind	sich erinnern	to remember
setzen	to place, set	sich setzen	to sit down
unterhalten	to entertain, sustain	sich unterhalten	to have a conversation
verlassen	to leave	sich auf etwas verlassen	to rely or count on something
verstehen	to understand	sich verstehen	to agree, get along
vorstellen	to introduce, present	sich vorstellen	with dative pronoun: to imagine

If Germans want to express a reflexive action and want to make absolutely sure it is understood as such, they will often add *selber* or *selbst* to the sentence (there's no difference between these two words). This way the listener can identify the reflexive nature of the action more easily.

> *Ich sehe mich im Spiegel. = Ich sehe mich selber im Spiegel.*
> I see myself in the mirror.

> *Er hat sich eingeladen. = Er hat sich selber eingeladen.*
> He has invited himself.

> *Ich wasche mir die Füße. = Ich wasche mir selbst die Füße.*
> I wash my feet myself.

 Getting to grips with reflexive verbs is predominantly a vocabulary exercise. Check the dictionary's entry whenever you are unsure how a reflexive pronoun affects the meaning of a sentence.

Exercise

Translate these sentences with the help of a dictionary.

1. Ein rechter Schütze hilft sich selbst. (from Wilhelm Tell by Friedrich Schiller)
2. Der brave Mann denkt an sich selbst zuletzt. (from Wilhelm Tell by Friedrich Schiller)
3. Er duscht sich jeden Tag.
4. Das Forschungsinstitut zieht nach Berlin um.
5. Der Schauspieler zieht sich um.
6. Stell dir vor, ich habe die Königin getroffen.
7. Stell mich bitte der Königin vor!
8. Holen wir uns noch ein Dessert?

9. Die Studenten freuen sich auf die Ferien.
10. Er hat sich seine Frage selbst beantwortet.
11. Erinnern Sie sich an die Vorgeschichte?
12. Haben Sie meinen Briefbeschwerer gesehen?

Vocabulary

ein rechter Schütze – a proper marksman

10.3 Appositions and phrases

A clause requires two components, a subject and a verb, in order to be complete. If a clause lacks either of these components it is incomplete and considered a phrase. Phrases are still separated by a comma from other clauses. Phrases are more common in spoken language and do not occur very often in written language. Most commonly they occur at the end of longer statements, because an author or speaker wants to add additional information to a statement.

> *Ich schlage vor, dass wir uns am Montag treffen, und zwar um acht Uhr.*
> I recommend that we meet on Monday, (in fact) at eight o'clock.

> *Ähnliche Beobachtungen wurden auch von anderen Forschern gemacht, z.B. Meyer et al (2014).*
> Similar observations were made by other scholars, e.g. Meyer et al (2014).

These sorts of additions are often introduced by *und zwar* or *z.B.* Since the previous clause was complete (the verbs *treffen* and *gemacht* signalled the ends of the clauses), a comma is inserted to separate any new information.

Appositions usually contain additional information that could have been placed in a longer relative clause, but hasn't been (most likely to keep the text shorter). Appositions usually consist of adjectives and nouns.

> *Das Buch, ein Harry-Potter-Roman, ist sehr spannend.*
> The book, a Harry Potter novel, is very exciting.

10.4 Summary of chapter

There are three points to summarise for this chapter.

1. Personal pronouns in German inflect with case and number. It is helpful to learn the translations of these.
2. Reflexive pronouns can be tricky. Often they can be ignored in a translation, sometimes they point to an action being reflexive (that otherwise

wouldn't be reflexive) and in some cases they change the meaning of an action. If you struggle with the comprehension of a sentence with a reflexive pronoun, it is best to check the dictionary entry for the verb. This can often clarify things.

3. Appositions and phrases are not "proper clauses," because they lack a subject and verb. They are often nested in a clause or at the end of a sentence. In both cases, commas will separate them.

Practice text: Glück im Unglück (1)

The following text is an adapted excerpt from a Spiegel Special dossier on the Cold War.

It contains a variety of linguistic features, among them prepositions, different tenses (including pluperfect), superlative, relative clauses, subordinate clauses, infinitive clauses and in general a fairly complex sentence structure where you will need to pay close attention to the cases of nouns.

The title is a German saying that does not relate to any particular part of the text.

Glück im Unglück

Nach dem Sieg über Hitler hatte das Bündnis der Westalliierten mit der Sowjetunion sein Ziel erreicht – und zerbrach. Zu groß waren die politisch-ideologischen Gegensätze gerade in Europa, dessen Osten Stalin seinem Imperium einverleibte. Anstatt zusammenzuarbeiten, wurden aus Partnern Feinde, es begann der Kalte Krieg.

Das besiegte Deutschland lag auch im Zentrum des Nachkriegsdramas – und machte in seinem westlichen Teil unter Führung von Kanzler Adenauer aus der Not eine Tugend. Der „Alte von Rhöndorf", wie seine Untertanen ihn mit anhänglichem Respekt nannten, war ein gewiefter Politiker. Dabei war Konrad Adenauer nicht gerade ein Meister ziselierter Rede. „Je einfacher denken", sagte er einmal, „ist oft eine wertvolle Gabe Gottes." Intellektuelle mögen sich geschüttelt haben, aber das einfache Volk verstand. Es verstand, dass es mit Adenauer aufwärts ging – und aufwärts hieß westwärts, einfach gedacht. Es verstand wohl auch, dass sich die Bundesrepublik ohne Adenauer vermutlich anders entwickelt <u>hätte</u> (would have). Vielleicht früh wiedervereinigt, aber dann nur zu Bedingungen Moskaus.

Adapted excerpt from: Bönisch, Georg (2008). "Glück im Unglück". In *SPIEGEL SPECIAL Geschichte. Der Kalte Krieg. Wie die Welt das Wettrüsten überlebte*. 3/2008. Spiegel Verlag. pp. 24–33.

Vocabulary

anhänglich – devoted, clingy
anstatt – instead of
aufwärts – upwards
Besatzungszone, die (-, -n) – occupied area
Bündnis, das (-ses, -se) – alliance
sich einverleiben (sep.v.) – to incorporate, swallow up
Feind, der (-(e)s, -e) – enemy
Gabe, die (-, -n) – gift, talent
Gegensatz, der (-es, Gegensätze) – contrast, opposition
gewieft– smart, crafty, experienced
Niederlage, die (-, -n) – defeat
sich schütteln – to shake, tremble, be agitated
Tugend, die (-, -en) – virtue
vermutlich – presumably, probably
wiedervereinigen (sep.v.) – to reunite
wohl auch – here: probably as well
ziseliert – chiselled, here: eloquent, detailed, nuanced

11 Prepositions; pronominal phrases; other uses of pronouns; word formation of nouns

11.1 Prepositions

German prepositions are relatively straightforward as long as you remember one thing: they do not translate very well. In general you will need to adapt translations to something suitable in English.

*Wir treffen uns **am** Bahnhof.*
We meet **at** the train station.

*Wir gehen **ins** Kino.*
We're going **to** the cinema.

There is usually no risk of misunderstanding a sentence due to a wrongly translated preposition.

 Prepositions are usually easy to deal with; they form one complete logical unit with the noun they refer to. If you look at any text you are working with as a puzzle that you have to assemble, prepositions are one puzzle piece that is easy to identify and to fit. The preposition will determine the case of the noun, though this usually doesn't matter to your translation. In a different metaphor you can view a prepositional phrase as a little isolated kingdom and the preposition as the gatekeeper.

*Wir wanderten **während des Gewitters**.*
We were hiking during the thunderstorm.

The phrase *während des Gewitters* is complete by itself and can be inserted anywhere in the complete puzzle that is your translation. *Während* is also an example of a preposition that does not have, unlike most prepositions, a locationary or directional sense, but a temporary one.

In German, prepositions are almost always placed before the noun they refer to. Words that can be placed between a preposition and the noun it refers to are usually: a determiner and/or an adjective. The big exception to this are participial constructions, which we'll deal with in chapter 14.

German prepositions fall into two categories: those with a fixed case (accusative, dative or genitive) and those with a flexible case depending on the situation (accusative or dative).

1. Common prepositions with genitive

The most common prepositions in this group are *dank*, *trotz*, *während* and *wegen*. Note that they are sometimes used with dative as well, especially in spoken German. Some genitive prepositions about locations will also be combined with the preposition *von*, effectively making it dative (because of the *von*; there are two examples of this among the exercises).

trotz	während	wegen
außerhalb	innerhalb	diesseits
jenseits	oberhalb	unterhalb
um... willen	dank	kraft

2. Common prepositions with dative

aus	außer	bei
gegenüber	mit	nach
seit	von	zu

3. Common prepositions with accusative

bis	durch	für
gegen	ohne	um
wider	entlang/lang	

The prepositions *entlang* and *lang* usually follow their nouns rather than precede them, although *entlang* can also precede a noun; it is then used with the genitive.

4. Prepositions with either accusative or dative

This is the smallest group of prepositions and the list here is complete; they occur very frequently in German. The dative case is used for stationary relationships or confined movements. The accusative is used for movements from one point to another, i.e. towards a specific goal. Interestingly, the prepositions *aus* and *zu* should logically go with accusative (because of the directional sense), but always go with dative.

an	auf	hinter
in	neben	über
unter	vor	zwischen

Long and short forms

Prepositions and articles can be compacted into one unit.

For example, *an dem* can be compacted to *am*. The m is a hint that the dative article *dem* was compacted with *an*. Another example would be *in das*, which can be compacted to *ins*. Again, the last letter (s) is the hint that the accusative article *das* was compacted with *in*.

Exercise

A. Look up the meaning of prepositions that you are unfamiliar with.
B. Contracted prepositions: work out the missing long forms (preposition + article) of the following prepositions. The bold line demarcates the beginning of colloquial forms (i.e. not "proper" German, but still used occasionally).

Short	Long	Short	Long
am	an dem	fürs	
ans		hinters	
beim		vorm	
im		unterm	
ins	in das	vors	
vom		übers	
zum		unters	
zur		hinterm	
hintern	hinter den	durchs	
ums		aufs	
untern		übern	

C. Translate these sentences.
   1. Statt eines Kanzlers haben wir in England einen Premier.
   2. Der Präsident steigt aus dem Auto.
   3. Anna blieb zwei Monate lang in der Entzugsklinik.
   4. Er kaufte ein Haus neben dem Haus seines Vaters.
   5. Haben Sie das Buch bei sich?
   6. Nach dem Essen trinken wir eine Tasse Tee.
   7. Die Luft wird immer verschmutzter wegen der vielen Autos.

8. Die ganze Klasse sitzt um einen Tisch.
9. Wir gehen ins Kino.
10. Die Sache liegt außerhalb meines Einflusses.
11. Wir treffen uns am Hauptbahnhof.
12. Das Römerlager lag diesseits des Rheins.
13. Sein Haus liegt außerhalb von Hamburg.
14. In seinem Werk „Jenseits von Gut und Böse" kritisiert Nietzsche veraltete Moralvorstellungen.
15. Peter fährt mit seinem Auto in den Parkplatz von Aldi.
16. Peter fährt mit seinem Auto im Parkplatz von Aldi.
17. Geh um Himmels willen nicht ohne deinen Regenschirm nach draußen.

Vocabulary

Entzugsklinik, die (-, -en) – rehab centre
veraltet – obsolete, outdated
verschmutzen – to pollute

D. Separable verbs and prepositions
    Sometimes a sentence can appear to have the same preposition twice (or simply too many). This is often due to a separable verb and not actually a preposition. There are sentences in C where this could have been done (but it has been omitted). Do you think you know in which sentences a separable verb could have been used to double up the prepositions and to make things clearer?

E. Implication for Reading Skills
    Look through the examples in C again. In which cases does the ability to determine the case of the preposition make a difference to the meaning of the sentence?

11.2 Pronominal adverbs

Words such as *davon, damit, darüber, hiermit, wovon, womit* are called pronominal adverbs. They bear resemblance to prepositions, but rather fulfil a pronominal role. They are formed by adding a prefix (da-, hier-, wo-) to a preposition. If the preposition begins with a vowel, the prefixes dar- or wor- are used instead.

In general, pronominal adverbs refer to the object or an action in either a previous or a following clause. They occur when a verb is typically used with a specific preposition (i.e. a phrasal verb), but this isn't followed up with a noun in the same clause. The noun or concept/action is then usually in the previous or next clause and the pronominal adverb links to this.

Here's an example where the pronominal adverb links to a noun in a previous clause.

> *Er hat **viele Probleme**. Wir haben lange **darüber** gesprochen.*
> He has many problems. We talked about it/them for a long time.

Compare this with an example where the link is in the next clause:

> *Er wartet **darauf**, dass die Sonne aufgeht.*
> He is waiting (for it/the fact) that the sun rises.

The verb *sprechen* (first example) is typically used with the preposition *über* when you want to express "to talk about something." Since the topic of the conversation is not explicitly mentioned in the second sentence, the dar- is added to the preposition and it signals to the reader that the topic is mentioned in an adjacent clause. The same could be achieved with a pronoun *(Wir haben lange über sie gesprochen.)*; it depends on the author or speaker which option he or she prefers. The only exception is that pronominal adverbs can only refer to things/ideas/thoughts; not to living beings.

Since the answer to the question "what is he waiting for?" (second example) is not given in the first clause, the *darauf* tells the reader that it will follow in the next clause. You could see this kind of pronominal adverb use as a subtle pointer for the reader that the answer/missing object will be found in the next clause.

How should I translate these pronominal adverbs?

When translating pronominal adverbs, you should try to find a suitable translation in English rather than a literal translation. Some pronominal adverbs can be rendered in English through constructions such as "for it/through the fact/in fact," but in general it is better to either not translate these pronominal adverbs at all, or to find a fitting English expression. As long as you remember that there is a link between the pronominal adverb and an object/action in another clause, and you can identify that link correctly, you should be able to interpret the sentence correctly.

> *Er hat sich **dadurch** diskreditiert, dass er eine frühere Veröffentlichung plagiiert hat.*
> He has discredited himself **by** plagiarising an earlier publication.

Exercise

Translate these sentences; try to find idiomatic expressions in English for the sentences with pronominal phrases.

1. Er hat Angst vor Spinnen.
2. Er hat Angst davor, dass Spinne ihn beißt.

3. Wir denken darüber nach, uns ein neues Auto zu kaufen.
4. Wir überlegen, uns ein neues Auto zu kaufen.
5. Machiavelli schreibt darüber, was für eine Art Herrscher länger an der Macht bleiben kann.
6. Machiavelli beschreibt, was für eine Art Herrscher sich länger an der Macht halten kann.
7. In meiner Dissertation beschäftige ich mich mit der Herrschaft der Habsburger in der Schweiz.
8. In meiner Dissertation geht es darum, wie die Herrschaft der Habsburger sich auf die Schweiz auswirkte.
9. Der Prophet spricht von dem Leben in der Zukunft.
10. Der Prophet spricht davon, wie man in der Zukunft lebt.

11.3 Other uses of determiners and pronouns

Words like *alle*, *viele*, *andere* can be used as determiners or pronouns. If used as a pronoun they are not capitalised.

> *Wir haben alles verloren.*
> We lost everything.

> *Trotzdem wollen viele immer mehr.*
> Still many always wants more.

Determiners such as *der*, *jeder*, *einer*, *mancher*, *wer*, *derjenige*, etc. can act as a pronoun, without any clear indication to which noun they refer. In these cases, additional words need to be added to make sense in English, for example "person" or "thing" if it is clear that this is what the pronoun implies. Otherwise, constructions such as "one," "the one," "he who," "she who" or "everyone," "someone," etc. need to be considered.

These forms occur most often in the masculine singular form, though feminine forms are possible. This type of construction is quite common in old sayings and rules or laws.

> *Einer, den wir beachten müssen, ist der Spieler auf der linken Seite.*
> One, whom we must watch, is the player on the left side. (*Einer* refers to *Spieler*, but this is not easily apparent.)

> *Der, der nichts zu verlieren hat, braucht die Niederlage nicht zu fürchten.*
> He who (The one who) has nothing to lose, does not have to fear defeat.

> *Wer stiehlt, ist zu bestrafen.*   A person who (Someone who) steals is to be punished.

Exercise

Translate these sentences.

1. Wer einmal lügt, dem glaubt man nicht.
2. Jeder kriegt, was er verdient.
3. Wer sich nicht selbst helfen will, dem kann niemand helfen. (Johann Heinrich Pestalozzi)
4. Ein Held ist einer, der tut, was er kann. Die anderen tun es nicht. (Romain Rolland)
5. Das, was wir aus Liebe tun, tun wir im höchsten Grade freiwillig. (Thomas von Aquin)
6. Ein jeder zählt nur sicher auf sich selbst. (from Wilhelm Tell by Friedrich Schiller)
7. Wer nicht mit mir ist, der ist wider mich. (from Wallenstein by Friedrich Schiller)
8. Jeder hat das Recht auf die freie Entfaltung seiner Persönlichkeit, soweit er nicht die Rechte anderer verletzt und nicht gegen die verfassungsmäßige Ordnung oder das Sittengesetz verstößt. (§2.1 German Basic Law)
9. Der, der ohne Sünde ist, soll den ersten Stein werfen. (This a simplified saying based on the Bible; compare it with the one in the introductory text to chapter 6).
10. Wer war Kaspar Hauser wirklich? Sein Fall war jedenfalls einer, der internationales Interesse erreichte.

Vocabulary

die verfassungsmäßige Ordnung – constitutional order
Sittengesetz, das (-es, -e) – moral law

11.4 Word formation of nouns

Have a look at the following words:

> *reinigen – das Reinigen – die Reinigung – die Reinheit – gereinigt – rein – das Reine – unrein – das Unreine – die Verunreinigung…*
>
> to clean – the cleaning – the cleaning/dry cleaner – purity – cleaned – pure – the pure – the impure – the impurity…

The words share a similar word stem – *rein* – and are related in meaning, yet they all have different meanings and are different types of words. In German, the relation between words is often quite visible and easy to identify. We will have a look here at some of the ways words are formed in German, with a focus on the creation of nouns. Many of these words' derivations have their own dictionary entry, but understanding the way these words are formed can be helpful and avoid confusion.

As a general rule, higher register texts tend to favour a nominal style (with many nouns) over a verbal style (that uses many verbs). You can expect to see more derived nouns in texts that were written by officials, academics and similar professionals.

Nominal style	Verbal style
Unsere Vorbereitung für die Konferenz hat begonnen. Our preparation for the conference has begun.	*Wir haben begonnen, uns für die Konferenz vorzubereiten.* We have started to prepare (ourselves) for the conference.
Die Durchsetzung der Regeln ist Priorität. The assertion of the rules is priority.	*Die Regeln müssen durchgesetzt werden.* The rules must be asserted.

Verb infinitives used as nouns

This is the most straightforward method of forming a noun out of a verb. The infinitive is capitalised to signal the new word type. These nouns are always neuter.

schwimmen – das Schwimmen
to swim – the swim/swimming

einkaufen – das Einkaufen
to shop – the (act of) shopping

Noun derivation through suffixes

Adding a suffix can turn almost any word into a noun. Common examples of such suffixes are -heit, -ung, -schaft, -erei, -nis.

dunkel – die Dunkelheit
dark – darkness

bearbeiten – die Bearbeitung
to process – the handling, processing

herrschen – die Herrschaft
to rule – the rule, sovereignty

wild – die Wildnis
wild – the wilderness

Diminutive forms are a special type of noun derivation used to show that something is a smaller version, or affection or belittlement (e.g. *das Männlein, das Häuschen*). If you want to know more about these forms, read the section in the appendix on diminutive forms (p. 207).

The suffixes -er/-ler/-ner usually denote a person who is doing something. These words are always masculine; the feminine forms would have an additional -in/-innen added to them.

>*fahren – der Fahrer*
>to drive – the driver

>*arbeiten – der Arbeiter*
>to work – the worker

>*die Kunst – der Künstler*
>the art – the artist

Suffixes ending in -ei (e.g. -erei, -lei) usually denote a repetitive action that is often – but not always – seen negatively.

>*hänseln – die Hänselei*
>to tease, pick on – the teasing

>*der Sklave – die Sklaverei*
>the slave – slavery

Adjectives used as nouns

Adjectives can be used as nouns as well. Their ending and gender depend on whether they are used to describe a person (masculine or feminine) or a thing/concept (neuter). If they are used to describe a person, it is often necessary to add "one" to the translation

>*der Alte* – the old one
>*die Grünen* – the green ones/the Green Party; a person from that party could be called either *die Grüne*, for a female person, or *der Grüne*, for a male person.
>*das Neue* – the new (thing)

Noun derivation through prefixes

Prefixes are less likely to change a word that is not a noun into a noun. They usually simply change the meaning of an existing noun.

Ge- can be used to create a noun of a repetitive activity, usually with a negative connotation.

>*reden – das Gerede*
>to talk – the chitchat

>*jammern – das Gejammere*
>to bemoan, lament – the moaning, lamenting

Erz-, Mit-, Nicht-, Un-, Ur-, Voll- are prefixes that have common meanings when applied to a word.

> *der Bewohner – der Mitbewohner*
> the inhabitant – the room- or housemate

> *der Schwimmer – der Nichtschwimmer*
> the swimmer – the non-swimmer

> *der Feind – der Erzfeind*
> the enemy – the arch enemy

> *das Ding – das Unding*
> the thing – the absurdity

Exercise

Which words are these examples derived from and how would you translate them?

1. das Unwetter
2. die Formalität
3. die Publikation
4. die Entscheidung
5. das Gezeter
6. die Schönheit
7. der Unfallfahrer
8. die Mitarbeiterinnen
9. die Rotverschiebung
10. die Schwarzmalerei
11. die Lautmalerei
12. das Eigentum
13. die Maskenbildnerin
14. die Vollmacht
15. die Exklusivität
16. der Urmensch
17. das Abstreiten
18. die Nichtakzeptanz

11.5 Summary of chapter

Here are five points to remember about this chapter.

1. Be flexible with the translation of German prepositions and look for a more idiomatic expression in English when required.
2. It is almost never important to know which case is used with a preposition.

3. Pronominal adverbs link sentences if the outcome/answer/response, etc. of an action is not given in the same but in an adjacent clause. They are often not needed in an English translation.
4. When determiners are used as pronouns on their own (i.e. with no reference to another noun), adding "one" or a contextual word (such as "person") to the translation is often necessary.
5. There is a great deal of flexibility in German when it comes to word formation. In order to avoid mistakes, pay attention to the word type, e.g. nouns (which are capitalised), verbs (position!) or adjectives.

Practice text: Ablasshandel

The following text deals with the practice of indulgences during the Middle Ages and Martin Luther's 95 Theses; the text features several elements from this chapter.

1. There are a number of difficult compound words in this text. If you are unsure of these, consult section 2.6 again.
2. There are a couple of tasks in the vocabulary section. Try to answer these before you attempt the translation of this text.

Ablasshandel

Vor dem Himmel kommt das Feuer – eine lange, schmerzhafte Reinigung von den aufgehäuften Sünden. Wer besondere Leistungen vollbrachte, konnte die Zeit im Fegefeuer verkürzen. Die Bescheinigung dafür war der Ablass: das Erlassen der Strafe für Sünden. Voraussetzung für den Straferlass war das Bekennen der Schuld in der Beichte.

Zusammen mit der Beichte bildete der Ablass eine Art Vertrag, der in Gottes Gericht wirksam wird. Ablässe wurden von der Kirche für Pilgerreisen, später auch gegen Geldzahlungen ausgegeben. Das Kaufen von Ablässen war attraktiv, doch es rief auch Protest hervor: Der Ablass sei (was) eine Anmaßung der Kirche. Nicht erst Luthers Reformbewegung fing hier an.

Der Ablass stammt aus einer Zeit, in der den Menschen bewusst war, dass sie unvollkommen sind und sich schuldig machen. Was konnte man also tun, um vor Gottes Gericht zu bestehen? Vorweggenommene Strafen durch Bußleistungen? Gute Taten, die über die Pflicht hinausgehen? Das Schuldbewusstsein des mittelalterlichen Menschen rechnete mit einem langen, schmerzhaften Feuer der Läuterung nach dem Tod. So wie Erz in der Schmelze gereinigt wird, reinigt das Fegefeuer die Seele, um in den Himmel eingehen zu können. Hier kann ein Ablass die Zeit verkürzen. Denn die Kirche besitzt einen Gnadenschatz: es sind die unzähligen guten Werke von Christus und den Heiligen, die alle weit mehr getan hatten, als zu ihrem eigenen Heil nötig war.

Die Kirche verstand sich als rechtmäßige Erbin Christi und aller Heiligen. Aus dieser Erbschaft speist sich der Ablass. Der Papst genoss das Privileg einen Generalablass auszugeben. Dieser war besonders attraktiv, denn er bedeutete nicht allein die Verkürzung der Fegefeuerstrafen, sondern die Erlösung jeglicher Feuerqual. Zur Zeit Martin Luthers konnte er gegen Geld an jedem Ort erwerben werden, an dem unter der Standarte des Papstes der Ablass verkündigt wurde – so auch bei Johann Tetzel in Jüterbog.

Besonders attraktiv war der Ablass des Johann Tetzel dadurch, dass er nach sozial gestaffelten Preisen ausgegeben wurde und auch für die Zukunft und für bereits Verstorbene galt. Hier setzte Luthers Kritik an: Der Papst und die Kirche haben, so Luther, keine Zugriffsmöglichkeiten auf die Seelen der Verstorbenen. Und welche Bedeutung hat Buße noch, wenn künftige Sünden schon „verrechnet" sind?

Adapted from: www.luther-tetzel-weg.de; published by: Pfarrer Bernhard Gutsche & Kirchengemeinde St. Nikolai Jüterbog.

Vocabulary tasks

- rechtmäßige Erbin Christi – rightful heir of Christ. Why is "Erbin" feminine?
- Bußleistung – This composite is not very common; try to find an adequate meaning.
- Gericht – This word has more than one meaning. Which one fits here?
- Gnadenschatz – The parts of this composite word are easily found in the dictionary, but what does it mean put together?
- rief – What is the infinitive of this?
- Schuldbewusstsein – The individual parts of this composite are easily found in a dictionary, but how would you translate the combination?
- verrechnen – This word has more than one meaning. Which one fits here?
- verstehen – You have probably already encountered this word before, but here it is used with *sich* and *als*. How can you translate this?
- vollbrachte – What is the infinitive of this word?

Vocabulary

Ablass, der (-es, Ablässe) – indulgence; in the teaching of the Roman Catholic Church, an indulgence is "a way to reduce the amount of punishment one has to undergo for sins"; in the Middle Ages this was through a financial transaction; in many cases it makes sense to translate it as plural in English even if it is singular in the German text.

anmaßen (sep.v.) – to assume/presume to do sth. (usually negative connotation)
Beichte, die (-,-n) – confession
etwas bekennen – to confess sth.
Bescheinigung, die (-,-en) – certification
Erlösung, die (-,-en) – deliverance, redemption, salvation
Erz in der Schmelze – ore in the furnace
etwas jmdm. erlassen – to exempt so. from sth., waive sth. for so.
Fegefeuer, das (-s,-) – purgatory [rel.]
Heil, das (-s, no plural) – salvation
künftig (auch: zukünftig) – future, in the future
Läuterung, die (-,-en) – cleaning, catharsis
Qual, die (-,-en) – pain, torture
schmerzhaft – painful
staffeln – to stagger, scale
Sünde, die (-n,-n) – sin
zugreifen (sep.v.) – to access sth., take hold
zwangsläufig – inevitably, unavoidably

12 Subjunctive I; reported speech

Der Student hat mir geschrieben, dass er krank sei.
The student wrote to me that he was sick.

Gott sei mit euch!
God be with you!

German has two subjunctive moods. In this chapter we will look at the uses of the subjunctive I.

12.1 Uses of the subjunctive I

The most common use of the subjunctive I is to express reported speech, i.e. when a statement from somebody else is reproduced. This use occurs mainly in high-quality news publications and academic writing, but it can also occur in less formal writing or even in speech. However, this is not the only use of the subjunctive I, it can also be used for giving advice or suggestions. Finally, while reported speech is the most common use for the subjunctive I, reported speech in German uses a mixture of the subjunctive I and subjunctive II forms for reported speech (this is explained further in 12.2). Here is quick contrast/summary of reported speech and subjunctive I.

Subjunctive I…	Reported speech…
…is most commonly used for reported speech.	…can be formed of both subjunctive I and subjunctive II forms.
…can be used to give advice or suggestions, or simply to express doubt and uncertainty.	…has some form of introduction that someone said/wrote/reported something.

1. Use of the subjunctive/reported speech to show distance (neutral citation or quote)

   *Professor X behauptet, er **habe** das Mutantengen gefunden.*
   Professor X claims, he found the mutant gene.

In this example, something is presented as the findings/view of somebody else. The author has not verified this and shows this by first introducing the clause with a typical introductory verb *(behauptet)* and second by using the subjunctive I form of *haben*. In formal writing, such as academic texts, reported speech occurs frequently and it usually does not carry any judgement or indication of doubt, but rather academic/journalistic/professional distance.

2. Use of subjunctive/reported speech to show doubt or uncertainty

Der Student hat mir geschrieben, dass er krank ist.
The student wrote to me that he is sick.

*Der Student hat mir geschrieben, dass er krank **sei**.*
The student wrote to me that he was sick.

The first example uses the indicative present tense form *ist* for the second clause. This indicates that the student is sick and that this is presented as a fact by the writer or speaker.

The second example uses the subjunctive I present tense form of *sein*, which is *sei*. This indicates that the information is relayed and not verified. Most importantly it is not presented as a fact and this creates some distance between the person making the claim (the student) and the person reproducing the message (the recipient of, presumably, an email). In a less formal setting, i.e. not a news item or an academic/high-quality publication, this would be seen by many as a sign that the author does not believe the student's claim. The setting in which this statement is done is therefore important.

In spoken German the subjunctive is rarely used except for the words *sei* and *seien;* as a result, if someone uses these highly recognisable words in spoken German, this will usually be seen as a conscious expression of doubt.

3. Subjunctive in older texts, church and recipes

In German, the subjunctive I is nowadays rarely used for anything other than reported speech. It used to be more commonly used for suggestions/advice and expressions of hope or when making predictions. You mostly find this use of the subjunctive I in older texts (usually around 100 years and more), in church sermons/prayers and in recipes.

*Man **nehme** eine Zwiebel und **hacke** diese…*
You shall/should take an onion and chop it…

*Vater unser im Himmel, geheiligt **werde** dein Name.*
Our Father in heaven, hallowed **be** thy name.

There is one idiomatic expression, *es sei gesagt*, which occurs more frequently. It can be translated as "it should be/needs to be said."

Reported speech in English

In English reported speech is often displayed by shifting the tense back. For example, the translation for the second sentence in part 2 could be "the student wrote me that he was sick." There is no other way to express the subjunctive I in English unless someone wants to insert words such as "allegedly, supposedly" or use the verb "claims" for a translation, in order to show clear distance between the claim. It is useful to remember that reported speech in both languages needs an introduction that someone said or wrote something, which helps to identify reported speech in English.

12.2 Subjunctive I forms in the present tense

There is a full set of conjugations for verbs in the present tense, but it is not used. You only need to know the following forms for the purpose of reading skills.

	sein	Any other verb, e.g. *haben*
3rd person singular	er/sie/es sei	er/sie/es habe (infintive stem + e)
3rd person plural	sie seien	Uses subjunctive II form for reported speech instead

The third person singular form of the subjunctive I is very regular for all verbs other than *sein*.

können	→ könn-	→ könne
Infinitive	Word stem	-e ending added

This means that even strong verbs that are irregular in their present tense singular form look like regular verbs in the subjunctive I (the 3rd person singular indicative form of *können* is *er/sie/es kann*).

Since 3rd person plural forms would look exactly like the indicative form for every verb other than *sein*, the subjunctive II form is used there (which will be looked at more closely in the next chapter).

Indicative: *Sie schreiben, dass sie die Hausaufgaben gemacht haben.*
They write that they have done the homework.

Subjunctive I (not used): *Sie schreiben, dass sie die Hausaufgaben gemacht haben.*

Reported speech: *Sie schreiben, dass sie die Hausaufgaben gemacht hätten.*
They write that they have (supposedly) done the homework.

Reported speech constructions are usually introduced by a short statement that makes it clear that the next statement is reported, such as "it is said, he wrote, they reported…" and similar. Here are some examples in German:

Der Spiegel schreibt, dass…
Frau Merkel sagte, sie…
Es wurde berichtet, dass…

This helps the reader understand that they are dealing with a report. Note that in German, these kinds of introduction can either be followed up by a subordinate clause (usually introduced by *dass*) or just a sequence of main clauses. Reported speech then continues typically for as long as the subjunctive I and II forms are used. Once the text reverts back to indicative forms, the quotation is usually over.

The first clue that you are dealing with a reported speech construction is usually context. Did someone start a clause with a statement that somebody said, replied, claimed, reported or wrote something? Check for these statements, as they will precede most reported speech passages.

12.3 Subjunctive I in the past tense

There is only one past tense for the subjunctive, which looks like a compound past. It is formed by combining a subjunctive I form of *haben* or *sein* with a past participle, similar to the indicative present perfect.

*Er hat mir geschrieben, dass er in Spanien **gewesen sei.***
He has written to me, that he had been in Spain.

*Die Nachrichten berichten, es **habe** neue Waldbrände in Kalifornien **gegeben.*** (Remember *es gibt*? This is the subjunctive I past tense form.)
The news reports, there have been new forest fires in California.

*Sie sagten, sie **hätten** das nicht **gewusst**.* (Remember: the subjunctive II forms are used for 3rd person plural reported speech, so we have *hätten* here instead of *haben*.)

They said, they hadn't known that.

Exercise

A. Which sentences are indicative; which are subjunctive?

	Indicative	Subjunctive
1. Er werde uns morgen anrufen.		
2. Der Dieb wird von der Polizei gesucht.		
3. Die Suppe ist stark gewürzt.		
4. Die Regeln seien ungerecht.		
5. Der Richter lege sein Amt nieder.		
6. Die Angeklagten hätten niemals ausgesagt.		

B. All of these sentences contain a subjunctive form; can you identify its use and translate them?

	Reported speech – neutral	Reported speech – doubt	Advice or suggestion
1. Albert Einstein sagte einst, Fantasie sei wichtiger als Wissen, denn Wissen sei begrenzt.			
2. Drum prüfe, wer sich ewig bindet, Ob sich das Herz zum Herzen findet. Der Wahn ist kurz, die Reu' ist lang. (Friedrich Schiller)			
3. Der Angeklagte behauptet, er habe kein Geld vom Kläger gestohlen.			
4. Die Zeitung berichtet, dass die Bundeskanzlerin ihre Teilnahme an dem Wirtschaftsgipfel abgesagt habe.			

5. Du hast mir eine kostbare Stunde gestohlen, sie werde dir an deinem Leben abgezogen! (from Die Räuber by Friedrich Schiller)			
6. Lang lebe der König!			
7. Der Student schrieb mir, er könne nicht an der Prüfung teilnehmen, weil er krank sei.			
8. Ohne eine Unterschrift könne der Scheck nicht eingelöst werden, sagte mir die Frau von der Bank am Schalter.			

Vocabulary

aussagen (sep.v.) – to give testimony, bear witness, predicate
drum – therefore, for that reason; the modern form is *darum*
prüfen – to investigate, check, test; here: question
Reue, die (-, no plural) – repentance, remorse
stehlen – to steal
teilnehmen (sep.v.) – to participate
Unterschrift, die (-, -en) – signature

Untrue statements in the past

When discussing a matter that is known to be factually incorrect, or a statement that is now known to be untrue, the reported speech in the past tense is usually the correct way of expressing this. The following example explains this:

> *Die sowjetische Regierung behauptete bis 1990, dass das Massaker im polnischen Katyn von deutschen Soldaten verübt worden **sei**.*
> The Soviet government claimed until 1990 that the massacre in Katyn in Poland had been perpetrated by German soldiers.

Because we now know that German soldiers did not carry out the massacre in Katyn – it was admitted by the Soviet government in 1990 – we couldn't use an indicative form for this statement. We have to use reported speech in the past tense for this statement.

12.4 Subjunctive I in the passive voice

The subjunctive I is easily combined with the passive. The indicative forms of the auxiliary verb are simply replaced by a subjunctive I form.

> *Die Nachrichten berichten, die Brücke **werde** heute wieder geöffnet.*
> The news reports the bridge will be opened again today.

> *Er sagte, der Artikel **sei** veröffentlicht worden.*
> He said the text had been published.

Practice text: Glück im Unglück (2)

In chapter 10 we looked at the first two paragraphs of this text; here is more of the same text. If you have already translated the first two paragraphs back in chapter 10, reread your translation before you continue with the new parts.

Glück im Unglück

Eines aber begriffen die meisten Menschen nicht: dass ihr Kanzler nur wenige Jahre nach dem Ende des Zweiten Weltkriegs, nach der totalen Niederlage, nach der völligen moralischen Diskreditierung durch die Verbrechen des Hitler-Regimes, davon sprach, dass das Land wieder Soldaten brauche. Adenauer, der nie als Soldat gedient hatte, trieb die Planungen für den Aufbau einer Armee zügig voran. Er scheute sich nicht, diese Arbeit einer kleinen Behörde zu übertragen, die eine Art Tarnnamen trug: „Zentrale für den Heimatdienst", ZfH.

Schon in seiner ersten Grundsatzrede als Vorsitzender der CDU in der britischen Besatzungszone, am 24. März 1946, hatte Adenauer konstatiert, Staat und Macht seien untrennbar verbunden, und Macht zeige sich am „sinnfälligsten und eindrucksvollsten" im Heer. Dieser Ton musste den Strategen der US-Armee durchaus gefallen haben. Denn sie spielten schon früh mit dem Gedanken, Deutschlands Armee wiederaufzubauen, um sie schnell in ein westeuropäisches System zu integrieren.

Adapted excerpt from: Bönisch, Georg (2008). "Glück im Unglück". In *SPIEGEL SPECIAL Geschichte. Der Kalte Krieg. Wie die Welt das Wettrüsten überlebte.* 3/2008. Spiegel Verlag. pp. 24–33.

Vocabulary

begreifen – to grasp, recognise, understand
Gedanke, der (-n, -n) – thought, idea
dienen – to serve
durchaus – quite, definitely, by all means
eindrucksvoll – impressive
gewieft – smart, crafty
sinnfällig – evident, obvious
übertragen – to transfer
untrennbar – inseparable
vorantreiben (sep.v.)– to push on/forward, to advance sth.

13 Subjunctive II; conditional sentences

The subjunctive II is used for dreams, wishes and hypothetical statements and, in the past tense, when talking about options in the past that are no longer valid. All of these statements have one thing in common: they are not factually true. For this reason, the subjunctive II forms are referred to as non-factual verb forms.

Indicative	Subjunctive II
Ich habe viel Geld. I have a lot of money. → Fact: I have a lot of money!	*Ich hätte gerne viel Geld.* I would like to have a lot of money. → Wish/dream: I do not have a lot of money.
Du rennst, weil die Polizei hinter dir her ist. You're running, because the police are after you. → Fact: The police are hard on your heels!	*Du rennst, als ob die Polizei hinter dir her wäre.* You're running as if the police were after you/in pursuit of you. → *Irrealer Vergleich* (unreal comparison): You're (only) running very fast.

In addition, the subjunctive II can also be used for polite statements and for reported speech. The polite forms are not used that much nowadays, but you will still hear them from time to time.

***Könnten** Sie bitte das Fenster aufmachen?*
Could you please open the window?

***Wärest** du so freundlich und **würdest** du bitte endlich die Musik ausmachen?*
Could you be so nice and finally turn the music off?

13.1 Subjunctive II forms

Every German verb has a subjunctive II form. These are either regular or irregular.

Weak verbs: indicative and subjunctive II forms

ich kaufe – ich kaufte	wir kaufen – wir kauften
du kaufst – du kauftest	ihr kauft – ihr kauftet
er/sie/es/man kauft – er/sie/es/man kaufte	sie/Sie kaufen – sie/Sie kauften

You will probably have noticed that these regular subjunctive II forms look exactly like the preterite forms. For this reason, they are rarely used. They can be very confusing and one can only understand from context whether such a form is preterite or the subjunctive II.

If you consider the sentence:

Er kaufte ein neues Auto.

Most people will translate this as "he bought a new car," assuming it is the much more common preterite tense. But if this is combined for example with a conditional clause, the context will point towards it being the subjunctive II:

Wenn er Geld hätte, kaufte er ein neues Auto.

This sentence would now be translated as "If he had money, he would buy a new car." It is still not very satisfying in terms of clarity and for that reason, Germans tend to express the subjunctive II with *würde* plus the infinitive of the verb instead (we'll explain that in a moment).

Strong verbs often have an umlaut added to them. Some examples of common verbs (3rd person singular) follow. The 3rd person singular form of the subjunctive also has an -e added to it, which helps distinguish it from the preterite form, where no ending is added to strong verbs. Except for the umlauts, the plural forms of the subjunctive II and the preterite look identical.

er nimmt – er nähme
er geht – er ginge

er findet – er fände
er bringt – er brächte
er kommt – er käme
er leidet – er litte
er liegt – er läge
er sieht – er sähe

and the modal verbs:

er kann – er könnte
er will – er wollte (same as preterite)
er soll – er sollte (same as preterite)
er darf – er dürfte
er muss – er müsste
er möge – er möchte
er wird – er würde

In most cases, strong verbs are easily recognisable as the subjunctive II, as the umlaut and the extra -e make them look different from the preterite forms.

Subjunctive II expressed with würde/translation in English

Every German verb can be also be expressed by using the subjunctive II form of *werden*: *würde* and the verb's infinitive. There is no difference in meaning between these forms.

In English, the subjunctive II is translated with "would," except for *wäre*, which is either "were" or "would be," *hätte*, which is "would have," *könnte*, which is "could," and *sollte*, which is "should."

1. Strong verbs
   Er tränke ein Bier.   =   *Er würde ein Bier trinken.*

   He would drink a beer.

2. Auxiliary verbs/modal verbs
   Er wäre König von England.   =   *Er würde der König von England sein.*

   He would be the king of England.
   Ich könnte das Haus kaufen.   =   *Ich würde das Haus kaufen können.*

   He could buy the house/he would be able to buy the house.

3. Weak verbs
   Er produzierte einen Film.   =   *Er würde einen Film produzieren.*

   He would produce a movie.

There is no difference in quality of expression or meaning. While Germans nowadays favour the *würde* + infinitive variant most of the time, you should be prepared to encounter more of the strong and weak versions without *würde* in older texts.

Commonly used subjunctive II forms

There are a few subjunctive II forms that you should know by heart and be able to recognise. These are *wäre*, *hätte*, *würde* and the modal verbs.

A few additional common strong verbs are listed here, but learning them by heart is not necessary.

wäre (would be)

	Singular		Plural			Singular		Plural	
1. Person	ich	wäre	wir	wären	1. Person	I	would be	we	would be
2. Person	du	wärst/ wärest	ihr	wäret	2. Person	you	would be	you	would be
3. Person	er/sie/ es	wäre	sie/Sie	wären	3. Person	he/she/it	would be	they/ you	would be

hätte (would have)

	Singular		Plural			Singular		Plural	
1. Person	ich	hätte	wir	hätten	1. Person	I	would have	we	would have
2. Person	du	hättest	ihr	hättet	2. Person	you	would have	you	would have
3. Person	er/sie/es	hätte	sie/Sie	hätten	3. Person	he/she/it	would have	they/ you	would have

würde (would)

	Singular		Plural			Singular		Plural	
1. Person	ich	würde	wir	würden	1. Person	I	would	we	would
2. Person	du	würdest	ihr	würdet	2. Person	you	would	you	would
3. Person	er/sie/ es	würde	sie/Sie	würden	3. Person	he/she/it	would	they/ you	would

Modal verbs

	könnten		wollen		sollen	
	Singular	Plural	Singular	Plural	Singular	Plural
1. Person	ich könnte	wir könnten	ich wollte	wir wollten	ich sollte	wir sollten
2. Person	du könntest	ihr könntet	du wolltest	ihr wolltet	du solltest	ihr solltet
3. Person	er/sie/es könnte	sie könnten	er/sie/es wollte	sie wollten	er/sie/es sollte	sie sollten

	dürfen		müssen		mögen	
	Singular	Plural	Singular	Plural	Singular	Plural
1. Person	ich dürfte	wir dürften	ich müsste	wir müssten	ich möchte	wir möchten
2. Person	du dürftest	ihr dürftet	du müsstest	ihr müsstet	du möchtest	ihr möchtet
3. Person	er/sie/es dürfte	sie dürften	er/sie/es müsste	sie müssten	er/sie/es möchte	sie möchten

Common irregular verbs *sehen, nehmen, gehen*

	sehen		nehmen		gehen	
	Singular	Plural	Singular	Plural	Singular	Plural
1. Person	ich sähe	wir sähen	ich nähme	wir nähmen	ich ginge	wir gingen
2. Person	du sähest	ihr sähet	du nähmest	ihr nähmet	du gingest	ihr ginget
3. Person	er/sie/es sähe	sie sähen	er/sie/es nähme	sie nähmen	er/sie/es ginge	sie gingen

Regular verbs *kaufen, arbeiten,* with and without *würde*

	kaufen		arbeiten	
	Singular	Plural	Singular	Plural
1. Person	ich kaufte	wir kauften	ich arbeitete	wir arbeiteten
2. Person	du kauftest	ihr kauftet	du arbeitest	ihr arbeitetet
3. Person	er/sie/es kaufte	sie kauften	er/sie/es arbeitete	sie arbeiteten

	würde + kaufen		würde + arbeiten	
	Singular	Plural	Singular	Plural
1. Person	ich würde kaufen	wir würden kaufen	ich würde arbeiten	wir würden arbeiten
2. Person	du würdest kaufen	ihr würdet kaufen	du würdest arbeiten	ihr würdet arbeiten
3. Person	er/sie/es würde kaufen	sie würden kaufen	er/sie/es würde arbeiten	sie würden arbeiten

Exercise

Identify the following forms. Which are indicative, which are subjunctive and which could be either preterite or the subjunctive II? The second example has two clauses, but uses the same mood in both clauses.

	Indicative	Both possible (preterite or subj. II)	Subj. II
1. Er arbeitete in einem Steinbruch.			
2. Wäre ich König, müsste ich nicht mehr jeden Morgen früh aufstehen.			
3. Wilhelm arbeitet in einem Büro.			
4. Der Artikel müsste noch dieses Jahr erscheinen.			
5. Wissenschaftler dürfen die Artikel dieses Journals nur online lesen und nicht ausdrucken.			
6. Viele Freiwillige nahmen an dem Experiment teil.			
7. Die Ergebnisse der Untersuchung erschienen in einem Onlinejournal.			
8. In den 1970er Jahren mussten Wissenschaftler alle Forschungsergebnisse in Printform lesen.			
9. Die Ergebnisse kamen nicht an.			

Vocabulary

ankommen (sep.v.) – to arrive
aufstehen (sep.v.) – to get up, to get out of bed
ausdrucken (sep.v.) – to print out
Steinbruch, der (-(e)s, Steinbrüche) – quarry

13.2 Subjunctive II in the past tense

Similar to the subjunctive I, there is only one past tense for subjunctive II, which looks like a compound past. It is formed by combining a subjunctive II form of *haben* or *sein* with a past participle, just as you would for the indicative present perfect.

The biggest difference is in meaning: the subjunctive II is used to make non-factual statements such as wishes and dreams, and the past tense of the subjunctive expresses options that are no longer possible, because for example the moment has passed.

> *Wenn ich Medizin **studiert hätte, wäre ich Arzt geworden**.*
> If I had studied medicine, I would have become a doctor.

13.3 Subjunctive II used for reported speech

As mentioned in chapter 12, reported speech in German uses subjunctive forms. When the indicative and the subjunctive I are indistinguishable, the subjunctive II form is used instead. This is always the case for the 3rd person plural forms of any verb other than the verb *sein*. This will impact on the translation. Take the following example:

> *Meine Eltern hätten ihr Haus verkauft.*
> My parents **would have** sold their house.

Without any introduction we would assume it is the subjunctive II and would translate *hätten* as "would have." However, if the example is preceded by an introductory clause that this is reported, we translate it differently, in this case with "had."

> *Mein Bruder behauptet, meine Eltern hätten ihr Haus verkauft.*
> My brother claimed (that) my parents **had** sold their house.

Identifying reported speech is therefore vital to get the correct meaning.

Exercise

Which forms are the subjunctive II and would be translated as such, e.g. with would/were/should/could...? Which are reported speech and which are indicative? Tick the correct box. In some cases, you can tick more than one box.

	Indicative	Subj. I/ II used as reported speech	Subj. II
1. Wäre ich der König von England, hätte ich viele Aufgaben.			
2. Mein Bruder hatte ein Ferienhaus auf Mallorca.			
3. Mein Bruder hätte gerne ein Ferienhaus auf Mallorca.			
4. Das müsste funktionieren.			
5. Sie hätten Italien besucht, wenn sie Geld für das Hotel gehabt hätten.			
6. Sie sagten, sie hätten Italien besucht.			
7. Der Spion durfte nicht in das Regierungsgebäude.			
8. Viele Kinder mussten in der Schule früher Latein lernen.			
9. Meine Frau wollte nicht nach Italien in Urlaub fahren.			
10. Man sagt, einem Dieb dürfe man nicht vertrauen.			
11. Diesen Dialekt könnten sie nicht verstehen, meinten die Studenten.			
12. Viele Menschen könnten mehr für die Umwelt tun.			

Vocabulary

Gebäude, das (-s, -) – building
Umwelt, die (-, -en) – environment

13.4 Subjunctive II in the passive voice

Like the subjunctive I, the subjunctive II is easily combined with the passive. The indicative forms of the auxiliary verb are simply replaced by a subjunctive II form.

Eine solche Biographie **würde** *nie gedruckt werden.* (The infinitive form of *werden* here stresses the future tense; *würde* plus *gedruckt* express the passive voice.)
Such a biography would never be printed.

Eine solche Biographie **wäre** *nie gedruckt worden.*
Such a biography would have never been printed.

Das **hätte** *nie veröffentlicht werden dürfen!*
That should have never been published!

13.5 Unreal comparative clauses

Er rannte, als ob der Teufel hinter ihm her wäre.
He ran, as if the devil was after him.

An unreal comparative clause is used for a comparison that is not true/real. If you look at the example just given, most people will understand right away that this comparison is not real (whether you believe in the devil or not). The comparative particle here is translated as "as if" to express this comparison. Note that *als ob* facilitates this understanding.

Sie tut so, als wäre sie etwas Besseres.
She acts (in such a way), as if she was something better (as if she was better than them/stands above them).

Two things are different in this sentence. First, a *so* has been added to the first clause as a linking word. You could translate this as "in such a way," but this can usually be omitted in English. In German it is usually added to make the reader/listener aware that a comparison is coming in the next part (i.e. it links the sentences logically together).

The second thing that has happened is that *wäre* has moved to the second position – which it shouldn't have! You would have expected it at the end of the clause in the fourth position. This is an idiomatic expression and an irregularity in German syntax that only occurs if *als* is used in this way without *ob*. Fortunately, you will only encounter this with these type of clauses.

Finally, *wie wenn* works exactly the same way as *als ob*.
There is no meaning difference between:

Sie tut so, als wäre sie etwas Besseres.
Sie tut so, als ob sie etwas Besseres wäre.
Sie tut so, wie wenn sie etwas Besseres wäre.

All three are translated as "she acts (in such a way), as if she was something better."

Exercise

Translate these sentences.

1. Manche Politiker lügen, als ob ihr Leben davon abhinge.
2. Er rennt, wie wenn er von der Tarantel gestochen wäre.[1]
3. Das Insekt legt sich reglos hin, als wäre es tot.

Vocabulary

von etwas abhängen (sep.v.) – to depend on sth.
reglos – motionless
stechen – to sting

13.6 Conditional sentences

As the name implies, a conditional sentence describes what action or consequence takes place if a certain condition is met. What makes these types of constructions unique is that they consist of two parts – the condition and the consequence. Conditional sentences can use either the subjunctive or the indicative.

The most basic conditional sentence begins with a *wenn* and uses a linking word such as *dann* to show the consequence.

> *Wenn es Samstag wäre, dann könnte ich lange schlafen.*
> If it were Saturday, then I could sleep long.

To shorten the sentence, the linking word is often omitted.

> *Wenn es Samstag wäre, könnte ich lange schlafen.*
> If it were Saturday, I could sleep long.

One specialty of these constructions, which is mirrored in English, is that the *wenn* can be omitted as well, if the verb is placed in the first position of the sentence.

> *Wäre es Samstag, könnte ich lange schlafen.*
> Were it Saturday, I could sleep long.

This is similar to questions and commands: placing the verb in the very start of the sentence alerts the listener or reader that a special construction is coming that is not a normal statement. The order of the two clauses can also be reversed, regardless of whether *wenn* is used or not:

> *Ich könnte lange schlafen, wäre es Samstag.*
> I could sleep long, were it Saturday.

Indicative vs. subjunctive in conditional sentences

The indicative is used in conditional sentences to describe rules or outcomes that are always true if the condition is met.

> *Immer wenn es regnet, werden die Straßen nass.*
> Whenever it rains, the streets get wet.

The statement is always true, as when it rains, streets will definitely get wet. The use of *immer wenn* further strengthens this aspect of something that is always true. A subtler example is:

> *Wenn es kalt ist, ziehe ich meine Jacke an.*
> If it is cold, I put on my jacket.

This is a very reasonable statement; we understand that if it is cold, it is a natural action to put on one's jacket. Therefore it is logical to put this in the indicative. Compare this with the subjunctive II version:

> *Wenn es kalt wäre, würde ich meine Jacke anziehen.*
> If it were cold, I would put my jacket on.

There is a very important difference to the previous example. In the subjunctive version, we have to assume that it is not cold, because the subjunctive always expresses something that is not real, either because it is impossible, cannot happen anymore or simply hasn't happened yet. Therefore we can phrase the meaning like this: "If it were cold, I would put my jacket on, but it isn't actually cold, so I won't put my jacket on."

If you struggle with the difference between conditional sentences using the indicative and the subjunctive, it is very helpful to fall back on this and to remind yourself that the subjunctive is a non-factual form, expressing something that is not true.

Sogar wenn, selbst wenn, falls

These forms occur most often with conditional sentences. They are variations of the typical *wenn – dann* structure.

Sogar wenn and *selbst wenn* have no difference in meaning; they simply intensify the condition by saying "even if."

> *Sogar wenn ich eine Gehaltserhöhung bekomme, habe ich nicht genug Geld zum Leben.*
> Even if I get a (salary) raise, I won't have enough money to live.

Falls can be translated as "in case." In some cases this makes more sense than *wenn* ("if").

> *Falls morgen die Sonne scheint, sollten wir eine Stunde früher in den Park gehen, weil es sehr voll werden wird.*
> In case the sun shines tomorrow, we should go to the park an hour earlier, because it will get very full.

Exercise

Translate these conditional sentences. Which ones are the indicative and which ones are the subjunctive and how does this affect your understanding of what they express?

1. Wenn es dunkel ist, geht die Notbeleuchtung an.
2. Mischt man Wasserstoffperoxid mit Trockenhefe, erhält man eine überraschende Reaktion.
3. Selbst wenn du der letzte Mensch auf der Erde wärest, würde ich nicht auf ein Date mit dir gehen.
4. Ich würde den Fisch bestellen, wäre er nicht so teuer.
5. Viele Menschen können sich ihre Hypothek nicht mehr leisten, wenn die Notenbank die Zinsen weiter erhöht.
6. Falls ich morgen nicht da bin, bitte ich Sie, an der neuen Unternehmensvision zu arbeiten.

Vocabulary

Hypothek, die (-, -en) – mortgage
Notenbank, die (-, -en) – central bank
Trockenhefe, die (-, -n) – dry yeast
Zins, der (-es, -en) – (financial) interest (almost always used in plural)

Practice text: **Wenn die Haifische Menschen wären**

This is a longer text exercise that is split into three parts. The first part looks only at a few selected verbs; the second part then focuses on translation of the text. A third part offers some comprehension questions related to the text. *Wenn die Haifische Menschen wären* is a parable by Bertolt Brecht, published as part of his *Geschichten von Herrn Keuner*. Brecht wrote these parables over a period of 30 years. The complete collection was published in 1956.

A. Preparation exercise for translation

Here are some examples from the text that will help you with the translation later on. Please write in the "Grammar" box any information you find helpful, such as the indicative, subjunctive I, subjunctive II, active or passive voice.

Line	Sentence	Grammar	Translation
1	Wenn die Haifische Menschen wären…		
3–4	[Sie] würden bauen.		
5	Sie würden dafür sorgen, dass…		
8	Wenn er sich verletzen würde,…		
8–9	Es würde gemacht.		
10	Es gäbe Feste.		
13–14	Sie würden brauchen.		
15	Sie könnten finden.		
16	Sie würden unterrichtet werden,		
17	…, dass es das Größte sei, …		
17–18	…, wenn es sich aufopfert.		
28	Der Unterschied bestehe.		
29	Sie sind stumm und schweigen.		
32	Er tötete.		
41	Sie strömten in die Haifischrachen.		
44	Es würde auch aufhören.		
47	Sie dürften die kleineren Fischlein auffressen.		

B. Translate the text.

1	«Wenn die Haifische Menschen wären», fragte Herrn K. die kleine
2	Tochter seiner Wirtin, «wären sie dann netter zu den kleinen Fischen?»
3	«Sicher», sagte er. «Wenn die Haifische Menschen wären, würden sie im
4	Meer für die kleinen Fische gewaltige Kästen bauen lassen, mit allerhand
5	Nahrung drin, sowohl Pflanzen als auch Tierzeug. Sie würden sorgen,
6	daß die Kästen immer frisches Wasser hätten, und sie würden überhaupt
7	allerhand sanitäre Maßnahmen treffen. Wenn zum Beispiel ein Fischlein
8	sich die Flosse verletzen würde, dann würde ihm sogleich ein Verband
9	gemacht, damit es den Haifischen nicht wegstürbe vor der Zeit. Damit die
10	Fischlein nicht trübsinnig würden, gäbe es ab und zu große Wasserfeste;
11	denn lustige Fischlein schmecken besser als trübsinnige. Es gäbe natürlich
12	auch Schulen in den großen Kästen. In diesen Schulen würden die Fischlein
13	lernen, wie man in den Rachen der Haifische schwimmt. Sie würden zum
14	Beispiel Geographie brauchen, damit sie die großen Haifische, die faul
15	irgendwo liegen, finden könnten. Die Hauptsache wäre natürlich die
16	moralische Ausbildung der Fischlein. Sie würden unterrichtet werden,
17	daß es das Größte und Schönste sei, wenn ein Fischlein sich freudig
18	aufopfert, und daß sie alle an die Haifische glauben müßten, vor allem,
19	wenn sie sagten, sie würden für eine schöne Zukunft sorgen. Man würde
20	den Fischlein beibringen, daß diese Zukunft nur gesichert sei, wenn sie
21	Gehorsam lernten. Vor allen niedrigen, materialistischen, egoistischen
22	und marxistischen Neigungen müßten sich die Fischlein hüten und es
23	sofort den Haifischen melden, wenn eines von ihnen solche Neigungen
24	verriete. Wenn die Haifische Menschen wären, würden sie natürlich auch
25	untereinander Kriege führen, um fremde Fischkästen und fremde Fischlein
26	zu erobern. Die Kriege würden sie von ihren eigenen Fischlein führen lassen.
27	Sie würden die Fischlein lehren, daß zwischen ihnen und den Fischlein der
28	anderen Haifische ein riesiger Unterschied bestehe. Die Fischlein, würden
29	sie verkünden, sind bekanntlich stumm, aber sie schweigen in ganz
30	verschiedenen Sprachen und können einander daher unmöglich verstehen.
31	Jedem Fischlein, das im Krieg ein paar andere Fischlein, feindliche, in
32	anderer Sprache schweigende Fischlein tötete, würden sie einen kleinen
33	Orden aus Seetang anheften und den Titel Held verleihen. Wenn die
34	Haifische Menschen wären, gäbe es bei ihnen natürlich auch eine Kunst.
35	Es gäbe schöne Bilder, auf denen die Zähne der Haifische in prächtigen
36	Farben, ihre Rachen als reine Lustgärten, in denen es sich prächtig
37	tummeln läßt, dargestellt wären. Die Theater auf dem Meeresgrund
38	würden zeigen, wie heldenmütige Fischlein begeistert in die Haifischrachen
39	schwimmen, und die Musik wäre so schön, daß die Fischlein unter
40	ihren Klängen, die Kapelle voran, träumerisch, und in allerangenehmste
41	Gedanken eingelullt, in die Haifischrachen strömten. Auch eine
42	Religion gäbe es ja, wenn die Haifische Menschen wären. Sie würde
43	lehren, daß die Fischlein erst im Bauch der Haifische richtig zu leben

44	begännen. Übrigens würde es auch aufhören, wenn die Haifische
45	Menschen wären, daß alle Fischlein, wie es jetzt ist, gleich sind. Einige von
46	ihnen würden Ämter bekommen und über die anderen gesetzt werden.
47	Die ein wenig größeren dürften sogar die kleineren auffressen. Das wäre
48	für die Haifische nur angenehm, da sie dann selber öfter größere Brocken
49	zu fressen bekämen. Und die größern, Posten habenden Fischlein würden
50	für die Ordnung unter den Fischlein sorgen, Lehrer, Offiziere, Ingenieure
51	im Kastenbau usw. werden. Kurz, es gäbe überhaupt erst eine Kultur im
52	Meer, wenn die Haifische Menschen wären.»

Brecht, Bertolt (1995). *Werke. Große kommentierte Berliner und Frankfurter Ausgabe,* Band 18: Prosa 3. Bertolt-Brecht-Erben/Suhrkamp Verlag.

Vocabulary

allerhand – all kinds of
Amt, das (-(e)s, Ämter) – office, official position
angenehm – pleasant, enjoyable, preferable
anheften (sep.v.) – to pin
auffressen (sep.v.) – to eat up
aufhören (sep.v.) – to end, stop
sich aufopfern (sep.v.) – to sacrifice oneself
Bauch, der (-(e)s, Bäuche) – belly
begeistert – enthusiastic
jmdm. etwas beibringen (sep.v.)– to teach sth. to so.
bekanntlich – generally well-known
einlullen (sep.v.) – to lull
erobern – to conquer
faul – lazy
feindlich – hostile
Flosse, die (-, -n) – fin
fremd – foreign, alien
freudig – cheerful, happily
Gehorsam, der (-s, no plural) – obedience
gewaltig – enormous
Haifisch, der (-s, -e) – shark
Hauptsache, die (-, -n) – the main thing
Held, der (-en, -en) – hero
sich vor etwas hüten – to beware of sth.
Kapelle, die (-, -n) – chapel, here: band, orchestra
Kasten, der (-s, Kästen) – box
Klang, der (-(e)s, Klänge) – sound
lehren – to teach
lustig – cheerful, funny, happy
Meer, das (-(e)s, -e) – sea, ocean
melden – to report
Neigung, die (-, -en) – inclination

nett – nice
niedrig – low, base
Orden, der (-s, -) – medal
Rachen, der (-s, -) – throat, jaws
riesig – huge
schweigen – to be silent
Seetang, der (-s, -e) – seaweed
sichern – to secure, ensure
sogleich – immediately
für etwas sorgen – to take care of sth.
strömen – to stream
stumm – mute, silent
träumen – to dream → träumerisch – dreamily
trübsinnig – melancholic
überhaupt – actually (can sometimes be omitted)
übrigens – by the way
untereinander – amongst themselves
Unterschied, der (-(e)s, -e) – difference
unterrichten – to teach, educate
verraten – to betray
Verband, der (-s, Verbände) – bandage
verletzen – to injure
voran – ahead
Wirtin, die (-, Wirtinnen) – landlady

C. *Further questions*

Grammatical questions

a. Look at the subjunctive II forms in the text. What forms could be mistaken for the preterite?
b. There are not just the subjunctive II forms used in the text. Look for the other forms in the text. What other forms are used and why?

Comprehension questions

c. What could the "boxes" that the sharks construct for the little fish represent?
d. What would the fish learn in school? What do you think is the point of that kind of "education" (roughly lines 11 to 24)?
e. What is said about war, art and religion?
f. What would happen to equality among fish and why? What is said about privileges?
g. What do you think is the political belief of the author? Find evidence for this in the text.

Note

1 The actual saying is a bit shorter: Er rennt, wie von der Tarantel gestochen.

14 Extended participial phrases

14.1 Extended participial phrases

Der von allen guten Geistern verlassene Mann.
The from all good spirits abandoned man. → The man that has been abandoned by all good spirits.

Participial phrases are essentially shorter relative clauses hidden in a complex construction formed primarily of participles and adjectives. These constructions vary, but have two common traits: first, there are usually many more words between the determiner and its noun than one would expect from English, and second, these constructions can be very difficult to spot and understand/translate correctly. English uses very short constructions like this, e.g. the writer born in 1895, the French-speaking county, the sugar-coated doughnut, but German tends to use longer and much more complex constructions.

Unlike most grammatical features in German, there is no single term used to describe these constructions. Typical names in German include *Partizipialphrasen*, *Partizipialattribute* or *Partizipialsatz*. Other German reading skills books also differ on the term used to describe these; interestingly they are united in using the term "adjective" instead of "participle." April Wilson (2007: 194) refers to the feature as "The Overloaded Adjective Constructions," Coles & Dodd (1997: 39, 60) as "Extended Adjective Phrases" and Alan Korb (2014: 226) as "Extended-Adjective Construction." The term in this book for this grammatical feature is "extended participial phrase," because the constructions tend to use participles as adjectives and because they do not form complete sentences but phrases.

First, we are going to build an extended participial phrase step by step. Keep track of the determiner *die* and its noun *Sprache* throughout this chart. They form the basis of any translation and essentially form a bracket around the rest of the construction.

Step	German	English	Comment
1	**Die Sprache.**	The language.	Note that without a verb this is not a proper sentence/clause but a phrase.
2	**Die** piktische **Sprache.**	The Pictish language.	Determiner – adjective – noun: a very typical construction.
3	**Die** heute ausgestorbene piktische Sprache.	The nowadays extinct Pictish language.	An adverb (*heute*) and a participle (*ausgestorbene*) have been added. We struggle to translate it properly in English, so we'll shift most of the information into a relative clause.
→	→ **Die** piktische **Sprache**, die heute ausgestorben ist.	→ The Pictish language, which is extinct nowadays.	This extra step makes it much easier to deal with the translation of this construction.
4	**Die** vermutlich mit dem Keltischen verwandte und heute ausgestorbene piktische **Sprache.**	The Pictish language, which is probably related to Celtic and which is extinct nowadays.	A second concept has been added to the construction ("probably related to Celtic"). The best translation is to put this in a relative clause as well.

We could go on and add additional pieces of information to our phrase, but at some point it becomes just too confusing and unintelligible. What you should notice, however, is that no matter how complex this construction becomes, the core of its meaning is still "the language."

When dealing with an extended participial phrase, always bear in mind that the original determiner and the noun it refers to form the key part of the meaning. Think of them as forming a bracket in which all the other information is located.

Dealing with an extended participial phrase takes place in two steps.

1. Identify the phrase: where it begins (determiner) and where it ends (noun).
2. Translate the phrase with the help of a relative clause.

An optional third step is to look for similar constructions in English (to, for example, avoid the relative clause or to "polish" your translation).

Some learners may feel confident enough to skip the relative clause and instead keep a translation more similar to the German construction.

> *Eine von Bäumen beschattete Hütte.*
> A tree-shaded hut.

Be careful with this! You can easily make unnecessary mistakes this way. Try to stick to the two steps described earlier and then, once you have a clear understanding of the phrase, opt for a simpler construction in English.

14.2 Identifying an extended participial phrase

In a nutshell, an extended participial phrase is characterised by having more words between the determiner and its noun, and often those words are also unexpected in that position.

> *Die in die Schule gehenden **Kinder**.*
> The children (who are) going to school.

After *die* we would expect a noun, or an adjective followed by a noun. We wouldn't typically expect four other words, of which one is another noun and one is a participle. In addition, after *die* we would certainly not expect a preposition (*in*), because this does not really make sense. In order to identify a participial phrase we therefore need to look for a construction, where a lot of words have been placed between the determiner and its noun.

There a couple of additional telltale signs as well.

- A determiner followed by a preposition, or a determiner followed by another determiner, are typical indications that a participial phrase is at hand.

> *Die das Haus verlassenden **Personen**.*
> The people (that are) leaving the house.

Note that the determiner can be replaced by a preposition or an adjective.

> ***Typische** das Verständnis erschwerende **Fehler** sind: …*
> Typical mistakes that complicate the comprehension are: …

- Participles used as adjectives are very common in this type of construction.

> *Der von allen gefürchtete **Tyrann**.*
> The tyrant, who is feared by all.

Note that these constructions can be formed with only a regular adjective as well (i.e. without a participle), but this is rather rare.

*Die für Deutsche und auch Österreicher typische **Nachspeise**.*
The dessert (which is) typical for Germans and Austrians as well.

- Prepositions occur very frequently in this type of construction as they link different nouns.
  *Der von der Zeitung „Die Zeit" veröffentlichte **Artikel**.*
  The article that has been published by the newspaper "Die Zeit."

14.3 Translating an extended participial phrase

Go through the following steps to translate an extended participial phrase:

1. Find the beginning and end of the phrase. It typically starts with an article, but sometimes an adjective can stand in for an article.
    *Ich schenke **meiner** an der Grippe erkrankten **Mutter** einen Blumenstrauß.*
    I give (as a gift) a bouquet of flowers to my mother, who has become ill with the flu.
    If the article is preceded by a preposition it makes sense to include that.
    *Ich gehe heute nicht **in die** wegen Schnee geschlossene **Schule**.*
    Today, I'm not going to the school, which has been closed because of snow. (In English we would use the preposition "to" and not "in.")

2. Translate the noun of the phrase first. This is your basic meaning.
    *Ich schenke **meiner** an der Grippe erkrankten **Mutter** einen Blumenstrauß.*
    I give my mother a bouquet of flowers.
    *Ich gehe heute nicht **in die** wegen Schnee geschlossene **Schule**.*
    Today, I'm not going to school.

3. Translate the rest of the phrase as a relative sentence.
    *Ich schenke **meiner** an der Grippe erkrankten **Mutter** einen Blumenstrauß.*
    I give (as a gift) a bouquet of flowers to my mother, who has become ill with the flu.
    *Ich gehe heute nicht **in die** wegen Schnee geschlossene **Schule**.*
    Today, I'm not going to the school, which has been closed because of snow. An alternative is to skip the relative pronoun and put the content just after a comma; as you can see in the following examples, this works quite well in some sentences (closed because of snow) and less in others (ill with the flu).*Ich gehe heute nicht **in die** wegen Schnee geschlossene **Schule**.*

Today, I'm not going to the school, closed because of snow.
Ich schenke **meiner** *an der Grippe erkrankten* **Mutter** *einen Blumenstrauß.*
I give (as a gift) a bouquet of flowers to my mother, ill with the flu.

4. Optional: if you want, you can consider adapting the translation to something that is more idiomatic or easier to understand.
   Ich gehe heute nicht **in die** *wegen Schnee geschlossene* **Schule.**
   Because the school is closed, due to snow, I'm not going in today.
   I'm not going to school today, as it's closed due to snow.
   Ich schenke **meiner** *an der Grippe erkrankten* **Mutter** *einen Blumenstrauß.*
   I give my mother, sick with the flu, a bouquet of flowers.
   My mother is sick with the flu and I give her a bouquet of flowers.

As tempting as it can be to skip step 3 and go straight to step 4, I recommend you do this step at least in your head, in order to avoid unnecessary mistakes. Remember, with German Reading Skills the aim is to get a correct understanding of the original text, not getting a perfect idiomatic translation.

"Unwrapping" a participial phrase from the back

 Sometimes it can be useful to "unwrap" complex participial phrases backwards. Translate the noun and its determiner first, then start with the last word of the phrase before the noun and work your way to the front, rather than starting with the first word of the phrase.

Die typischen und nur durch internationale Hilfe zu bezwingenden sozialen Probleme.	???
Die Probleme.	The problems.
Die sozialen Probleme.	The social problems.
Die zu bezwingenden sozialen Probleme.	The social problems that can/must/ should* be countered.
Die nur durch internationale Hilfe zu bezwingenden sozialen Probleme.	The social problems that can only be countered through international support.
Die typischen und nur durch internationale Hilfe zu bezwingenden sozialen Probleme.	The social problems that are typical and can only be countered through international support.

* The choice of modal verbs will be explained along with fake passive constructions in chapter 15. We'll choose "can" as a translation for now.

As you can see in the previous example, we work our way backwards from the noun, starting with *sozialen* and then continuing with each piece of the puzzle. This way we arrive with relative ease at a correct understanding of the construction.

This approach can sometimes be useful if you are stuck on a more complex participial phrase. In the example, we could have put *sozialen* in the relative clause of our translation ("the problems, which are social"), but this wasn't necessary for the understanding and "the social problems" is shorter and easier to understand.

Exercises

A. Easy extended participial phrases

1. Der in der Zeitung „Die Zeit" am 14. August erschienene Artikel...
2. Der in Frankfurt geborene Schriftsteller...
3. Der laut lachende Mann ging aus dem Zimmer.
4. Der Dieb fand den in einem Tresor versteckten Schmuck nicht.
5. Das sehr schlecht erzogene Kind gibt nur freche Antworten.
6. Die vor ein paar Stunden am Herzen operierte Frau schläft noch ruhig.
7. Das bis Weihnachten ausgebuchte Hotel hat einen sehr guten Ruf.
8. Die an ihrer Neutralität festhaltende Schweiz vermittelt in der Krise.
9. Das sich stets im Dunkeln fürchtende Kind kommt nachts immer zu den Eltern.
10. Die fröhlich vor sich hinzwitschernden Vögel sitzen auf den Bäumen.

B. Intermediate extended participial phrases

1. Die Universität hat ihren Ursprung in einem Jahrhunderte alten Kloster, das auf einem Berg liegt.
2. Der mit einem Preis ausgezeichnete und vielzitierte Artikel ist bahnbrechend.
3. Die bisher existierenden internationalen Abkommen spielen eine bedeutende Rolle im Welthandel.
4. Die von der Wichtigkeit des technologischen Fortschritts überzeugten Südkoreaner haben in der Unterhaltungselektronik eine Spitzenposition.
5. Vor dem Fall der Mauer gab es zwei unabhängig voneinander existierende Ordnungen, Ost und West.
6. Zu diesem Schluss kam eine von einem internationalen Forscherteam unternommene und kürzlich veröffentlichte Studie.
7. Eine neue Untersuchung belegt, dass von Menschen heimlich konsumiertes und als Urin ausgeschiedenes Kokain ins Trinkwasser gelangt.
8. Dies ist ein von der EU und anderen öffentlichen Geldgebern finanziertes Forschungsprojekt.
9. Der genauso brutale wie hässliche Polizist wagte es nicht, Johannes zu verhaften.

10. Auf leisen wie geschickten Pfoten schlich die Katze in der durch den Vollmond erhellten Nacht davon.
11. Zuvor war Johannes von der mächtigen und weithin gefürchteten, gelegentlich sogar gehassten Königin in den Palast bestellt worden.

Vocabulary

bahnbrechend – groundbreaking
davonschleichen (sep.v.) – to sneak away
erhellen – to illuminate
festhalten (sep.v.) – to hold on, retain
gelangen – to end up, reach
geschickt – dexterous, nimble, skilled
hassen – to hate
vor sich hinzwitschern (colloquial construction; sep.v.) – to chirp, to be busy with chirping
Pfote, die (-, -n) – paw
verhaften – to arrest
etwas wagen – to dare (to do) sth.
zuvor – before/at an earlier time

Advanced/difficult extended participial phrases can be found in chapter 15.

Practice text: Erstes Flugblatt der Weißen Rose

The *Weiße Rose* (White Rose) was a resistance group in the Third Reich that was active primarily in the Munich region between June 1942 and February 1943. They wrote a total of six leaflets in which they denounced the actions of the Nazis and urged others to join the resistance. Following the arrest of the siblings Sophie and Hans Scholl at the University of Munich, many members of their group were executed. The legacy of the *Weiße Rose* is well known in Germany today.

The first four leaflets were sent to a selected group of intellectuals (students, professors, book merchants, etc.). Here is an excerpt from the first leaflet they wrote.

It contains three extended participial phrases and a number of difficult words. The second paragraph (*"Wenn das deutsche Volk..."*) is one extremely long and complex sentence, so much that the authors themselves had to insert a hyphen to restart their thoughts. Break the sentence down into individual clauses, locate the single main clause and combine them slowly one by one for better comprehension. Check the vocabulary section for advice on *geworden sind* before you begin. In general it makes sense with this text to break the long German sentences down into smaller English sentences – as long as the meaning is the same, this is not a concern. **This text is very difficult!**

Flugblatt I

Nichts ist eines Kulturvolkes unwürdiger, als sich ohne Widerstand von einer verantwortungslosen und dunklen Trieben ergebenen Herrscherclique "regieren" zu lassen. Ist es nicht so, daß sich jeder ehrliche Deutsche heute seiner Regierung schämt, und wer von uns ahnt das Ausmaß der Schmach, die über uns und unsere Kinder kommen wird, wenn einst der Schleier von unseren Augen gefallen ist und die grauenvollsten und jegliches Maß unendlich überschreitenden Verbrechen ans Tageslicht treten?

Wenn das deutsche Volk schon so in seinem tiefsten Wesen korrumpiert und zerfallen ist, daß es, ohne eine Hand zu regen, im leichtsinnigen Vertrauen auf eine fragwürdige Gesetzmäßigkeit der Geschichte das Höchste, das ein Mensch besitzt und das ihn über jede andere Kreatur erhöht, nämlich den freien Willen, preisgibt, die Freiheit des Menschen preisgibt, selbst mit einzugreifen in das Rad der Geschichte und es seiner vernünftigen Entscheidung unterzuordnen - wenn die Deutschen, so jeder Individualität bar, schon so sehr zur geistlosen und feigen Masse geworden sind, dann, ja dann verdienen sie den Untergang.

Wenn jeder wartet, bis der andere anfängt, werden die Boten der rächenden Nemesis unaufhaltsam näher und näher rücken, dann wird auch das letzte Opfer sinnlos in den Rachen des unersättlichen Dämons geworfen sein. Daher muß jeder einzelne seiner Verantwortung als Mitglied der christlichen und abendländischen Kultur bewußt in dieser letzten Stunde sich wehren, soviel er kann, arbeiten wider die Geißel der Menschheit, wider den Faschismus und jedes ihm ähnliche System des absoluten Staates. Leistet passiven Widerstand - Widerstand -, wo immer Ihr auch seid, verhindert das Weiterlaufen dieser atheistischen Kriegsmaschine, ehe es zu spät ist, ehe die letzten Städte ein Trümmerhaufen sind, gleich Köln, und ehe die letzte Jugend des Volkes irgendwo für die Hybris eines Untermenschen verblutet ist. Vergeßt nicht, daß ein jedes Volk diejenige Regierung verdient, die es erträgt!

Wir bitten Sie, dieses Blatt mit möglichst vielen Durchschlägen abzuschreiben und weiterzuverteilen!

Vocabulary

zur geistlosen und feigen Masse geworden sind – the verb here, *zu etwas werden*, is rather tricky. You can translate it with "become," but then need to skip the *zu* in your translation, or you opt for a different translation.

etwas abschreiben (sep.v.) – to copy something, usually by hand

alsdann – thereupon

Durchschlag, der (-(e)s, Durchschläge) – carbon copy

feig – cowardly, craven

fortschreiten (sep.v.) – to progress

zu etwas gereichen – to honour, benefit; this word is difficult to translate here in this context.

leichtsinnig – careless, lightheaded

Mitläufer, der (-s, -) – follower

Mißbilligung, die (-, -en) – disapproval

etwas preisgeben (sep.v.) – to relinquish sth., to disclose

rächen – to avenge

Schleier, der (-s, -) – veil, haze

Schmach, die (-, no plural) – disgrace, humiliation

Trieb, der (-(e)s, -e) – urge, drive, desire

unaufhaltsam – inexorable

verwerflich – reprehensible, repugnant

Widerstand leisten – to put up resistance

15 *Ersatzpassiv* constructions and other fake passive constructions

German has a number of other ways of expressing the passive that do not involve *werden* or *sein* and/or a participle. These constructions share in common that they look like an active construction, but can be translated in the passive voice.

15.1 *Man*

As mentioned in chapter 9, constructions with *man* can often be translated as a passive construction.

> *In der Schule lernt man Rechnen.*
> In school one learns counting (maths). → In school, counting is learned.

15.2 *Sein* + *zu* + infinitive

This construction is comparatively common in German, and it is used both in spoken language and in higher register written language. It usually includes a sense of need, urgency or advice and the translation can vary on the context. Note that the infinitive in these constructions cannot be translated as an infinitive and that the *zu* plays an important role in this construction.

The typical translation for *sein* + *zu* + infinitive is "this or that can/must/should be done."

> *Die Vokabeln sind am besten bis Montag zu lernen.*
> The homework should best be learned by Monday.

> *Die Hose ist bei mindestens 60 Grad zu waschen, damit die Flecken rausgehen.*
> The trousers must be washed at at least 60 degrees, in order to get the stains out.

> *Die Rechnung ist noch zu bezahlen, ich habe genug Geld.*
> The bill can still be paid; I have enough money.

The construction also occurs occasionally in academic writing, especially in introductions to statements. Occasionally you might also see the *ist* replaced by a *sei*, its subjunctive I form, without this having any bearing on its meaning.

> *Es ist darauf hinzuweisen,...*
> It must/should be pointed out,...

> *Wobei zu betonen sei,...*
> At the same time it should be stressed,...

15.3 *-bar* and *-lich*

The suffixes *-bar* and *-lich* express ability – something can be done or is possible.

> *Die Pizza ist noch essbar.*
> The pizza is still edible.

These constructions can usually be translated as a passive construction ("something can or cannot be done"), i.e. "The pizza can be eaten."

> *Seine Aussage ist nicht verständlich.*
> His statement is not comprehensible./His statement cannot be understood.

Exercise

Translate these sentences. Many of them can be translated in more than one way. What would the passive voice version be?

1. Max Webers Texte sind oft schwer verständlich.
2. Man darf nicht vergessen, dass manche Texte Max Webers zuerst als Reden gehalten worden sind.
3. Die Beleidigung unserer Religion ist nicht hinnehmbar.
4. Solche Aussagen sind in Zukunft unbedingt zu vermeiden.
5. Vorsicht! Die Vase ist sehr zerbrechlich.
6. Was ist noch dazu zu sagen?
7. Die Regeln zu den Ruhezeiten sind leicht einzuhalten.
8. Man kann nicht immer ein Held sein, aber man kann immer ein Mann sein. (Johann Wolfgang von Goethe)

Vocabulary

etwas einhalten (sep.v.) – to observe, hold, comply with sth.
etwas hinnehmen (sep.v.) – to accept sth., put up with sth.
zerbrechen – to shatter, break

15.4 *Lassen* and other verbs and constructions that can carry a passive meaning

A number of verbs can carry a passive meaning even though they are used without *werden* or a participle.

Sich lassen + infinitive

When combined with a reflexive pronoun and an infinitive, *lassen* carries a passive meaning most of the time, similar to "can be done."
Compare the following two examples:

> *Sie lassen die Kunden nur bar bezahlen.*
> They only let the customers pay with cash.

> *Die Rechnung lässt **sich** nur bar bezahlen.*
> The bill can only be paid with cash.

This construction always consists of *sich lassen* and an infinitive. Essentially it is the same as a passive construction with *können*, i.e.:

> *Die Rechnung kann nur bar bezahlt werden.* = *Die Rechnung lässt sich nur bar bezahlen.*
> The bill can only be paid with cash.

Gehören

Gehören can be used with a participle to express the passive. These expressions are often colloquial and usually mean that something "should be done."

> *Das gehört verboten.*   That should be banned.

Bekommen and kriegen

Bekommen and *kriegen* can be translated with a passive construction, especially if everything else makes barely any sense or is almost incomprehensible. They often take a role similar to *werden* in these sentences and will be teamed up with a participle. These expressions are also often colloquial.

> *Die Studenten bekommen/kriegen die deutsche Grammatik erklärt.*
> The German grammar is being explained to the students.
> (as opposed to: "The students get the German grammar explained").

Exercise

A. Translate these sentences.

1. Die Schlussfolgerung des Autors lässt sich nicht nachvollziehen.
2. Es ist weiterhin darauf hinzuweisen, dass sich aus diesem Datensatz keine zuverlässigen Informationen lesen lassen.
3. Bekommt man eine ernsthafte Frage gestellt, sollte man aufrichtig und ehrlich antworten.
4. Die Falschmeldung gehört richtiggestellt.
5. Wo es Not tut, lässt sich alles wagen.
6. Der Insasse im offenen Vollzug bekommt von morgens bis abends Ausgang. (Note that *Ausgang* is not "exit" here.)

Vocabulary

wo es Not tut – where there is need

aufrichtig – sincere, earnest, honest
Falschmeldung, die (-, -en) – hoax, false report
Insasse, der (-n, -n) – inmate
Schlussfolgerung, die (-, -en) – conclusion, deduction, argumentation
Vollzug, der (-(e)s, Vollzüge) – execution, carrying out; here: prison
zuverlässig – reliable

Reflexive and phrasal verbs

Reflexive verbs can also have a passive meaning especially when they denote an accomplishment or activity. Examples include verbs such as *sich ärgern*, *sich fürchten*, *sich freuen*, *sich schämen*.

Phrasal verbs that use a verbal noun (especially when ending in -ung) often have a passive meaning.

This includes verbs such as *erfahren, erhalten, gehen, gelangen, kommen, stehen* and they usually have little meaning without the phrasal noun.

Exercise

B. Translate these sentences. Some of these might have a passive meaning.

1. Es ärgert mich sehr, wenn jemand nicht zu einem Meeting kommt.
2. Die Befürchtungen haben sich bestätigt.
3. Die Verbrechen der Kolonialherren sind in Vergessenheit geraten.
4. Die Reihenfolge der Agendapunkte steht nicht zur Debatte.
5. Für solche Aussagen sollte man sich schämen.
6. Das Urteil hat weithin Ablehnung gefunden.
7. Der Prozess hat durch die Veränderungen Perfektion erfahren.
8. Die Tickets für das Konzert verkauften sich schneller als erwartet.
9. Auch heute noch interessieren sich viele Forscher für die Werke der Klassik.
10. Wo befindet sich der Ausgang?

15.5 Advanced/difficult extended participial phrases

Here are some (even) more difficult extended participial phrases. They are in this chapter, as some of them make use of *zu* to show that something needs to be done or should be done.

If *zu* is combined with a present participle, it describes the possibility or necessity of doing something.

In order to explain this, let's have a look at a common German word, *der Auszubildende*, an apprentice.

The verb *ausbilden* means "to train or educate someone." A job training or apprenticeship in German is called *die Ausbildung*. As you would expect, the person entering such training still has to be trained. Once they are finished, they are trained, i.e. *ausgebildet*. The past participle *ausgebildet* shows the completeness of the task.

In order to express that someone is to be trained/should be trained, we can use the fake passive construction from 15.2 "*sein + zu +* infinitive" and say that *Die junge Person ist auszubilden*; "the young person is to be trained/should be trained." Because *ausbilden* is a separable verb, the particle *zu* is placed in between the separable prefix and the verb.

If we want to express this in an extended participial construction, we can say *die auszubildende Person*; "the person that is to be trained."

Exercise

Translate the following sentences!

1. Das Hypertext Transfer Protocol (HTTP) ist als Grundstein des Internets aus der heutigen, vom Internet dominierten Welt nicht mehr wegzudenken. Ursprünglich von Tim Berners-Lee und seinem Team in der Schweiz entwickelt, hat es den rasanten, beispiellosen und unwiderruflichen Siegeszug des modernen World Wide Webs ermöglicht. (Very difficult, don't despair!)
2. Die in dieser Situation anzuwendende Lösung ist offensichtlich.
3. Die als altmodisch und patriarchalisch angreifbaren Ansichten der religiösen Hardliner sind heutzutage nicht mehr zu verteidigen.
4. Ein plötzlich möglich gewordener Durchbruch in der Stammzellentherapie wird durch unzeitgemäße Gesetze gehemmt.
5. Die von dir angeblich im Zug gefundene Jacke sieht verdächtig wie die von mir verlorene Jacke aus.
6. Ein Bergsteiger wird noch immer vermisst. Die zu seiner Rettung zusammengestellte und ihn noch immer suchende Suchmannschaft ist bislang erfolglos geblieben.
7. Das so lange und heftig umkämpfte Problem des Rechtes im Neuen Testament scheint mir angefasst zu sein.
8. Der festzunehmende Verbrecher ist bewaffnet und gefährlich.
9. Die Thesen der von Rudolf Sohms 1892 erschienen, aber noch heute bewegenden und faszinierenden Arbeit über das Kirchenrecht bestimmen nach wie vor die aktuelle Debatte.

10. Die seltsame Struktur des Satzes ist genau wie die seiner alsbald zu nennenden Parallelen meines Wissens kaum je betrachtet worden.
11. Die, die die neue und demokratisch gewählte Regierung stürzen wollen, gehören der dem alten General treuen Garde an.

Practice text: Lion Feuchtwanger "An den Bewohner meines Hauses"

This is an excerpt from an open letter written by the Jewish writer Lion Feuchtwanger; it was published in March 1935 in the exile newspaper *Pariser Tagesblatt*. It is addressed to the inhabitant of his house in Berlin, Herr X. The tasks following the text do not require a complete translation of the text, but if you choose to do so for practice, you can find a sample translation in the answer key.

1	**An den Bewohner meines Hauses Mahlerstrasse 8 in Berlin**
2	Ich weiß nicht, wie Sie heißen, mein Herr, und auf welche Art Sie in den
3	Besitz meines Hauses gelangt sind. Ich weiß nur, daß vor zwei Jahren die
4	Polizei des Dritten Reiches mein gesamtes bewegliches und unbewegliches
5	Vermögen beschlagnahmt und der Reichsaktiengesellschaft für
6	Konfiskation des Vermögens politischer Gegner (Aufsichtsratsvorsitzender
7	Minister Göring) überwiesen hat. Ich erfuhr das aus einem Schreiben des
8	Hypothekengläubigers. Sie teilten mir erläuternd mit, die Rechtsprechung
9	des Dritten Reichs verstehe, wenn es sich um das konfiszierte Vermögen
10	politischer Gegner handle, unter ,Vermögen' nur die Aktiva. Trotzdem
11	also mein Haus und meine Bankkonten, die die Hypothek um ein
12	Vielfaches überstiegen, konfisziert seien, sei ich verpflichtet, die
13	Hypothekenzinsen genauso wie meine deutschen Steuern aus meinem im
14	Ausland neu zu erwerbenden Vermögen weiter zu bezahlen. Sei dem wie
15	immer, jedenfalls sitzen jetzt Sie, Herr X, in meinem Haus, und ich habe
16	nach der Auffassung deutscher Richter die Zinsen zu zahlen.
17	Wie gefällt Ihnen mein Haus, Herr X? Lebt es sich angenehm darin? Hat
18	der silbergraue Teppichbelag der oberen Räume bei der Plünderung durch
19	die S.A.-Leute sehr gelitten? Mein Portier hat sich damals in diese oberen
20	Räume geflüchtet, die Herren wollten sich, da ich in Amerika war, an ihm
21	schadlos halten, der Teppichbelag ist sehr empfindlich, und Rot ist eine
22	kräftige Farbe, die schwer herauszubringen ist. Auch der Gummibelag des
23	Treppenhauses war nicht gerade für die Stiefel von S.A.-Leuten berechnet.
24	Wenn er sehr gelitten hat, wenden Sie sich am besten an die Firma Baake.
25	Was fangen Sie nicht mit den beiden Räumen an, die meine Bibliothek
26	enthielten? Bücher, habe ich mir sagen lassen, sind nicht sehr beliebt in
27	dem Reich, in dem Sie leben, Herr X, und wer sich damit befaßt, gerät
28	leicht in Unannehmlichkeiten. Ich zum Beispiel habe das Buch Ihres

29	‚Führers' gelesen und harmlos konstatiert, daß seine 140 000 Worte
30	140 000 Verstöße gegen den deutschen Sprachgeist sind. Infolge dieser
31	meiner Feststellung sitzen jetzt Sie in meinem Haus. Manchmal denke
32	ich darüber nach, wofür man wohl im Dritten Reich die Büchergestelle
33	verwenden könnte. Seien Sie vorsichtig, falls Sie sie herausreißen
34	lassen, daß die Mauer nicht darunter leidet.
35	Und was haben Sie mit dem Terrarium angefangen? Hat man wirklich
36	meine Schildkröten und meine Eidechsen totgeschlagen, weil ihr Besitzer
37	‚fremdrassig' war? Und haben die Blumenbeete und der Steingarten sehr
38	gelitten, als die SA-Leute meinen krumm und lahm geschlagenen Portier
39	durch den Garten verfolgten, wie er sich in den Wald flüchtete?
40	Lassen Sie mein Haus nicht verkommen, Herr X. Pflegen Sie es, bitte,
41	ein bißchen.
42	Mit vielen guten Wünschen für unser Haus
43	*Lion Feuchtwanger*

Vocabulary

Ausland, das (-(e)s, no plural) – overseas, abroad
sich mit etwas befassen – to concern oneself with sth.
Belag, der (-(e)s, Beläge) – covering, film, coat, surface
berechnen – to estimate, calculate, charge
beschlagnahmen – to confiscate
beweglich und unbeweglich – mobile and immobile, movable and fixed;
    here: active and passive
bisschen – a little, a little bit, a few
Büchergestell, das (-s, -e) – book shelf
erfahren – to experience, find out
erwerben – to acquire, purchase, earn, gain
feststellen (sep.v.)– to assert, determine, state
flüchten – to flee
Gläubiger, der (-s, -) – creditor
Hypothek, die (-, -en) – mortgage
jedenfalls – anyway, in any case, at any rate
etwas pflegen – to take care of sth., look after sth.
schadlos – harmless; here: to compensate for sth., to take advantage of so.
Steuer, die (-, -n) – tax
totschlagen (sep.v) – to beat to death
übersteigen – to exceed, outstrip
Unannehmlichkeit, die (-, -en) – inconvenience
verfolgen – to chase, persecute

verkommen – to deteriorate; here: to become rundown
Vermögen, das (-s, -) – wealth, assets
Wunsch, der (-es, Wünsche) – wish

Tasks

A. The following sentences could all be translated with a passive voice construction. Try to work out possible passive voice translations.

  1. Line 3: Ich weiß nicht, wie Sie heißen.
  2. Lines 21–22: Rot ist eine kräftige Farbe, die schwer herauszubringen ist.
  3. Lines 26–27: Bücher, habe ich mir sagen lassen, sind nicht sehr beliebt in dem Reich, in dem Sie leben, Herr X.
  4. Lines 31–33: Ich denke darüber nach, wofür man im Dritten Reich die Büchergestelle verwenden könnte.
  5. Lines 35–36: Hat man wirklich meine Schildkröten und meine Eidechsen totgeschlagen?

B. Translate the following two extended participial constructions.

  1. Ich bin verpflichtet, die Hypothekenzinsen genauso wie meine deutschen Steuern aus meinem im Ausland neu zu erwerbenden Vermögen weiter zu bezahlen.
  2. Haben die Blumenbeete und der Steingarten sehr gelitten, als die SA-Leute meinen krumm und lahm geschlagenen Portier durch den Garten verfolgten, wie er sich in den Wald flüchtete?

C. Comprehension questions

  1. What happened two years ago?
  2. What is the irony regarding Feuchtwanger's mortgage interest?
  3. What happened to Feuchtwanger's porter and what cynical advice is given to the recipient of the letter in regard to the carpets and floor coverings?
  4. Why did the SA people not beat or arrest Feuchtwanger?
  5. Lines 25–31: Why does Feuchtwanger believe that the recipient of the letter might remove the library from the house? What did Feuchtwanger do and what was the result of this?
  6. For what reason were the reptiles in Feuchtwanger's terrarium killed?
  7. The phrase *infolge dieser meiner Feststellung* seems rather difficult, but can be translated in a simple fashion. How?

16 Strategies for dealing with longer and older texts

In this chapter we will look at some general advice on how to deal with complex, long and demanding texts as well as older texts, i.e. texts that do not use the typical language one would encounter in modern day writing. Much of this advice focuses on reading for academic purposes, i.e. reading research monographs or journal articles written in German, but can be adapted to other purposes, such as those that journalists or novelists might have when researching background material for their work or reading material in German for pleasure.

16.1 Reading to the level of understanding required

One of the biggest constraints any researcher faces is available time. Reading a text in a non-native language – in this case German – will take more time than reading a text in one's native language. It is therefore paramount to make the most of the available time and to avoid wasting time on a very long text that is not crucial for the project you are working on.

Before working on a text, it is best to start by asking yourself what it is that you want to achieve by reading a text:

- What insight do I hope to gain from this text?
- How do I expect this insight to fit into the overall knowledge I have of the topic?
- How will the comprehension of this text further my ability to complete my research project?
- How much of this text do I need to know? All of it, parts of it, or only a very specific part?

To illustrate this, I've used the made-up example of a researcher, Maggie, and show four situations she could find herself in when looking at new texts that she could read.

Situation A. *"I have already read a lot about topic X. At this stage, not all texts that I read contain new information. I want to know if this text contains anything new."*

A good approach for Maggie would be to start by skim reading the text. Skim reading involves looking for words and structures of a text that are recognisable and can be easily understood. Maggie's extensive knowledge of the topic will have provided her with a good deal of cognates, phrases, names and dates that will aid her in that. This is especially true for specialised jargon, which she can either identify from the English cognate or that she has encountered before in German. Recurring nouns that are typical for a certain topic will stick out of the text as they are capitalised in German. A good way to start is by reading summaries and headings; if the text has an abstract, a blurb, a contents page or a conclusion, start with these. From there, continue with chapter and section headings in order to pinpoint parts of the text that could be of interest. You do not want to read everything in detail at this stage, rather you want to jump from a part that you understand mostly to another part and see if there is anything in there that is worthy of more of your time or a close reading. It is a good idea to use markers on the text (if you are allowed to) – little adhesive tags, etc. Electronic document readers often provide similar methods for taking notes. Keep in mind that German sentence structure is different from English and that verbs often form verbal brackets; a lot of verb parts will therefore be at the end of clauses, unlike in English.

Situation B. *"I'm not sure what this text is about and if it is relevant at all to my topic."*

The first step in this case would be to scan the text for nouns, dates and names that are repeated. Since these words are capitalised and stick out, they can be quickly identified. Look for any vocabulary that seems somewhat specialised and consult a dictionary if necessary to see if it could point you towards a particular topic or a stream of discussion within your field. This will allow you to pinpoint sections of the text that might be relevant for you. Sometimes word families can be identified, i.e. words such as *reinigen – rein – Reinigung*, which would widen your scope beyond just nouns. As in the previous situation, it is a good idea to start with any sort of summaries and with headlines or captions.

Scanning becomes difficult if an author uses several different terms for the same concept, as you can miss the repetition in those cases. In this case you might have to look up a few more nouns to see if there is some overlap of meaning.

Situation C. "I know this text is important for my research."

If you are researching a certain author's work in German, you will know that some texts need to be read closely. You can follow the steps laid out at the beginning of this book, which will guide you through the typical stages of working with a text and help you gain a deep and thorough understanding of the text.

"Five steps towards understanding a text"

There is some general guidance on how to work towards understanding a text on p. xii. Be sure to read if you are not familiar with its content.

Situation D. "My professor told me to read this. I have no idea what it is about."

This is probably the worst-case scenario, as it can be very time-consuming. You need to start first with some scanning of the text to gain a better overview of the topic, general content and structure of the text. Once you have arrived at a rudimentary understanding of what the text is about, re-evaluate how it fits in with your overall aims and then proceed to a close reading if necessary.

Sometimes **reading for pleasure** is similar to this situation. You may have heard about a novel that is very good and feel that you want to practise your German while enjoying the novel. In this case, it can still make sense to read the blurb, to get a bit of an idea of the setting of the novel, but in most cases you will not want to read anything that could be considered a spoiler. You will also not want to do any or extensive scanning of the text, as again this would ruin the experience. As a result, you will probably find the first chapters challenging, but as you progress in the story and your knowledge of vocabulary and background knowledge build up, things will become easier. Finally, if you ever really struggle with a novel and find it too difficult to read, do not give up completely, but maybe try a different novel. The style of some authors is simply more difficult to read than that of others and it would be a pity if you let one bad experience ruin the fun for you.

The following chart summarises several of the points made here:

	Topic (familiar/unfamiliar; extensive/little or no knowledge)	
Level of understanding required (general structure/ thorough understanding)	Familiar topic/extensive knowledge & general structure → **Skim reading** to get an overview of the structure of the text and most relevant parts	Unfamiliar topic/little or no knowledge & general structure → **Scanning**, to collect key words and to find central passages related to topic; possible re-evaluation later
	Familiar topic/extensive knowledge & thorough understanding → **Close reading**	Unfamiliar topic/little or no knowledge & thorough understanding → Cursory **scanning** to gain information on possible topic and key words; followed by **close reading**

Worst case scenario?

Mistakes in the German text!

Although it is very rare for academic texts or other published material, grammatical mistakes can occur in written texts. The worst kinds are those that affect the subject–verb agreement. There is no particular helpful advice I can give if this happens, except to prepare yourself mentally for when this happens and to encourage you to trust yourself a bit. If you have made it this far to chapter 16 and you follow the basic steps to the letter – slowly building up a structure and isolating all unnecessary parts – you should trust your instincts in those cases where you cannot decode a sentence because of a possible mistake on behalf of the author.

16.2 Dealing with archaic language use in older texts

You may have already come across German that looked slightly different (spelling, endings) or used unfamiliar vocabulary or vocabulary with meaning that differed from the one you found in your dictionary. Like other languages, German has developed over time and some of those changes have been more profound or comprehensive than others. Modern German is usually referred to as *Hochdeutsch* (High German) and has been around since as early as the

15th century; the invention of the printing press by Johannes Gutenberg in the middle of the 15th century and the translation of the Bible into German by Martin Luther in the first half of the 16th century were important developments that shaped the language that is used today. Other changes came by convention and were enforced gradually through school education. Unfortunately, even a text that is "only" 100 years old will often feel old-fashioned and have different, archaic spellings or uses of words.

Grammar and spelling reforms have taken place several times and the last one, in 1996, streamlined a lot of spelling to bring it into line with the underlying grammar. This last reform was made legally binding in Germany and Austria, and other countries with a German-speaking population have followed suit.

For German Reading Skills, the German Orthography Reform from 1996 has little impact (mostly it just recognised that *dass* used to be spelt as *daß*).

Here are some of the more frequent differences that you need to be aware of.

Dative

> ...*aus dem engen Kreise...*
> *Die Indier sind von großem, schlanken Wuchse.*

There used to be a rule in German that singular nouns in the dative case should have an e added to them if the genitive form of that word ends in -(e)s. This rule is no longer applied, but the e is still sometimes used with some phrases, for example *im Zuge der Ermittlungen* or *am Tage*. You will often find that in older texts singular dative forms have an e added. For the purposes of reading a German text, this does not make things more difficult, if anything it makes things slightly easier (as you have another way of identifying the dative case).

The use of the ß

> *dass/daß*

The spelling reform in 1996 brought a lot of spelling in line with the underlying grammar. For example, words that have an inflected article or preposition are now capitalised, such as *vor Kurzem* (in many cases the old version remains a correct alternative).

The use of ss and ß is now tied to the pronunciation of a word. If the vowel is short, ss will be used (e.g. *der Fluss* – the river); if a vowel is long, ß will be used (e.g. *der Fuß* – the foot). This has had an effect on the spelling of one very common word in German: *daß* is now spelled *dass*, and this is the only correct way of spelling it nowadays.

It is also noteworthy that Swiss German does not use the ß (instead ss is used).

More frequent use of the subjunctive I and II

> *...daß es mit der poetischen Gabe keine so seltene Sache **sei**...*

The use of the subjunctive I for guesses and advice was more common than it is nowadays. These uses are usually not for reported speech (the practice text contains some occurrences of this). In addition, both the subjunctive I and II sometimes translate as "shall," which is uncommon in English nowadays.

Alternative meanings of words

> *Der **brave** Mann denkt an sich zuletzt.* (instead of *mutige*)
> *Er **erkannte** sie aber nicht, bis sie ihren Sohn gebar.* (instead of *vollendete* or *vollzog*)

Some words will have a different meaning from what you have learned or from what your dictionary tells you. In these cases it can be useful to consult a more comprehensive dictionary that lists old meanings of words. However, more frequently you will encounter words you know, where the translation is slightly different. Here you will need to rely on your deductive skills to surmise the meaning from the context. The practice text contains a number of these occasions for verbs such as *müssen* or *kommen*.

In addition, prepositions can also be used differently than expected:

> *Wir haben jetzt **an** den ›Philokteten‹ ein herrliches Beispiel.* (instead of *mit*)
> *...**ans** dem engen Kreise.* (instead of *aus*)

Alternative spellings and old word forms

> *...es **sey** die Farbe, die...* (instead of *sei*)
> *Die Luft, die sie **einathmen**.* (instead of *einatmen*)

Different spellings can throw you off especially if a text is also in an unfamiliar script. These differences seem to occur most often with the letters i/y, t/th; but double consonants (or lack thereof) and other "irregularities" can occur. Depending on the education of the author and the age of the text, these differences can range from very subtle to almost every second or third word.

Sometimes you will also encounter old word forms that are not typically used in modern German. These can be very tricky to deal with, especially if they are also spelled differently or combine words that look or sound familiar. Here are some examples:

> *...in diesen pedantischen **Dünkel**...*
> This has nothing do to with the words *dunkel* or *Dunkelheit*, but means "arrogance." The word is still part of the modern German dictionary, but its use is extremely rare.

*Ihre Angst **ward** immer größer.*
Thanks to fairy tales such as the Brothers Grimm, the form *ward* is still widely recognised and understood. The modern form of this word is *wurde*, the preterite of *werden*. It is not connected to *war*, the preterite form of *sein*.

*...die **mehrsten** Weiber...*
This is what the logical superlative of the comparative form *mehr* would be if it existed in modern German. The correct form nowadays is *meisten*.

If you encounter such a word, you should try a combination of research and deduction.

- Can you identify parts of the word that look familiar?
- Have you considered the context in which the word is used? Does this point to a meaning?
- Has your search in dictionaries or the Internet found anything? You may not find a dictionary entry, but perhaps a blog post asks the same question or a different text uses the same word, from which you can deduce its possible meaning.

Punctuation

Punctuation in German has not always been as clear-cut and precise as it is today. The use of the comma is of special importance here, as it is such a great help for determining where one clause ends and another starts. Unfortunately, in older texts you will see more commas that are placed according to the author's "feel," rather than the sentence structure. Other punctuation differences (such as the colon) have no impact on the understanding of a text.

German Fraktur

Finally, the traditional Germanic script Fraktur can prove challenging to read for those unfamiliar with it. Even then, poor print or deterioration due to age can make documents partly illegible; some symbols (for example umlauts, s or ligatures) also vary depending on the age of the document. Charts of the German Fraktur alphabet are widely available on the Internet and it is helpful to have period-correct printouts alongside the text you are trying to read.

Practice text: Gespräche mit Goethe

Johann Peter Eckermann: Gespräche mit Goethe in
den letzten Jahren seines Lebens - Kapitel 80

»Ich sehe immer mehr,« fuhr Goethe fort, »daß die Poesie ein
Gemeingut der Menschheit ist und daß sie überall und zu allen Zeiten
in Hunderten und aber Hunderten von Menschen hervortritt. Einer
macht es ein wenig besser als der andere und schwimmt ein wenig
länger oben als der andere, das ist alles. Der Herr von Matthisson muß
daher nicht denken, er wäre es, und ich muß nicht denken, ich wäre
es, sondern jeder muß sich eben sagen, daß es mit der poetischen Gabe
keine so seltene Sache sei, und daß niemand eben besondere Ursache
habe, sich viel darauf einzubilden, wenn er ein gutes Gedicht macht.
Aber freilich, wenn wir Deutschen nicht ans dem engen Kreise unserer
eigenen Umgebung hinausblicken, so kommen wir gar zu leicht in
diesen pedantischen Dünkel. Im Bedürfnis von etwas Musterhaftem
müssen wir immer zu den alten Griechen zurückgehen, in deren
Werken stets der schöne Mensch dargestellt ist. Alles übrige müssen
wir nur historisch betrachten und das Gute, so weit es gehen will, uns
daraus aneignen.«

»Darin«, fuhr Goethe fort, »waren nun wieder die Griechen so groß,
daß sie weniger auf die Treue eines historischen Faktums gingen, als
darauf, wie es der Dichter behandelte. Zum Glück haben wir jetzt an
den ›Philokteten‹ ein herrliches Beispiel, welches Sujet alle drei großen
Tragiker behandelt haben, und Sophokles zuletzt und am besten.
Dieses Dichters treffliches Stück ist glücklicherweise ganz auf uns
gekommen; dagegen von den ›Philokteten‹ des Äschylus und Euripides
hat man Bruchstücke aufgefunden, aus denen hinreichend zu sehen ist,
wie sie ihren Gegenstand behandelt haben. Wollte es meine Zeit mir
erlauben, so würde ich diese Stücke restaurieren, so wie ich es mit dem
›Phaëton‹ des Euripides getan, und es sollte mir keine unangenehme
und unnütze Arbeit sein.

Bei diesem Sujet war die Aufgabe ganz einfach: nämlich den Philoktet
nebst dem Bogen von der Insel Lemnos zu holen. Aber die Art, wie
dieses geschieht, das war nun die Sache der Dichter, und darin konnte
jeder die Kraft seiner Erfindung zeigen und einer es dem andern
zuvortun. Der Ulyß soll ihn holen; aber soll er vom Philoktet erkannt
werden oder nicht, und wodurch soll er unkenntlich sein? Soll der Ulyß
allein gehen, oder soll er Begleiter haben, und wer soll ihn begleiten?
Beim Äschylus ist der Gefährte unbekannt, beim Euripides ist es der
Diomed, beim Sophokles der Sohn des Achill. Ferner, in welchem
Zustande soll man den Philoktet finden? Soll die Insel bewohnt sein

oder nicht, und wenn bewohnt, soll sich eine mitleidige Seele seiner angenommen haben oder nicht? Und so hundert andere Dinge, die alle in der Willkür der Dichter lagen und in deren Wahl oder Nichtwahl der eine vor dem andern seine höhere Weisheit zeigen konnte. Hierin liegt's, und so sollten es die jetzigen Dichter auch machen, und nicht immer fragen, ob ein Sujet schon behandelt worden oder nicht, wo sie denn immer in Süden und Norden nach unerhörten Begebenheiten suchen, die oft barbarisch genug sind und die dann auch bloß als Begebenheiten wirken. Aber freilich ein einfaches Sujet durch eine meisterhafte Behandlung zu etwas zu machen, erfordert Geist und großes Talent, und daran fehlt es.«

Available online as part of Project Gutenberg: http://gutenberg.spiegel.de/buch/gesprache-mit-goethe-in-den-letzten-jahren-seines-lebens-1912/80 (accessed 14/02/2019)

Vocabulary

Philoktetes – In Greek mythology, Philoctetes is the son of a Greek king. He participates in the Trojan War on the side of the Greeks and is famous as a hero and accomplished archer. On the return home, Ulysses exiles him on an island; the exact reason why he is exiled is unclear (there are different accounts of the story).

There are also several plays around the story of Philoctetes, which, in the case of Sophocles' tragedy, are centred around his life on the island of Lemnos, where Ulysses revisits him after ten years of exile.

Begebenheit, die (-, -en) – event, incident
Bruchstück, das (-(e)s, -e) – fragment
das pedantische Dünkel – pedantic arrogange; *Dünkel* is very rarely used nowadays
sich etwas auf etwas einbilden (sep.v.) – pride oneself on sth., be vain about sth.
Gabe, die, (-e, -n) – talent, ability
Gefährte, der (-n, -n) – companion
Faktum, das (-s, Fakten) – not very common for: factum, fact
Mitleid, das (-(e)s, no plural) – mercy, pity, sympathy/compassion
Sujet, das (-s, -s) – an object or topic of artistic contemplation/work; subject
unkenntlich – unrecognisable
unnütz – useless
Zustand, der (-s, Zustände) – state, condition

Additional practice texts

Here are four additional practice texts. Except for the third text, all of these have tasks other than translation – either grammatical or comprehension.

Text 1: Völker der Welt!

This is a shortened version of a public speech given by the mayor of West Berlin, Ernst Reuter, on 9 September 1948 during the Berlin Blockade by the Soviet army. During this time, the city relied completely on airlifts from the Western Allies to avoid starvation. Reuter gave the speech at a rally in front of the *Reichstagsgebäude*, in front of hundreds of thousands of worried West Berliners.

Völker der Welt! Schaut auf diese Stadt!

Wenn heute dieses Volk von Berlin zu Hunderttausenden hier aufsteht, dann wissen wir, die ganze Welt sieht dieses Berlin. Denn verhandeln können hier schon nicht mehr die Generale, verhandeln können schon nicht mehr die Kabinette. Hinter diesen politischen Taten steht der Wille freier Völker, die erkannt haben, dass hier in dieser Stadt ein Bollwerk, ein Vorposten der Freiheit aufgerichtet ist, den niemand ungestraft preisgeben kann.

Wer diese Stadt, wer dieses Volk von Berlin preisgeben würde, der würde eine Welt preisgeben, noch mehr, er würde sich selber preisgeben, und er würde nicht nur dieses Volk von Berlin preisgeben in den Westsektoren und im Ostsektor Berlins. Nein, wir wissen auch, wenn sie nur könnten, heute stünde das Volk von Leipzig, von Halle, von Chemnitz, von Dresden, von all den Städten der Ostzone, so wie wir auf ihren Plätzen und würde unserer Stimme lauschen ?

Ihr Völker der Welt, ihr Völker in Amerika, in England, in Frankreich, in Italien! Schaut auf diese Stadt und erkennt, dass ihr diese Stadt und dieses Volk nicht preisgeben dürft und nicht preisgeben könnt! Es gibt nur eine

---

> Möglichkeit für uns alle: gemeinsam so lange zusammenzustehen, bis
> dieser Kampf gewonnen, bis dieser Kampf endlich durch den Sieg über
> die Feinde, durch den Sieg über die Macht der Finsternis besiegelt ist!

Tasks

Grammar and comprehension tasks

1. Who does Ernst Reuter address in his speech beyond the audience directly in front of him?
2. What does West Berlin represent according to Ernst Reuter (first paragraph)?
3. The second paragraph states the consequences of relinquishing West Berlin. What would these be? Why is the use of the subjunctive II noteworthy in the second paragraph and what does it imply in the sentence underlined?
4. According to Reuter there is only one option. What is the option?
5. Who is meant by *Macht der Finsternis*?

Vocabulary

besiegeln – to seal
lauschen – to eavesdrop, listen to

Text 2: „Ich habe doch nichts zu verbergen"

This is an essay on the role of data protection in the modern world. A complete translation of this text is not necessary; instead complete the grammar and comprehension questions that follow.

1	„Ich habe doch nichts zu verbergen"
2	Ein Großteil der Debatte über die Zukunft von Datenschutz und Big
3	Data kreist um die verbreitete, jedoch selten hinterfragte Annahme,
4	dass es sich beim Datenschutz lediglich um ein[en] Schutzschild
5	gegen Eingriffe des Staates, der Medien oder Großunternehmen
6	handele. Daher wird oft davon ausgegangen, dass Verletzungen der
7	Privatsphäre einmalige Vorkommnisse aufgrund irgendeines Lecks
8	seien: Vertrauliche persönliche Informationen werden plötzlich mit
9	einem viel größeren Personenkreis geteilt; was einst ein Geheimnis
10	war, wird auf einmal allgemein bekannt – und lässt sich nicht wieder
11	geheim machen; und so weiter.

12	In dieser Logik gelten Verletzungen der Privatsphäre merkwürdiger-
13	weise als eher flüchtige Ereignisse, die eigentlich auf die Enthüllung
14	eines größeren Geheimnisses zielen – eines entwickelten Guts, das
15	durch verschiedene Datenschutzmaßnahmen gesichert werden soll.
16	Wer also annimmt, dass hinter der schützenden Schicht aus Recht oder
17	Konvention kein solches Gut existiert, hat auch kein Problem damit,
18	wenn sich die flüchtigen Verletzungen der Privatsphäre häufen: Ist im
19	„Tresor unserer Privatsphäre" nichts zu holen, ist es egal, wie oft die
20	Bank überfallen wird. Dies ist das theoretische Gerüst, auf das sich die
21	nichtssagende, dennoch überall anzutreffende Phrase stützt: „Ich habe
22	doch nichts zu verbergen."

23	Ein Problem dieser Argumentation ist, dass sie sich vor allem auf die
24	Vergangenheit, nicht aber auf die Zukunft bezieht. Sie ist hilfreich, um
25	„statische" Güter vor einmaligen Angriffen zu schützen, nicht aber, um
26	im Einklang mit den eigenen Prinzipien und Werten eine Vorstellung
27	von zukünftigen, dynamischen Schutzgütern zu entwickeln. Doch was
28	ist, wenn das wahre Ziel von Datenschutz darin besteht – statt einen gut
29	ausgestalteten Datenbestand an Geheimnissen vor ständigen Angriffen
30	zu schützen –, gute Bedingungen für die Herausbildung einer neuen,
31	zukunftsorientierten Identität zu schaffen, die unabhängig ist von den
32	zahlreichen Beschränkungen durch Staat und Großunternehmen? Mit
33	anderen Worten: Was ist, wenn Datenschutz nicht primär das Ziel hat,
34	sicherzustellen, dass wir verbergen können, was wir verbergen wollen,
35	sondern uns allen zu erlauben, das zu sein, was wir sein könnten –
36	sogar in einer Zeit, in der die Räume zum Experimentieren schrump-
37	fen, weil die Bedürfnisse der Geheimdienste stetig wachsen und sich
38	die Geschäftsmodelle von Konzernen laufend weiterentwickeln?

39	Wenn dies tatsächlich der Fall ist, wenn es also nicht so sehr um die
40	Wahrung unserer Geheimnisse geht, sondern um die Wahrung aus-
41	gedehnter offener Räume, in denen wir weiterhin mit verschiedenen
42	Ideen, Lebensstilen und Identitäten experimentieren können, dann
43	funktioniert das „Ich-habe-doch-nichts-zu-verbergen-Argument"
44	nicht mehr, denn es erfasst nicht den eigentlichen Gegenstand, um
45	den es bei der Aufgabe von Privatsphäre geht. Stattdessen müsste die
46	Parole aktualisiert werden in „Ich habe doch nichts zu tun" oder „Ich
47	habe doch nichts zu wollen", was eine passende Beschreibung der von
48	Byung-Chul Han analysierten „Müdigkeitsgesellschaft" sein könnte:
49	Die Aufgabe des eigenen Raums zum Experimentieren bedeutet die
50	Aufgabe jeder Ambition, das eigene Leben selbst zu bestimmen – also
51	die stillschweigende Akzeptanz des Status quo.

Excerpt from: Morozov, Evgeny (2015). "Ich habe doch nichts zu verber-gen". In *Aus Politik und Zeitgeschichte, 11-12/2015*. BPB. pp. 3–7.

Vocabulary

Big Data, (die) – big data; usually used without an article
Datenschutz, der (-(e)s, no plural) – data protection
flüchtig – fleeting
sich häufen – to accumulate, heap up
Leck, das (-s, -s) – leak
lediglich – merely, solely, only
Tresor, der (-s, -e) – the safe, strong box
vertraulich – confidential

Tasks

A. The text contains a number extended participial phrases. Translate them.
1. Line 3: die verbreitete, jedoch selten hinterfragte Annahme
2. Lines 20–21: die nichtssagende, dennoch überall anzutreffende Phrase
3. Lines 28–29: einen gut ausgestalteten Datenbestand
4. Lines 30–31: einer neuen, zukunftsorientierten Identität
5. Lines 40–41: ausgedehnter offener Räume
6. Lines 47–48: der von Byung-Chul Han analysierten „Müdigkeits-gesellschaft"

B. How do you translate the following verb construction?
1. Lines 10–11: und lässt sich nicht wieder geheim machen;
2. Lines 39–40: wenn es also nicht so sehr um die Wahrung unserer Geheimnisse geht,…

C. How are the modal verbs in the following passage translated?
Lines 45–48: Stattdessen müsste die Parole aktualisiert werden in „Ich habe doch nichts zu tun" oder „Ich habe doch nichts zu wollen", was eine passende Beschreibung der „Müdigkeitsgesellschaft" sein könnte.

D. Comprehension questions.
1. Lines 2–6: What is a common misconception? Why is the subjunctive I used here?
2. Lines 16–22: Summarise what the argument *Ich habe doch nichts zu verbergen* means.
3. Lines 23–24: What is the problem that the author talks about here?
4. Lines 24–38: The author counters the simple statement *Ich habe doch nichts zu verbergen* from the first paragraph by offering a new dimension and a new role of data protection. What are this dimension and aim?
5. Lines 39–45: What do we need in order to experiment with different ideas, lifestyles and identities? What is the consequence for the argument *Ich habe doch nichts zu verbergen*?
6. Lines 49–51: What is the serious consequence of not defending and/or fighting for data protection?

Text 3: Matthäus 1: 18–25

In this biblical text you will find the following tenses: present tense, preterite, perfect, future and pluperfect. Its main feature though is the archaic or unusual use of some of the vocabulary; pay attention especially to the underlined words. The text is taken from the New Testament, Mt 1: 18–25 (23 has been omitted). If you struggle with the text, have a look in an English-language Bible for guidance.

> Mit der Geburt Jesu Christi war es so: Maria, seine Mutter, war mit Josef verlobt; noch bevor sie zusammengekommen waren, zeigte sich, dass sie ein Kind erwartete – durch das Wirken des Heiligen Geistes. Josef, ihr Mann, der <u>gerecht</u> war und sie nicht <u>bloßstellen</u> wollte, beschloss sich in aller Stille von ihr zu trennen. Während er noch darüber nachdachte, erschien ihm ein Engel des Herrn im Traum und sagte: „Josef, Sohn Davids, fürchte dich nicht, Maria als deine Frau zu <u>nehmen</u>; denn das Kind, das sie erwartet, ist vom Heiligen Geist. Sie wird einen Sohn gebären; ihm sollst du den Namen Jesus geben; denn er wird sein Volk von seinen Sünden erlösen." Dies ist alles geschehen, damit sich erfüllte, was der Herr durch den Propheten gesagt hat. (..)
>
> Als Josef erwachte, tat er, was der Engel des Herrn ihm befohlen hatte, und <u>nahm</u> seine Frau zu sich. Er <u>erkannte</u> sie aber nicht, bis sie ihren Sohn gebar. Und er gab ihm den Namen Jesus.

Vocabulary

erfüllen – to fulfil
gebären – to give birth
geschehen – to happen
Traum, der (-(e)s, Träume) – dream
Wirken, das (-s, no plural) – act, effect

Tasks

A. Find an example for each of the following tenses:
   - present tense
   - preterite
   - perfect
   - pluperfect
   - future

B. Translate the text and pay special attention to the translation of the underlined words.

Text 4: Von den 95 Thesen zum Augsburger Religionsfrieden

Finally, here is a longer text with a comprehensive and difficult test of your abilities. The questions focus on grammar and comprehension tasks; a complete translation of the text is not required. The text fits thematically with the text from chapter 11.

1	**Von den 95 Thesen zum Augsburger Religionsfrieden**
2	Zu Beginn des 16. Jahrhunderts bildete das westliche Europa einen
3	kulturellen Raum, der von verbindenden Traditionen geprägt war –
4	allen voran die lateinische Sprache, die in der transnationalen und
5	gelehrten Kommunikation dominierte. Auch einige religiöse Praktiken
6	waren exklusiv in der westlich-lateinischen Christenheit verwur-
7	zelt, etwa die Kreuzzüge, der Pflichtzölibat der Priester, der rechts-
8	verbindlich geforderte Gehorsam gegenüber dem Bischof von Rom
9	oder das Bußwesen, das bestimmte Vergehen mit exakt tarifierten
10	Kompensationsleistungen belegte. Dasselbe galt für den Ablass. Bei
11	diesem seit dem Hochmittelalter ausgebauten Heilsinstitut handelte
12	es sich um eine Verkürzung oder gar gänzliche Aufhebung zeitlicher
13	Sündenstrafen, die, sofern sie nicht zu Lebzeiten abgetragen wurden,
14	vor der Erlösung im Fegefeuer gebüßt werden mussten. Die attrak-
15	tiven Plenarablässe, die in der Regel gegen Geldzahlungen die totale
16	Sündenvergebung (plena remissio peccatorum) gewährten, konnte nur
17	der Papst spenden und wurden in großen Kampagnen europaweit und
18	seit der Erfindung des Buchdrucks Mitte des 15. Jahrhunderts weithin
19	einheitlich propagiert.
20	(..)
21	Als der Augustinermönch Martin Luther am 31. Oktober 1517 mit der
22	Veröffentlichung von 95 Thesen in Wittenberg und ihrer Versendung
23	an den obersten kirchlichen Würdenträger im Heiligen Römischen
24	Reich deutscher Nation, Albrecht von Brandenburg, Erzbischof von
25	Mainz und Magdeburg, die Ablasspraxis infrage stellte, rührte er also
26	an die zentrale Frage nach der menschlichen Identität aus und vor
27	Gott. Luther war davon überzeugt, dass der Ablass die jedem Christen
28	gebotene stetige Buße aushöhle, also die Umkehr zu einer Gottes
29	Geboten entsprechenden Lebensführung. Anstatt die Christen auf den
30	Weg der Nachfolge ihres leidenden Heilandes zu führen, gewähre ihnen
31	der Ablass trügerische Sicherheiten und verlogene Erleichterungen.
32	Das Evangelium, das die bedingungslose göttliche Gnade gegenüber
33	dem wegen seiner Gottferne verzweifelten Sünder verkünde, werde
34	durch ein Heilsangebot entwertet, das jedem – unabhängig von seiner

35	inneren Haltung – nur aufgrund des Erwerbs eines Ablassbriefes
36	den Erlass von Fegefeuerpein und den Eintritt in den Stand der
37	ewigen Seligkeit zuerkenne. Auch wenn der Bettelmönch aus dem
38	Augustinereremitenorden keineswegs der erste Theologe war, der den
39	Ablass angriff, so war seiner Kritik doch eine beispiellose Wirkung
40	beschieden. Dies hing zum einen damit zusammen, dass Luther den
41	Ablass gleichsam „von innen", vom Grundverständnis des christlichen
42	Glaubens und der entsprechenden sittlich-religiösen Haltung der
43	Buße her attackierte. Zum anderen erlangten seine Thesen durch den
44	Buchdruck eine für ihn selbst völlig überraschende Verbreitung und
45	wurden ungemein zügig innerhalb Deutschlands, aber auch in anderen
46	europäischen Ländern rezipiert.

| 47 | **Ein Reformer wird zum Reformator** |

48	Zum Zeitpunkt der Veröffentlichung der 95 Thesen war sich Luther
49	noch nicht darüber im Klaren, dass ein Angriff auf den Ablass auf
50	eine Infragestellung der Papstgewalt hinauslaufen musste. Denn der
51	Stellvertreter Christi auf Erden erhob den Anspruch, über einen „Schatz
52	der Kirche" (thesaurus ecclesiae) zu verfügen, in dem die Verdienste
53	Christi und der Heiligen gesammelt waren; kraft der ihm übertragenen
54	Schlüsselgewalt konnte er nach Belieben darüber verfügen. Verbindliche
55	Lehrentscheidungen zum Ablass hatte die römische Kirche jedoch
56	noch nicht dogmatisiert. Insofern hoffte Luther zunächst, dass sich
57	der Papst seine Kritik an der marktschreierischen Ablasspropaganda
58	des Dominikaners Johann Tetzel zu eigen machen werde. Nach
59	der Thesenpublikation setzte eine lebhafte Publizistik ein: Luther
60	führte literarische Auseinandersetzungen mit Tetzel und einer stetig
61	wachsenden Zahl weiterer Apologeten der römischen Papstkirche.
62	Neben der Frage des Ablasses rückten allgemeine Probleme der
63	Gnaden- und der Sakramentenlehre, des Verhältnisses von biblischer
64	Norm und kirchlicher Tradition, der Autorität der Kirchenväter, der
65	Päpste und der Konzilien ins Zentrum der theologischen Debatten.
66	Nach und nach ergriffen andere Theologen und Autoren aus dem
67	Laienstand verdeckt oder offen Partei für Luther; andere sorgten
68	dafür, dass Luthers Schriften umgehend nachgedruckt und europaweit
69	verbreitet wurden.

Excerpt from: Kaufmann, Thomas (2016). "Meilensteine der Reformation. Von den 95 Thesen zum Augsburger Religionsfrieden". In *Aus Politik und Zeitgeschichte 52/2016*. BPB. pp. 8–14.

Vocabulary

Ablass, der (-es, Ablässe) – indulgence
Erlass, der (-es, -e) – here: absolution
Gehorsam, der (-s, no plural) – obedience
Heilsinstitut, das (-s, -e) – here: a promise of salvation
Lehre, die (-, -n) – teaching(s)
rechtsverbindlich – legally binding
übertragen – to transfer
Vergebung, die (-, no plural) – forgiveness
Zölibat, der (-s, no plural) – celibacy
zügig – quick, rapid

Part 1 – Grammar (45 marks)

Task A (8 marks)

Give the cases of the following nouns <u>as they appear in the text</u>.

1. Lines 2–3: einen kulturellen Raum
2. Line 4: die lateinische Sprache
3. Line 9: bestimmte Vergehen
4. Lines 14–15: die attraktiven Plenarablässe
5. Line 22: ihrer Versendung
6. Line 27: die jedem Christen
7. Line 33: wegen seiner Gottferne
8. Lines 42–43: der Buße

Task B (4 marks)

Identify whether the main verb in the following sentences is the indicative or subjunctive I.

	Indicative	Subjunctive I
1. Lines 10–11: Bei diesem seit dem Hochmittelalter ausgebauten Heilsinstitut handelte es sich um eine Verkürzung oder gar gänzliche Aufhebung zeitlicher Sündenstrafen.		
2. Lines 27–28: dass der Ablass die jedem Christen gebotene stetige Buße aushöhle,		
3. Lines 34–37: das jedem (..) nur aufgrund des Erwerbs eines Ablassbriefes (..) den Stand der ewigen Seligkeit zuerkenne.		
4. Lines 62–65: Neben der Frage des Ablasses rückten allgemeine Probleme der Gnaden- und der Sakramentenlehre (..) ins Zentrum der theologischen Debatten.		

Task C (6 marks)

Identify the tenses and whether the form is active or passive (1 mark for the tense, 1 mark for active/passive)

	Tense	Active	Passive
1. Lines 33–34: werde durch ein Heilsangebot entwertet			
2. Lines 56–58: dass sich der Papst seine Kritik an der marktschreierischen Ablasspropaganda des Dominikaners Johann Tetzel zu eigen machen werde.			
3. Lines 68–69: dass Luthers Schriften umgehend nachgedruckt und europaweit verbreitet wurden.			

Task D (9 marks)

Do the following adjectives qualify a noun, verb or another adjective?

Line 4: transnationalen	☐ qualifies a noun	☐ qualifies a verb	☐ qualifies another adjective
Line 6: exklusiv	☐ qualifies a noun	☐ qualifies a verb	☐ qualifies another adjective
Lines 7–8: rechtsverbindlich	☐ qualifies a noun	☐ qualifies a verb	☐ qualifies another adjective
Line 8: geforderte	☐ qualifies a noun	☐ qualifies a verb	☐ qualifies another adjective
Line 9: exakt	☐ qualifies a noun	☐ qualifies a verb	☐ qualifies another adjective
Line 12: zeitlicher	☐ qualifies a noun	☐ qualifies a verb	☐ qualifies another adjective
Line 18: weithin	☐ qualifies a noun	☐ qualifies a verb	☐ qualifies another adjective
Line 19: einheitlich	☐ qualifies a noun	☐ qualifies a verb	☐ qualifies another adjective
Line 67: offen	☐ qualifies a noun	☐ qualifies a verb	☐ qualifies another adjective

Task E (15 marks)

Identify the beginning (the determiner) and the end of the extended participial phrases in the following sentences (1 mark) and translate them (2 marks for a correct translation; 1 mark for a partially correct translation).

1. Lines 10–14: Bei diesem seit dem Hochmittelalter ausgebauten Heilsinstitut handelte es sich um eine Verkürzung oder gar gänzliche Aufhebung zeitlicher Sündenstrafen, die, sofern sie nicht zu Lebzeiten

abgetragen wurden, vor der Erlösung im Fegefeuer gebüßt werden mussten.

2. Lines 27–29: Luther war davon überzeugt, dass der Ablass die jedem Christen gebotene stetige Buße aushöhle, also die Umkehr zu einer Gottes Geboten entsprechenden Lebensführung.

3. Lines 32–37: Das Evangelium, das die bedingungslose göttliche Gnade gegenüber dem wegen seiner Gottferne verzweifelten Sünder verkünde, werde durch ein Heilsangebot entwertet, das jedem – unabhängig von seiner inneren Haltung – nur aufgrund des Erwerbs eines Ablassbriefes den Erlass von Fegefeuerpein und den Eintritt in den Stand der ewigen Seligkeit zuerkenne.

4. Lines 43–46: Zum anderen erlangten seine Thesen durch den Buchdruck eine für ihn selbst völlig überraschende Verbreitung und wurden ungemein zügig innerhalb Deutschlands, aber auch in anderen europäischen Ländern rezipiert.

5. Lines 50–54: Denn der Stellvertreter Christi auf Erden erhob den Anspruch, über einen „Schatz der Kirche" (thesaurus ecclesiae) zu verfügen, in dem die Verdienste Christi und der Heiligen gesammelt waren; kraft der ihm übertragenen Schlüsselgewalt konnte er nach Belieben darüber verfügen.

Task F (3 marks)

What do the following determiners refer to?

1. Line 40: <u>dies</u>
2. Line 44: für <u>ihn</u>
3. Line 54: <u>er</u>

Part 2 – Reading comprehension (30 marks)

Task A (18 marks)

Determine whether the following statements are true or false?

Lines 2–5: Zu Beginn des 16. Jahrhunderts bildete das westliche Europa einen kulturellen Raum, der von verbindenden Traditionen geprägt war – allen voran die lateinische Sprache, die in der transnationalen und gelehrten Kommunikation dominierte.

		True (T) or False (F)
1.	All of Western Europe could be considered one cultural region.	
2.	All written communication took place in Latin.	

Lines 10–19: Dasselbe galt für den Ablass. Bei diesem seit dem Hochmittelalter ausgebauten Heilsinstitut handelte es sich um eine Verkürzung oder gar gänzliche Aufhebung zeitlicher Sündenstrafen, die, sofern sie nicht zu Lebzeiten abgetragen wurden, vor der Erlösung im Fegefeuer gebüßt werden mussten. Die attraktiven Plenarablässe, die in der Regel gegen Geldzahlungen die totale Sündenvergebung (plena remissio peccatorum) gewährten, konnte nur der Papst spenden und wurden in großen Kampagnen europaweit und seit der Erfindung des Buchdrucks Mitte des 15. Jahrhunderts weithin einheitlich propagiert.

		True (T) or False (F)
3.	The practice of indulgences was expanded and refined in the Middle Ages.	
4.	Indulgences were used to reduce the risk of fires.	
5.	Indulgences were available all over Europe.	
6.	The printing press allowed the spread of indulgences as a form of propaganda.	
7.	There was a variety of practices regarding indulgences in place across Europe.	

Lines 21–27: Als der Augustinermönch Martin Luther am 31. Oktober 1517 mit der Veröffentlichung von 95 Thesen in Wittenberg und ihrer Versendung an den obersten kirchlichen Würdenträger im Heiligen Römischen Reich deutscher Nation, Albrecht von Brandenburg, Erzbischof von Mainz und Magdeburg, die Ablasspraxis infrage stellte, rührte er also an die zentrale Frage nach der menschlichen Identität aus und vor Gott.

		True (T) or False (F)
8.	The publication of Luther's 95 theses was not limited only to Wittenberg.	
9.	Abrecht von Brandenburg was a high-ranking person in the church at that time.	

Lines 27–29: Luther war davon überzeugt, dass der Ablass die jedem Christen gebotene stetige Buße aushöhle, also die Umkehr zu einer Gottes Geboten entsprechenden Lebensführung.

		True (T) or False (F)
10.	Luther did not promote penance as a way of dealing with one's sins.	

Lines 29–37: Anstatt die Christen auf den Weg der Nachfolge ihres leidenden Heilandes zu führen, gewähre ihnen der Ablass trügerische Sicherheiten und verlogene Erleichterungen. Das Evangelium, das die bedingungslose göttliche Gnade gegenüber dem wegen seiner Gottferne verzweifelten Sünder verkünde, werde durch ein Heilsangebot entwertet, das jedem – unabhängig von seiner inneren Haltung – nur aufgrund des Erwerbs eines Ablassbriefes den Erlass von Fegefeuerpein und den Eintritt in den Stand der ewigen Seligkeit zuerkenne.

		True (T) or False (F)
11.	Christians should follow the example of their saviour when it comes to penance.	
12.	Indulgences effectively deceive worshippers.	
13.	Distance from God can make sinners feel more relaxed.	
14.	Indulgences (in order to work) still require a sinner to feel remorse or regret for their actions.	

Lines 50–54: Denn der Stellvertreter Christi auf Erden erhob den Anspruch, über einen „Schatz der Kirche" (thesaurus ecclesiae) zu verfügen, in dem die Verdienste Christi und der Heiligen gesammelt waren; kraft der ihm übertragenen Schlüsselgewalt konnte er nach Belieben darüber verfügen.

		True (T) or False (F)
15.	*Schatz der Kirche* denotes the material wealth of the church.	
16.	The pope has the keys to the church vault.	

Lines 54–58: Verbindliche Lehrentscheidungen zum Ablass hatte die römische Kirche jedoch noch nicht dogmatisiert. Insofern hoffte Luther zunächst, dass sich der Papst seine Kritik an der marktschreierischen Ablasspropaganda des Dominikaners Johann Tetzel zu eigen machen werde.

		True (T) or False (F)
17.	The indulgences could be criticised because they were not protected by church dogma.	
18.	Johann Tetzel was known to stand in market places and advertise indulgences in a loud voice.	

Task B (12 marks)

Comprehension questions

1   What information is given about Luther in regard to his background and actions? What two factors contributed to the distribution of his writing? Were the results and the feedback within the measures of what he had expected? (5 marks)

Lines 37–46: Auch wenn der Bettelmönch aus dem Augustinereremitenorden keineswegs der erste Theologe war, der den Ablass angriff, so war seiner Kritik doch eine beispiellose Wirkung beschieden. Dies hing zum einen damit zusammen, dass Luther den Ablass gleichsam „von innen", vom Grundverständnis des christlichen Glaubens und der entsprechenden sittlich-religiösen Haltung der Buße her attackierte. Zum anderen erlangten seine Thesen durch den Buchdruck eine für ihn selbst völlig überraschende Verbreitung und wurden ungemein zügig innerhalb Deutschlands, aber auch in anderen europäischen Ländern rezipiert.

2   According to the following passage, Luther's theses were a direct attack on whom and why? (2 marks)

Lines 48–54: Zum Zeitpunkt der Veröffentlichung der 95 Thesen war sich Luther noch nicht darüber im Klaren, dass ein Angriff auf den Ablass auf eine Infragestellung der Papstgewalt hinauslaufen musste. Denn der Stellvertreter Christi auf Erden erhob den Anspruch, über einen „Schatz der Kirche" (thesaurus ecclesiae) zu verfügen, in dem die Verdienste Christi und der Heiligen gesammelt waren; kraft der ihm übertragenen Schlüsselgewalt konnte er nach Belieben darüber verfügen.

3   Summarise what happened after the publication of Luther's 95 theses? (5 marks)

Lines 58–69: Nach der Thesenpublikation setzte eine lebhafte Publizistik ein: Luther führte literarische Auseinandersetzungen mit Tetzel und einer stetig wachsenden Zahl weiterer Apologeten der römischen Papstkirche. Neben der Frage des Ablasses rückten allgemeine Probleme der Gnaden- und der Sakramentenlehre, des Verhältnisses von biblischer Norm und kirchlicher Tradition, der Autorität der Kirchenväter, der Päpste und der Konzilien ins Zentrum der theologischen Debatten. Nach und nach ergriffen andere Theologen und Autoren aus dem Laienstand verdeckt oder offen Partei für Luther; andere sorgten dafür, dass Luthers Schriften umgehend nachgedruckt und europaweit verbreitet wurden.

Appendix

Grammar terminology explained

Term	Explanation	Examples
Adjective	An adjective gives more information about a noun or an action, for example how something looks or how something is done.	Green, fair, old
Adverb	An adverb gives more information about a verb, adjective or clause on how, when or why something was done.	Well, hardly, really, very
Case	Cases are used in many languages to show the function (or role) of a noun in a sentence, such as subject, object or possession.	My father, to **whom** I need to speak. The pope**'s** new book.
Clause	A clause is a part of a sentence that has its own subject and finite verb. Main clauses are complete on their own and can stand alone. Other clauses, such as relative or subordinate clauses, rely on a main clause to make sense.	Peter washes his car (main clause), which he bought last week (relative clause).
Comparative	A comparative is an adjective form that compares something.	Better, faster, smaller
Conjugation	Conjugation is a term used for the inflection of verbs. The endings of different verb forms show agreement with the subject and can also change for mood, tense or voice.	He **has** a car. We **had** a car.
Declension	Declension is a term used for the inflection of nouns or adjectives.	child, child**ren**
Diphthong	If two vowels are used to create a new sound, this is called a diphthong.	"au" in augment; "oi" in oil

Inflection	Inflection is when part of a word is changed to reflect its grammatical use or modify its meaning. Inflections can for example show whether a word is singular or plural, its case, the tense or the mood. The core part of the word usually stays the same or is at least recognisable.	I cook, I cooked, I have cooked, I had cooked. Car, cars. I am given, I was given.
Monophthong	If one vowel has one single sound, this is called a monophthong.	a, e, i, o, u, y
Mood (indicative/ subjunctive mood)	The term mood is used to differentiate factual statements (indicative) from non-factual statements (subjunctive).	Indicative: I am Subjunctive: (if) I were
Noun	A noun is a word that describes an object, thing, thought or person, whether concrete or abstract.	man, car, government
Participle	A participle is the third form of a verb (after the present tense and the preterite form). It describes something that is complete or done. Participles are often used with an auxiliary verb. German, unlike English, has two participles; the past participle (or participle II) is the more important one that is described here.	broken, gone, washed, destroyed
Person	The term person is typically used with verbs to describe who is doing something.	1st person forms: I, we 2nd person forms: you 3rd person forms: he, she, it, they
Possessive	The possessive shows that someone or something has ownership of someone or something. Usually this is shown with either a possessive adjective or a genitive case.	Possessive adjectives are words such as "his, my, your, our." "My father's car" is an example of the genitive case in English.
Prefix	A prefix is a short particle that is added to the front of a word to change its meaning.	Normal, abnormal
Preposition	Prepositions give information about nouns in regard to location, direction, time, or, occasionally, manner.	**Under** the table, **in** the car, **with** a knife
Pronoun	A pronoun stands in for another noun or a noun phrase.	Peter is my brother. **He** is six years old.

Strong and weak	"Strong" is another term for "irregular," such as an irregular verb. "Weak" is another term used for "regular."	Strong verb: I go, I **went** Weak verb: I cook, I cooked
Suffix	A suffix is a short particle that is added to the end of a word to change its meaning. Sometimes this changes the type of word, e.g. a verb can become a noun.	to govern, govern**ment**, home, home**less**
Superlative	A superlative is an adjective form that shows the highest/best/worst version.	Highest, best, worst
Verb	A verb is a word that describes an action or process.	go, cooking, washed
Voice (active/passive voice)	Voice is a term that is used with active and passive constructions. In active voice sentences, the focus is on who (agent) does what (action). In passive sentences, the focus is on the action, not the agent.	Active voice: I eat the cake. Passive voice: The cake is being eaten.

Difficult or tricky words and constructions

Word	Possible meanings	What makes it tricky?
all/alle/alles	all, everybody, everything	The word *all* can have several meanings. It can be used as a subject or object. However, since it is not capitalised it can be difficult to spot.
als/wie/wenn	als – as, than, when wie – as, how, such as wenn – if, when	There is a lot of meaning overlap between these three words. *Als* means "as" in most cases; it means "than" when it is used for comparisons; when it is used as a conjunction (often with a past tense verb) it can mean "when." *Wie* means "how," but it can also mean "as" in comparisons, but is only used for comparing something that is equal or similar. *Wenn* means "if" most of the time; it means "when" when it describes events that always or regularly occur. ***Als** ich in Italien lebte, war ich genauso alt **wie** du heute.* When I lived in Italy, I was exactly as old as you are. ***Wenn** es dunkel ist, geht die Notbeleuchtung an.* When it is dark, the emergency lighting turns on.

doch	still, however	One of the more difficult words to fully grasp in German is the word *doch*, because its meaning is highly contextual and difficult to express in English. Often it simply stresses or underlines a point. It can often make sense to omit it in a translation. *Doch auch das brachte keine Linderung.* Still, that did not bring relief. *Er hat das **doch** nicht gewusst.* He * didn't know that. (It is best to omit the translation here; possible translations would be: really, indeed, however.)
einig/eigen/ einzig	einig – united, agreed, some eigen – own, peculiar einzig – only, single	These words look very similar and can easily be confused; they all have different meanings (the list on the left is not complete). *Einige Menschen haben einen sehr **eigenen** Geschmack.* Some people have a very peculiar taste.
erst	only, first	The words *zuerst* and *erstens* always mean "first," but *erst* means "only" most of the time. Confusingly, it can mean "first" as well. *Ich gehe **erst** auf die Toilette, dann in die Kabine.* I go to the toilet first, then to the cabin.
etwa/etwas	etwa – approximately, about, roughly etwas – something	These words look similar, but have very different meanings. *Etwas* can be abbreviated in a dictionary.
es	it	*Es* can be used as a pronoun, referring to a previous noun. *Ich suche mein Hemd. Wo ist **es**?* I'm looking for my shirt. Where is it? It can be used as an impersonal subject or object in a clause, mainly to complete this clause. *Morgen regnet **es**.* Tomorrow it will rain. Finally, it can refer to a complete clause. ***Es** ist gesund, vegetarisch zu leben.* It is healthy, to live vegetarian.

je... desto/ umso...	the more... the more	The word *je* has different functions and meanings (e.g. "ever, per"). It can be used for comparisons by combining it with *desto* or *umso* in a second clause. The typical telltale sign for this use is an adjective in a comparative form. **Je** *schneller das Auto fährt,* **desto** *größer der Benzinverbrauch.* The faster the car drives, the bigger the fuel consumption.
lassen	to let	*Lassen* can be used in constructions that express the passive voice. See chapter 15 for more information on this.
lauter	louder, many, a lot of	If *lauter* is the comparative of the adjective *laut*, it means "louder." However, it can also be a synonym to *viele*. **Lauter** *Lügner hier!* A lot of liars here! Finally, there is a very rare meaning of *lauter* that means "pure" or "clean."
nicht/nichts	nicht – not nichts – nothing	These two words can be easily confused.
noch	still, else weder... noch – neither... nor noch nicht – not yet	What makes *noch* tricky is that it changes its meaning depending on other words in a sentence. On its own, a translation as "still" or "else" is usually fitting. With *weder* in another clause, the meaning becomes "neither... nor." If combined with *nicht*, the meaning changes to "not yet."
so	so, such, this way, in this manner	*So* can be difficult to translate, as it can have different meanings and/or functions. It is often advisable to start with the translation "so" and see how this fits, and if a more idiomatic English expression is possible. In many cases, *so* will be a linking word between conditional clauses and can be omitted in English translations. Here are some examples of *so* in sentences: *Die Blumen sind* **so** *schön.* The flowers are so beautiful. *Er hat das* **so** *gemacht.* He did that this way (in this manner). **So** *eine Aussage ist fragwürdig.* Such a statement is questionable. *Es scheint* **so***, als ob es heute nicht mehr regnen wird.* It seems (so), as if it won't rain anymore today.

sowohl... als auch	and, as well as	*Sowohl... als auch* can be translated as "as well as," but often it is just a more elaborate way of saying "and." *Er ist sowohl müde als auch hungrig.* He is tired as well as hungry. He is tired and hungry.
um	around, in order to, at	*Um* can be a preposition meaning ("around") or, when used with a time, "at." It can also introduce an extended infinitive clause as a special kind of conjunction. In those cases it can be translated as "in order to." *Wir gehen früh ins Bett, **um** morgen früh **um** sechs Uhr fit zu sein. Wir wollen morgen früh **um** den See joggen.* We go to bed early, in order to be fit/ready tomorrow morning at six o'clock. We want to jog around the lake tomorrow morning.
zu	to, too, towards	*Zu* can be a particle for verbs ("to"), for adjectives ("too") or a preposition with the dative case (to, towards).
zwar	although, though, indeed, in fact	When used on its own, *zwar* often means "although, even if, though." When used with "und," it usually is better translated as "indeed" or "in fact." *Es ist **zwar** nicht richtig, aber auch nicht komplett falsch.* Although it is not correct, it is also not completely wrong. *Wir gehen ins Kino, **und zwar** um acht Uhr.* We are going to the cinema, in fact at 8 o'clock.

Diminutive forms

A diminutive form shows that a noun is either a smaller version of it or it shows endearment/affection. In some cases it can also show belittlement, and some of these forms are old-fashioned or only used regionally.

In German, you create these forms by adding a suffix. This also changes the gender of the word to neuter. The most common suffixes are:

- chen: das Tischchen, das Männchen, das Autochen, das Städtchen;
- lein: das Fräulein, das Männlein, das Äuglein, das Büchlein.

Some regional variants include:

– li (mainly in Switzerland): das Brüderli;
– le/la (mainly in Swabian dialect): das Kätzle, die Kätzla (plural);
– erl(e) (mainly in Bavaria and Austria): das Stüberl, das Brüderle;
– je/sche (mainly in the Palatinate dialect): das Vögelsche.

There are some words that are formally diminutive forms, but have their own meaning in the dictionary:

das Mädchen – the girl
das Fräulein – Miss, unmarried woman; rarely used nowadays as it is considered sexist
das Märchen – fairy tale; the original word *die Mär* is rarely used
das Brötchen – a roll, not a "little bread"
das Männchen/Weibchen – there words are usually used to describe animal gender
das (Grill-)Hähnchen – lit. a little cockerel; this is usually used to describe a cooked or roasted chicken
das Meerschweinchen – a guinea pig

Numbers, cardinal numbers, dates and time

Numbers

In German, double-digit numbers, except for eleven and twelve, are pronounced or spelled out "in reverse," with the last digit before the second-to-last digit. This carries over if a number is "something"-thousand.

The use of the dot and comma is the opposite of English usage. Large numbers use a dot instead of a comma to help readers read it correctly e.g. the English number 22,000 would be 22.000 in German. Fractions use a comma instead of a dot, e.g. the English number 1.99 would be 1,99 in German.

Millionen is "millions" in English, but *Milliarden* is "billions," nine zeros, and *Billionen* is "trillions" (12 zeros). The next large number is *Billiarde* (quadrillion, 15 zeros) and then *Trillion* (quintillion, 18 zeros). The word to watch out for is *Billion*, as it is a false friend to the English "billions."

1	eins
2	zwei
3	drei
4	vier
5	fünf
6	sechs
7	sieben
8	acht
9	neun
10	zehn
11	elf
12	zwölf
13	dreizehn
14	vierzehn
...	
20	zwanzig
21	einundzwanzig
22	zweiundzwanzig
...	
133	einhundertdreiundreißig
...	
335	dreihundertfünfundreißig
...	
2.356	zweitausenddreihundertsechsundfünfzig
...	
43.934	dreiundvierzigtausendneunhundertvierundreißig
...	
2,5 Millionen	"zwei Komma fünf Millionen"

Cardinal numbers

For cardinal numbers (first, second, third...), German follows a straightforward system of adding "-te" to the numbers 2–19 and "-ste" to the numbers from 20 onwards. There are three irregular forms: "first" is *erste*, "third" is *dritte* and "seventh" is *siebte*. The adverb versions of these words add -ns to the end: erstens, zweitens, drittens... (firstly, secondly, thirdly...).

Number	Cardinal number	English equivalent cardinal number
eins	erste	first
zwei	zweite	second
drei	dritte	third
vier	vierte	fourth
fünf	fünfte	fifth
...		
einundzwanzig	einundzwanzigste	twenty-first

Dates

There are a couple of conventions around dates. The following are all acceptable ways to show a date in German:

Freitag, 4. Januar 2019	Freitag, der vierte Januar 2019	Friday, 4th of January 2019
Düsseldorf, den 4. Januar 2019	Düsseldorf, den vierten Januar 2019	Düsseldorf, 4th of January 2019
04.01.2019	(der) vierte erste 2019	4th of January 2019

In the numerical date, the day comes before the month. There is often a comma between individual location/date/time entries.

Years are pronounced a bit differently from "normal" numbers, similar to English.

1922 – neunzehnhundertzweiunzwanzig
2019 – zweitausendneunzehn

Time

In general, Germans use the 24-hour clock rather than the 12-hour clock that is common in the UK and the US. In spoken language or in more colloquial writing, you will find the 12-hour clock, but without any "am" or "pm" (context provides the required information).

The preposition *um* is used in time stamps. It is translated as "at." The word *Uhr*, lit. clock, usually means "o'clock," but in some cases it is not necessary to include it in a translation. Time stamps such as *12:05 Uhr* or *12:05* are both read out loud as *zwölf Uhr fünf*, i.e. *Uhr* is read out before the minutes even if it is not in the written text.

It is important to remember that *um* has different meanings and only means "at" when it is used to describe time.

Wir treffen uns um 8.
We meet at eight.

Das Meeting beginnt um 16.30 Uhr. (sechzehn Uhr dreißig)
The meeting begins at 4.30 pm.

Um wie viel Uhr treffen wir uns?
At what time do we meet?

On dictionaries

The choice of dictionary should depend on personal preference, the typical application and the required mobility. What this means is that those working mainly in one place do not have to consider portability as much as those travelling to libraries or archives. In general, some dictionaries have some strong points over others, and there are excellent online resources as well as printed dictionaries available.

Online dictionaries have many benefits and appear at first as the best choice in the 21st century. First, as they are non-physical they are highly "portable," and many have dedicated apps for use on mobile devices. With an online dictionary you can quickly access a huge amount of words and many dictionaries are connected to text corpora to give examples or can show different grammatical forms. A printed dictionary is naturally more limited by space in what it can contain. Second, many online dictionaries are able to find the more common inflected and conjugated forms of words, including irregular words. While this might make them seem like the best choice there are a few aspects where they are inferior to printed dictionaries. First, you need an Internet connection in order to access them. While this might seem irrelevant in the 21st century, those researchers who have had to work through archival material in a basement or a remote archive/library, or who visited a location abroad where their mobile phone company couldn't provide data access, will know that this is not always the case. And then there are situations, where one expected to have Internet access, but it turned out to not be the case. A busy library with poor Wi-Fi reception or speed due to too many users can also ruin a carefully planned research trip.

Second, some online dictionaries simply have too much information and either do not organise it in a useful way, or are simply misleading. Editors of printed dictionaries, on the other hand, have often thought very carefully about how to organise the information in the most accessible and concise way, which often helps with difficult words.

Third, larger printed dictionaries often include charts of irregular verb forms and other grammatical information that can often be very helpful for the purpose of Reading Skills.

In summary, the best approach is often to have access to both an online and a printed dictionary.

I personally use the following online dictionaries on a regular basis and have had, in general, good experience with them (please note that I am not affiliated with any of these webpages):

> Leo: https://www.leo.org/
> Beolingus: https://dict.tu-chemnitz.de/
> Linguee: https://www.linguee.com

Regarding printed dictionaries, it is important to strike a balance between portability and range and, if in doubt, I usually recommend students to "go big rather than small." If you go for a dictionary that is too small, the dictionary will not be useful for the purposes of German Reading Skills, as some words and explanations required for higher register language will be missing. Unfortunately, while the biggest, hardcover dictionaries cover the most words and terms (and provide more explanation), they are also large and unwieldy for travelling. Depending on your aims and needs, you might need to find a compromise. I have used most of the large bilingual dictionaries on the market – Cassell's, Collins, Langenscheidt and Oxford – and have found little difference between the newer versions.

Working at a desk, I personally prefer the very large "Collins Complete and Unabridged Dictionary" or the "Oxford German Dictionary" (previously called "Oxford Duden German Dictionary"); the Collins dictionary has a clearer and simpler typeface and text layout, which some people will prefer, while the Oxford dictionary typically has slightly more examples in the text. For portability, I prefer the "Langenscheidt Standard Dictionary German–English," or the Collins mid-size dictionaries. You can also get some great deals on older or used versions, but make sure it is an edition that includes the changes of the German spelling reform from 1996, and always make sure it is a bilingual dictionary, as there are monolingual dictionaries as well (especially from Langenscheidt, since it is a German publisher). You should take the claims of how many words (references, entries) they cover with a pinch of salt, as there are different ways of counting these. If you can, I would recommend visiting a local library or bookstore and browsing through some of them to see what you prefer.

Sometimes you might be looking for words that are very old or that seem to have a meaning that is different from the one your dictionary tells you. In this case, I have occasionally found the German edition of the website Wiktionary helpful, as it explains the origin and development of a word. The Duden website might also be helpful.

Wiktionary: https://de.wiktionary.org
Duden (monolingual): http://www.duden.de/woerterbuch

Additional grammar charts

Case declension chart 1: definite articles

	Masculine	Feminine	Neuter	Plural
Nominative	der Mann	die Frau	das Auto	die Kinder
Accusative	den Mann	die Frau	das Auto	die Kinder
Dative	dem Mann	der Frau	dem Auto	den Kindern
Genitive	des Mannes	der Frau	des Autos	der Kinder

Case declension chart 2: indefinite articles

	Masculine	Feminine	Neuter	Plural
Nominative	ein Mann	eine Frau	ein Auto	einige Kinder
Accusative	einen Mann	eine Frau	ein Auto	einige Kinder
Dative	einem Mann	einer Frau	einem Auto	einigen Kindern
Genitive	eines Mannes	einer Frau	eines Autos	einiger Kinder

Adjective declension chart – definite articles, indefinite articles, no articles

	Masculine nouns	Feminine nouns	Neuter nouns	Plural nouns
Nominative	der kleine Mann ein kleiner Mann kleiner Mann	die kleine Frau eine kleine Frau kleine Frau	das kleine Auto ein kleines Auto kleines Auto	die kleinen Kinder viele kleine Kinder kleine Kinder
Accusative	den kleinen Mann einen kleinen Mann kleinen Mann	die kleine Frau eine kleine Frau kleine Frau	das kleine Auto ein kleines Auto kleines Auto	die kleinen Kinder viele kleine Kinder kleine Kinder
Dative	dem kleinen Mann einem kleinen Mann kleinem Mann	der kleinen Frau einer kleinen Frau kleiner Frau	dem kleinen Auto einem kleinen Auto kleinem Auto	den kleinen Kindern vielen kleinen Kindern kleinen Kindern
Genitive	des kleinen Mannes eines kleinen Mannes kleinen Mannes	der kleinen Frau einer kleinen Frau kleiner Frau	des kleinen Autos eines kleinen Autos kleinen Autos	der kleinen Kinder vieler kleiner Kinder kleiner Kinder

Conjugation chart 1a: sein

	Indicative		Subjunctive II	
Present tense	ich bin du bist er/sie/es ist	I am you are he/she/it is	ich wäre du wär(e)st er/sie/es wäre	I would be you would be he/she/it would be
	wir sind ihr seid sie sind	we are you are they are	wir wären ihr wäret sie wären	we would be you would be they would be
Preterite/ past tense	ich war du warst er/sie/es war	I was you were he/she/it was	ich wäre gewesen du wär(e)st gewesen er/sie/es wäre gewesen	I would have been you would have been he/she/it would have been
	wir waren ihr wart sie waren	we were you were they were	wir wären gewesen ihr wäret gewesen sie wären gewesen	we would have been you would have been they would have been

Participle: gewesen

Conjugation chart 1b: sein in the subjunctive I

	Subjunctive I	
Present tense	ich sei du sei(e)st er/sie/es sei wir seien ihr seiet sie seien	Translation dependent on context
Past tense	ich sei gewesen du sei(e)st gewesen er/sie/es sei gewesen wir seien gewesen ihr seiet gewesen sie seien gewesen	

Conjugation chart 2: haben

	Indicative		Subjunctive II	
Present tense	ich habe du hast er/sie/es hat	I have you have he/she/it has	ich hätte du hättest er/sie/es hätte	I would have you would have he/she/it would have
	wir haben ihr habt sie haben	we have you have they have	wir hätten ihr hättet sie hätten	we would have you would have they would have
Preterite/ past tense	ich hatte du hattest er/sie/es hatte	I had you had he/she/it had	ich hätte gehabt du hättest gehabt er/sie/es hätte gehabt	I would have had you would have had he/she/it would have had
	wir hatten ihr hattet sie hatten	we had you had they had	wir hätten gehabt ihr hättet gehabt sie hätten gehabt	we would have had you would have had they would have had

Participle: gehabt

Conjugation chart 3: werden

	Indicative		Subjunctive II	
Present tense	ich werde du wirst er/sie/ es wird	I become you become he/she/ it becomes	ich würde du würdest er/sie/ es würde	I would (become) you would (become) he/she/ it would (become)
	wir werden ihr werdet sie werden	we become you become they become	wir würden ihr würdet sie würden	we would (become) you would (become) they would (become)
Preterite/ past tense	ich wurde du wurdest er/sie/ es wurde	I became you became he/she/it became	ich wäre geworden du wär(e)st geworden er/sie/es wäre geworden	I would have become you would have become he/she/it would have become
	wir wurden ihr wurdet sie wurden	we became you became they became	wir wären geworden ihr wäret geworden sie wären geworden	we would have become you would have become they would have become

Participle: geworden

Conjugation chart 4: indicative active and passive voice (weak verb)

	Active voice		Passive voice	
Present tense	ich höre du hörst er/sie/es hört	I hear you hear he/she/it hears	ich werde gehört du wirst gehört er/sie/es wird gehört	I am heard you are heard he/she/it is heard
	wir hören ihr hört sie hören	we hear you hear they hear	wir werden gehört ihr werdet gehört sie werden gehört	we are heard you are heard they are heard
Preterite	ich hörte du hörtest er/sie/ es hörte	I heard you heard he/she/ it heard	ich wurde gehört du wurdest gehört er/sie/es wurde gehört	I was heard you were heard he/she/it was heard
	wir hörten ihr hörtet sie hörten	we heard you heard they heard	wir wurden gehört ihr wurdet gehört sie wurden gehört	we were heard you were heard they were heard
Present perfect	ich habe gehört du hast gehört er/sie/es hat gehört	I have heard you have heard he/she/it has heard	ich bin gehört worden du bist gehört worden er/sie/es ist gehört worden	I have been heard you have been heard he/she/it has been heard
	wir haben gehört ihr habt gehört sie haben gehört	we have heard you have heard they have heard	wir sind gehört worden ihr seid gehört worden sie sind gehört worden	we have been heard you have been heard they have been heard
Past perfect	ich hatte gehört du hattest gehört er/sie/es hatte gehört	I had heard you had heard he/she/ it had heard	ich war gehört worden du warst gehört worden er/sie/es war gehört worden	I had been heard you had been heard he/she/it had been heard
	wir hatten gehört ihr hattet gehört sie hatten gehört	we had heard you had heard they had heard	wir waren gehört worden ihr wart gehört worden sie waren gehört worden	we had been heard you had been heard they had been heard
Future	ich werde hören du wirst hören er/sie/es wird hören	I will hear you will hear he/she/it will hear	ich werde gehört werden du wirst gehört werden er/sie/es wird gehört werden	I will be heard you will be heard he/she/it will be heard
	wir werden hören ihr werdet hören sie werden hören	we will hear you will hear they will hear	wir werden gehört werden ihr werdet gehört werden sie werden gehört werden	we will be heard you will be heard they will be heard

Future II	ich werde gehört haben du wirst gehört haben er/sie/es wird gehört haben	I will have heard you will have heard he/she/ it will have heard	ich werde gehört worden sein du wirst gehört worden sein er/sie/es wird gehört worden sein	I will have been heard you will have been heard he/she/ it will have been heard
	wir werden gehört haben ihr werdet gehört haben sie werden gehört haben	we will have heard you will have heard they will have heard	wir werden gehört worden sein ihr werdet gehört worden sein sie werden gehört worden sein	we will have been heard you will have been heard they will have been heard

Participle: gehört

Conjugation chart 5: subjunctive I active and passive voice

Note: these forms are only used if they are distinguishable from the indicative form. If not, the subjunctive II form is used.

The English translation is dependent on context.

	Active voice	Passive voice
Present tense	ich höre du hörest er/sie/es höre wir hören ihr höret sie hören	ich werde gehört du werdest gehört er/sie/es werde gehört wir werden gehört ihr werdet gehört sie werden gehört
Past tense	ich habe gehört du habest gehört er/sie/es habe gehört wir haben gehört ihr habt gehört sie haben gehört	ich sei gehört worden du seiest gehört worden er/sie/es sei gehört worden wir seien gehört worden ihr seiet gehört worden sie seien gehört worden

Conjugation chart 6: subjunctive II active and passive voice (weak verb)

	Active voice		Passive voice	
Present tense	ich hörte du hörtest er/sie/ es hörte	I would hear you would hear he/she/it would hear	ich würde gehört du würdest gehört er/sie/es würde gehört	I would be heard you would be heard he/she/it would be heard
	wir hörten ihr hörtet sie hörten	we would hear you would hear they would hear	wir würden gehört ihr würdet gehört sie würden gehört	we would be heard you would be heard they would be heard
Present tense with *würde*	ich würde hören du würdest hören er/sie/es würde hören	I would hear you would hear he/she/it would hear		
	wir würden hören ihr würdet hören sie würden hören	we would hear you would hear they would hear		
Past tense	ich hätte gehört du hättest gehört er/sie/ es hätte gehört	I would have heard you would have heard he/she/it would have heard	ich wäre gehört worden du wärest gehört worden er/sie/es wäre gehört worden	I would have been heard you would have been heard he/she/it would have been heard
	wir hätten gehört ihr hättet gehört sie hätten gehört	we would have heard you would have heard they would have heard	wir wären gehört worden ihr wäret gehört worden sie wären gehört worden	we would have been heard you would have been heard they would have been heard

Answer key

Alternative translations or additional words that could be inserted in translation have been added in brackets. Text behind the full stop of an answer (in brackets as well) is further explanation, hints or advice.

Chapter 1

1.1

THIS EXAMPLE SHOWS YOU HOW YOU CAN MAKE SENSE OF TEXTS WHERE SOME INFORMATION IS EITHER MISSING OR OBSCURED. IN THE BEGINNING YOU MAY HAVE FOUND IT HARD TO FIGURE OUT THIS PATTERN BUT AS YOU CONTINUE TO READ YOU FIND THAT IT BECOMES EASIER

1.2

Bruder – brother; Brüder – brothers; fallen – to fall; fällen – to fell; heilt – heals; hielt – held; Kuchen – cake; Küchen – kitchens; Leid – suffering; Lied – song; Meise – tit (a type of bird); mies – grotty, bad; Reise – trip, journey; Riese – giant; Tochter – daughter; Töchter – daughters; Vater – father; Väter – fathers; weise – wise; Wiese – meadow; zahlen – to pay; zählen – to count

1.4

A. braun – brown; sechs – six; hart – hard; Land – land; Markt – market; lang – long; warm – warm; oft – often; jung – young; roh – raw; mehr – more; Ende – end;

B. 1. Germany lies in Europe. It has nine neighbouring countries. The capital is Berlin.

2. At the University of Ulm students study Natural Sciences, Politics, History, Philosophy, Music, Art, Theology, English Studies and German Studies. What do you study?

C. geben – to give; über – over; haben – to have, halb – half

voll – full; bevor – before; der Vater – father; vier – four
helfen – to help; scharf – sharp; offen – open; der Pfeffer – pepper
denken – to think; die Erde – earth; das Ding – thing; der Tanz – dance
alt – old; die Mutter – mother; selten – seldom; tot – dead
das Wasser – water; besser – better; vergessen – to forget (if you replace ss
with tt you get a word very similar in sound to "forgotten"); groß – great
zehn – ten; sitzen – to sit; das Herz – heart; zu – to
zwölf – twelve; zwei – two; zwanzig – twenty
das Licht – light; hoch – high; die Sicht – sight; das Recht – right
machen – to make; sprechen – to speak; das Buch – book; suchen – to seek
kalt – cold; der Kanzler – the chancellor; kommen – to come; klar – clear
windig – windy; der Tag – day
jung – young; das Jahr – year
der Freund – friend; die Zunge – tongue; die Nacht – night; hassen – to hate;
die Straßenlaterne – street lantern; der Ellenbogen – elbow; durch – through;
fliegen – to fly; der Fiebertraum – feverish dream; die Dornenkrone – crown
of thorns; die Leiter – ladder; die Katze – cat; beide – both; die Erdnuss –
peanut (lit. earthnut, which is not too different from groundnut, another
name for a peanut)

Chapter 2

2.3

1. To drink a lot of alcohol is not healthy.
2. I have the permission to publish the article.

2.4

spinnen – to be crazy or bonkers; to spin (a thread); Spinnen (noun) – spiders; Fahrer (noun) – driver; fahren – to drive; licht – sparse, thin, bright; Licht (noun) – light; los – loose, off; Los (noun) – fate, lottery or raffle ticket; das Dritte Reich (noun) – Third Reich (an example of a noun where the adjective is also capitalised)

2.5

der Autofahrer – motorist; der Schreibtisch – desk; der Zeigefinger – index finger; die Studentenermäßigung – student discount; der Hörsaal – lecture hall or lecture theatre; der Abfalleimer – rubbish bin; die Bohrmaschine – drill; der Werbespruch – advertising slogan; der Buchladen – book store; die Glühbirne – light bulb (lit. glowing pear; if you look at the shape of a classic light bulb you can see the reference); die Nagelfeile – nail file; die Kirschmarmelade – cherry marmalade; das Motorboot – motor boat; der

Deutschlehrer – German teacher; der Verkehrsunfall – traffic accident; das Milchgesicht – milksop, rookie; die Gesichtsmilch – face crème; das Rindfleischetikettierungsüberwachungsaufgabenübertragungsgesetz – a law (Gesetz) to transfer (Übertragung) the task(s) (Aufgabe(n)) of monitoring (Überwachung) the labelling (Etikettierung) of beef (Rindfleisch); Rindfleisch is also a compound noun (lit. cattle or cow meat)

2.6

A.

Person	kommen	wohnen	machen	schreiben	trinken
ich	komme	wohne	mache	schreibe	trinke
du	kommst	wohnst	machst	schreibst	trinkst
er, sie, es	kommt	wohnt	macht	schreibt	trinkt
wir	kommen	wohnen	machen	schreiben	trinken
ihr	kommt	wohnt	macht	schreibt	trinkt
sie, Sie	kommen	wohnen	machen	schreiben	trinken

B. Conjugation charts for *sein*, *haben* and *würden* are listed in the chapter 2 and in the appendix.

C.

Person	sprechen	vergessen	sehen	essen	nehmen
ich	spreche	vergesse	sehe	esse	nehmen
du	sprichst	vergisst	siehst	isst	nimmst
er, sie, es	spricht	vergisst	sieht	isst	nimmt
wir	sprechen	vergessen	sehen	essen	nehmen
ihr	sprecht	vergesst	seht	esst	nehmt
sie, Sie	sprechen	vergessen	sehen	essen	nehmen

Person	fallen	laufen	schlafen	stoßen	gefallen
ich	falle	laufe	schlafe	stoße	gefalle
du	fällst	läufst	schläfst	stößt	gefällst
er, sie, es	fällt	läuft	schläft	stößt	gefällt
wir	fallen	laufen	schlafen	stoßen	gefallen
ihr	fallt	lauft	schlaft	stoßt	gefallt
sie, Sie	fallen	laufen	schlafen	stoßen	gefallen

The forms from verbs whose stem ends in –s or –ß can look confusing, as the second and third person singular look the same. Also, the forms of *nehmen* look unusual.

D. rate – 1.p. singular; verstehen – 1.p. plural & 3.p. plural & infinitive; kündigt – 3.p. singular & 2.p. plural; lügst – 2.p. singular

E.

Person	gründen	töten	arbeiten	binden
ich	gründe	töte	arbeite	binde
du	gründest	tötest	arbeitest	bindest
er, sie, es	gründet	tötet	arbeitet	bindet
wir	gründen	töten	arbeiten	binden
ihr	gründet	tötet	arbeitet	bindet
sie, Sie	gründen	töten	arbeiten	binden

Introductory text: Languages in the European Union (January 2019)

The European Union has 28 member states and uses 24 different languages as official working languages. (lit. as official "official languages" and working languages). According to §24 AEUV, all EU citizens have the right to contact European institutions in one of the 24 languages. The answer is in this language.

European institutions translate all important documents into all 24 official languages. However, the European Union uses primarily English, German and French internally.

The European Union supports language diversity. Every European is supposed to learn not only his mother tongue and English, but also an adoptive language. The European Union also supports minority languages, these (lit. that) are languages such as for example Luxembourgish, Yiddish, Romany or Irish, which only few people in the European Union speak. One can also write to the European Union in the "half-official" languages Catalan, Basque, Galician, Scots Gaelic or Welsh, but they are not official languages. In addition, there are special situations (lit. to this come special situations) such as for example Russian in the Baltic States or Turkish in Cyprus. There are many people in these countries, who speak these languages as their mother tongue or frequently in everyday life.

The most common mother tongue in the European Union is German with 18% of the citizens. In second place is (lit. stands) French with 14% and in third place English and Italian with 13% each. However, because 51% of all EU citizens speak English, English is the most popular language in the European Union.

Chapter 3

3.1

Mann – m, Männer; Terminus – m, Termini; Detail – n, Details; Publikation – f, Publikationen; Messer – n, Messer

3.2

Vater – m; Mutter – f; Sohn – m; Bär – m; Bärin – f; Polizist – m; Krankenschwester – f; Ärztin – f

They are easy to guess because they either refer to real human beings or, in the case of bear, follow the same rules as for people. In addition, the –in ending points to a feminine gender.

A.

Article		Article	
f	Weisheit	m	Terminator
f	Illusion	f	Frucht
f	Physik	m	Futternapf
n	Dokument	m	Lieferant
f	Hänselei	f	Atrophie
f	Baustelle	n	Gebirge

B.

Article		Article	
n	Gerede	f	Hypothek
n	Eigentum	m	Kommunismus
f	Krankheit	m	Schmetterling
f	Garage	f	Geographie
f	Distanz	m	Teppich
f	Politik	n	Parlament
f	Rarität	m	Honig
n	Klima	m	Topf
m	Rotor	f	Nachbarschaft

3.4

Kartoffeln, Gurken, Zwiebeln, Eier, Wienerwürste

3.5

	Masculine	Feminine	Singular	Plural
Fahrer	X		X	X
Fußballspielerinnen		X		X
Ritter	X		X	X
Krankenschwester		X	X	
Krankenpflegerin		X	X	
Physikerin		X	X	
Deutsche	X	X	X	
Poet	X		X	

Fahrer and *Ritter* could be singular or plural.
The gender of *Deutsche* is unclear without further information.

3.6

Am Samstag geht Peter mit seinem Bruder Max ins Kino. a, c, d
Fan rennt auf Spielfeld beim Superbowl. a, b
Deutschland lässt Brasilien beim Endspiel keine Chance. b, d

3.7

1. verstehe; 2. hat; 3. fahren; 4. begrüßt; 5. leben & sprechen; 6. muss & übersetzen; 7. schreibt; 8. wohnst; 9. kann... sprechen; 10. hat... vergessen.

3.8

A.
1. einschalten; I turn the TV on.
2. umschalten; I switch to a different channel.
3. anziehen; The man puts on a warm jacket.
4. umziehen; The family moves into a new apartment.
5. hervorziehen/ziehen; The cat pulls the mouse out of the hole.
6. hören; We listen to music.
7. aufhören; We stop with the music.
8. aufladen; I charge my mobile phone.
9. einladen; I invite Peter to the party.

10. laden; I load my pistol.
11. vorladen; The court summons the witness with the letter.
12. zusammenleben; We (will) live five years together, before we marry.
13. weggehen; I am going out again tonight (Easy to understand, but there are quite a lot of things going on here. First, the present tense here is used for a plan, so a future tense makes sense in English. Second, *weggehen* is lit. go away; finally, *heute Abend* and *noch einmal* have been rendered more idiomatic here.)
14. zurückkommen; I (will) come back before midnight.
15. vorkommen; Different sounds occur in nature to a large extent.
16. ausgehen; One acts on the assumption of the hypothesis (it is assumed) that tigers have become almost extinct.
17. as above; the German sentence uses a nested clause to show how the separable prefix could be in a different place of the sentence.
18. ausmachen & zumachen; Don't forget to turn the light off and close (shut) the door! (A shortened version of the German sentence would be: *Vergiss nicht, das Licht aus- und die Tür zuzumachen!*).

B. Underlined: verbs; in bold: main clause
   1. **Er sieht die Katze im Garten,** obwohl es Nacht ist. He sees the cat in the garden, although it is night.
   2. Weil er schon seit Tagen nichts gegessen hat, **sieht er dünn aus.** Because he has eaten nothing for days, he looks thin.
   3. Während er nach Hause geht, **fängt es an** zu regnen. (The infinitive can be considered its own clause. It doesn't have to be separated by a comma.) While he goes home, it starts to rain.
   4. **Er parkt sein Auto in der Wiesenstraße,** obwohl es verboten ist und er kein Geld für eine Strafe hat. He parks his car in the Wiesenstraße, although it is forbidden and he doesn't have money for a ticket (lit. he has no money for a punishment).
   5. **Niemand weiß,** dass Herr Steiner der Dieb ist. Nobody knows, that Mr Steiner is the thief.
   6. **Warum rufen wir nicht an** und fahren dann hin? Why don't we call and then drive there?
   7. Die deutsche Sprache korrekt auszusprechen, **finden viele Ausländer schwer.** (The first clause is an infinitive clause.) Many foreigners find it difficult to pronounce the German language correctly.
   8. Wie meine Mutter das gemacht hat, **ist ein Rätsel.** It is a mystery how my mom has done that.

Practice text: Redewendungen und Aphorismen von Friedrich Schiller

Friedrich Schiller is a world-famous German author. Many of his works are known internationally. It is not surprising that he has also had an influence on the German language. Even today, there are many expressions and wise sayings in German (originating) from his works.

From Wilhelm Tell:
Every street leads to the end of the world.
God only helps (then), when humans don't help anymore.
He must come through this narrow way (lit. hollow alley). (This saying is often used to state that there are no alternatives available.)
The lake smiles, invites (one) for a bath.

The old (things) fall, the time changes, and new life blooms from the ruins.

From Wallenstein:
Long speech, short message. (Lit. short sense; it means someone talked a great deal for a rather simple or short message).
The stars don't lie.

From Mary Stuart:
What one doesn't give up, one has not lost (What isn't given up, isn't lost).
I am better than my reputation.
A deep meaning lives in the old customs.

From Die Räuber:
Sleep and death are just twins.

From Das Lied von der Glocke:
The eye of the law is watching.
Where raw forces preside without sense (are at work without sense).

From Kabale und Liebe:
Sinners and evil spirits shy away from the light of the world.

From Der Parasit:
The appearance rules the world and justice exists (lit. is) only on the stage.

Chapter 4

4.1

B. a) Peter darf keine Nüsse essen.
   b) Maria muss in die Schule gehen.
   c) Morgen soll es regnen.
   d) Wir wollen ins Theater gehen.
   e) Ich kann Französisch sprechen.

C. f)   The girl cannot go to the theatre.
   g)   I am supposed to do the homework.
   h)   Christina does not have to go to the cinema (Christina needn't go to the cinema).
   i)   Christina is not allowed to go to the cinema.
   j)   A good thing needs time (lit. a while; the saying means "good things take a while/you can't rush them".)

4.2

A. a)   I like classical music.
   b)   I would like to listen to classical music.
   c)   That may be the reality.

B.

   1. a; 2. c; 3. c; 4. d; 5. a; 6. b; 7. c

4.3

A.

	addresses one person	addresses a group of people
Frag nicht so viel!	X	
Tragt bitte die Tüten ins Haus!		X
Können Sie bitte die Fenster aufmachen?	X	X
Gehen Sie bitte in den Hörsaal!	X	X
Finde deine Schwester!	X	
Glaubt nicht alles, was ihr hört!		X
Öffnen Sie bitte das Gesangbuch auf Seite 41!	X	X
Geht nicht allein aus dem Haus!		X
Mach niemandem die Tür auf!	X	

B. 1. b; 2. a; 3. c; 4. a
C. In order as they occur: Gießen...ab; abkühlen; schneiden...klein; hacken...klein; Schneiden...klein; Hacken...klein; Schmecken...ab.

Practice text: Da steh' ich nun, ich armer Tor

The tragedy "Faust" is the best-known work by Johann Wolfgang von Goethe. The play is about Doktor Faust, a scientist. (This is one of the idiomatic expressions with "es".) He is already very educated and knows a lot, but it is not enough. He wants to know all the secrets of the world. Only then can he be happy. He therefore closes a deal with the devil. The devil is called "Mephisto" in Goethe's Faust. If the devil can make Doktor Faust happy, he is supposed to get Faust's soul.

Now I have indeed studied Philosophy, Law and Medicine and unfortunately also Theology with intense effort (lit. hot effort).
Here I stand now, I poor fool, and I am as clever as (I was) before.
I'm a Magister (I got a Master of Arts) and Doctor even
and for ten years long I have been tricking my students (led them by the nose)
– upwards, downwards, criss-cross.
And I see, that we cannot know anything.
That just about wants to burn my heart!
(The last line is often completely rephrased in translations, for example "which is why I feel completely undone".)

Chapter 5

5.2

1. Der Unterhändler; 2. die Sekretärin; 3. die Tochter (The hint here is that there is an additional n on *Herr Keuner*, which suggests a case different from nominative. *Der Gastwirtin* can be ruled out (it is a feminine word), which leaves only *die Tochter* as a possible subject. The most difficult part about this sentence is that *Herr Keuner* is in the most likeliest position for the subject and it does not have an article, which makes it difficult to rule it out as the subject.)

5.3

A.

	Nominative	Accusative	Both cases possible
die Frau			X
diesen Tisch		X	
der Hut	X		
die Sprachen			X
das Buch			X
den Raben		X	
das Mädchen			X
die Studenten			X
die Hunde			X

B. 1. Saffron makes the cake yellow.
   2. Children and drunks speak the truth.
   3. The researchers publish the results.
   4. The dog eats the bird.
   5. The dog eats the bird. (Subject and object have swapped position in the German sentence, but the meaning has not changed.)
   6. The bird eats the dog.
   7. One introduced the Gregorian calendar in the 16th century in the Holy Roman Empire (The Gregorian calendar was introduced...).
   8. One should not wake sleeping dogs.
   9. What little Hans does not learn, grown-up Hans won't learn anymore. (The equivalent saying in English is "you can't teach an old dog new tricks.")
   10. Everything has an end, only the sausage has two.

5.4

1. One should not praise the day before the evening.
2. I give the dog a bone.
3. The professor answers the questions for the students.
4. The study helps the research field.
5. The voter should better not trust the politician.
6. Let's send the manuscript to the publisher (publishing house)!
7. The man buys a bag for the woman.
8. Who still gives trust to the liar? (Who still trusts the liar?)
9. A lot is missing for the healthy one, for the sick one only one thing (The healthy lacks/craves many things, the sick one only one thing).
10. Age does not protect from love, but love protects from aging.

5.5

1. I give the neighbour's dog a bone.
2. We remember the victims of the Second World War.
3. The son of the pastor (the pastor's son) is not in the church.
4. Peter's wife knocks on the door.
5. We are waiting for the letter from the publisher.
6. I am searching for my wife's bag.
7. The children of the revolution still want (crave) the validation of the parents.
8. You are supposed to eat your bread in the sweat of your face, because you are earth and you are supposed to become earth (You shall eat your bread in the sweat of thy brow, for you are dust and will become dust).
9. (He) who does not value the Pfennig (penny, cent, little coin...), is not worthy of the Taler (silver coin, pound, dollar...).
10. This book is definitely not the last (ultimate) conclusion of wisdom.

5.7

A. 1. Bei Neumond (D) steht der Mond (N) im Schatten (D) der Erde (G). During new moon, the moon stands (is) in the shadow of the earth.

2. Das Krokodil (N) beißt dem Kasper (D) das Bein (A) ab. The crocodile bites the leg off the fool. (This is an example where the dative has been used for possession, even if the genitive (*das Bein des Kaspers*) would have been the more accurate choice.)

3. Weder mein Lehrer (N) noch mein Kursbuch (N) kennen die Antwort (A) auf die Frage (A). Neither my teacher nor my course book know the answer to the question.

4. Die Musterlösung (N) für diese Aufgabe (A) ist unklar. The sample solution for this exercise is unclear.

5. Die Indianer (N) jagen keine Büffel (A) mehr. The Indians (Native Americans) don't hunt buffalos anymore.

6. Der Professor (N) will den Studenten (D) das Problem (A) nicht erklären. The professor does not want to explain the problem to the students.

7. Man wächst mit den Aufgaben (D). One grows with the tasks.

8. Der Freund (N) der Verlobten (Genitive Plural!) sendet der Mutter (D) der Braut (G) eine E-mail (A). The friend of the engaged couple sends the mother of the bride an email.

9. Wir sind die Kinder (N) Gottes (G). We are God's children.

10. Keine Antwort (N) ist auch eine Antwort (N). No answer is also an answer.

11. Der Dativ (N) ist dem Genitiv (D) sein Tod (N). The dative is the death of the genitive.

12. Ich spreche weder Französisch (A) noch Spanisch (A), dafür aber Russisch (A). I speak neither French nor Spanish, but I speak Russian. (You can omit *dafür* in the translation.)

13. Den Vorbereiteten (D) überrascht nichts. Nothing is surprising for the prepared (Nothing suprises the prepared).

14. Sag niemals nie! Never say never!

B. 1. Solche Fehler (A) <u>korrigiert</u> die Lehrerin (N, subject) so oft, dass sie die Fehler (A) manchmal schon <u>übersieht</u>.

2. Obwohl Universitäten (N, subject) in Europa meistens keine Privatinstitutionen (N) <u>sind</u>, <u>verbreiten</u> sich marktwirtschaftliche Ideen (N, subject) auch dort, wo man (subject) es (A) nicht <u>erwartet</u>.

Practice text: Oropos und die Graer

The priest of Amphiaraus is supposed to move into the holy site at the end of winter and is supposed to hold out there until the beginning of the next winter, so that he is at the site at least 10 days every month. The holy site is located distant from the city Oropos in the mountains; in Winter not many visitors of the dream oracle were to be expected: so the priests determined the beginning and end of the season in advance, similar to a seaside resort, and made them known to the public once and for all. The priest has a civil occupation aside from his honorary post and lives in the city, of course. It is therefore impossible for him to be in the temple the entire season. The following instructions provide pious visitors with the possibility to sacrifice (make sacrifices) even in the absence of the priest, but for the (an) oracle he had to be present without doubt. Therefore he is supposed to preside over his position (act out his role) at least every third day on average.

Comprehension questions: 1. c; 2. b; 3. a; 4. a, b, c ,d, f

Chapter 6

6.1

1. I am calling, in order to reserve a table in a restaurant.
2. This they said, however, in order to tempt him.
3. In order to get a promotion, the researcher has to publish many articles.
4. He calls, in order to invite his friend to a party.

6.3

The Nibelungenlied tells in two parts the story of the murder of Siegfried by Burgundian kings and of the revenge of his wife Kriemhild against the murderers.

Siegfried possessed mythical abilities (invisibility/camouflage cape, invulnerability) and a mythical gold treasure (Nibelungenhort). He was given the hand of the Burgundian king's sister Kriemhild only under the condition, that he supported his future brother-in-law Gunther with the courting of the Icelandic queen Brünhild - who was also equipped with supernatural strength. Gunther and Siegfried secretly changed roles in a competition. Gunther won the competition through this trick and he could marry Brünhild. This led years later to a fight between Kriemhild and Brünhild and to an insult to the queen. Hagen, King Gunther's advisor, solved this conflict through the sneaky murder of Siegfried. The widow Kriemhild later married the Hun king Etzel. Through this marriage Kriemhild gained the possibility (opportunity) to plan her revenge: she invited her brothers and Hagen into the Hun territory. Because Hagen recognised the danger, he appeared with a large army. Kriemhild provoked an attack and even used Etzel's and her small son as bait. In two days and three nights, thousands of Huns and Burgundians died in the fights. In the end, Kriemhild killed the murderer Hagen herself with Siegfried's sword. However, she was not allowed to do this without the permission of the king. For this deed, Kriemhild herself was killed.

6.4 Introductory text: Jesus und die Ehebrecherin

Frühmorgens aber <u>kam</u> Jesus wieder in den Tempel und alles Volk <u>kam</u> zu ihm und er <u>setzte</u> sich und <u>lehrte</u> sie. Da <u>brachten</u> die Gelehrten und die Pharisäer eine Frau, beim Ehebruch <u>ergriffen</u>, und <u>stellten</u> sie in die Mitte und <u>sprachen</u> zu Jesus: „Meister, man <u>hat</u> diese Frau beim Ehebruch auf frischer Tat <u>ertappt</u>. Mose <u>hat</u> uns im Gesetz <u>befohlen</u>, solche Frauen zu <u>steinigen</u>. Was <u>sagst</u> du?" Das <u>sagten</u> sie aber, um ihn zu <u>versuchen</u>. Jesus <u>richtete</u> sich <u>auf</u> und <u>sprach</u> zu ihnen: „Wer unter euch ohne Sünde <u>ist</u>, der <u>werfe</u> den ersten Stein auf sie." Als sie das <u>hörten</u>, <u>gingen</u> sie <u>hinaus</u>, einer nach dem anderen. Und Jesus <u>blieb</u> allein mit der Frau und <u>sprach</u> zu ihr: „Wo <u>sind</u> sie, Frau? <u>Hat</u> dich niemand <u>verdammt</u>?" Sie aber <u>sprach</u>: „Niemand, Herr." Jesus aber <u>sprach</u>: „So <u>verdamme</u> ich dich auch nicht. <u>Geh hin</u> und <u>sündige</u> hinfort nicht mehr."

In the German text, the preterite is used for the narrative and the present perfect is used for spoken language.

Jesus and the adulteress

Early in the morning Jesus came back into the temple and all the people came to him and he sat down and taught them. Then the scribes and Pharisees brought him a woman caught in adultery, and they put her in the middle and said to Jesus: "Master, this woman was caught in the act of adultery. In the law Moses commanded us to stone such women. What do you say?" They said this however, in order to tempt him (to set a trap for him). Jesus stood up and said to them: "He that is without sin shall throw the first stone."("He who among you is without sin, may throw the first stone.") When they heard this, they went outside, one after the other. And Jesus stayed alone with the woman and said to her: "Woman, where are they? Has no one condemned you?" "No one, sir," she said (however). "Then I do not condemn you either. Go and sin no more (hereinafter)."

6.6

Infinitive	Preterite	Participle
beißen	biss	gebissen
schneiden	schnitt	geschnitten
reiten	ritt	geritten
binden	band	gebunden
singen	sang	gesungen
trinken	trank	getrunken

fallen	fiel	gefallen
lassen	ließ	gelassen
blasen	blies	geblasen
tragen	trug	getragen
schaffen	schuf	geschaffen
waschen	wusch	gewaschen
lesen	las	gelesen
sehen	sah	gesehen
vergessen	vergas	vergessen
nehmen	nahm	genommen
sterben	starb	gestorben
sprechen	sprach	gesprochen
schreiben	schrieb	geschrieben
entscheiden	entschied	entschieden
steigen	stieg	gestiegen
fliehen	floh	geflohen
verlieren	verlor	verloren
schießen	schoss	geschossen
schwimmen	schwamm	geschwommen
wissen	wusste	gewusst
kennen	kannte	gekannt

6.7

1. angerufen; The police has called.
2. stationiert; The soldiers are stationed in the barracks.
3. no participle; Many people have to adapt to new circumstances in old age.
4. gehabt; I learn swimming in my free time. As a child I never had the chance. (Lit. As a child I have never had the chance.)
5. gebaute & zerstört; An earthquake has destroyed the house built in 1960.
6. beantwortet & geantwortet; Why have you not answered my question? Karl has answered my questions right away. (The verbs *antworten* and *beantworten* are synonyms.)
7. Verliebt & verlobt & verheiratet; "In love (lit. fallen in love), engaged and married" is a pop song by Peter Alexander.
8. mitgebracht; Has nobody brought a screwdriver along?

9. ausgegangen; On Saturday evening, many people went out in the inner city/downtown. (The translation of *Innenstadt* can differ widely depending on which city we are talking about.)
10. no participle; We are not allowed to (we must not) forget the invitation.

6.8

A. 1. Many people had already booked their holiday. (pluperfect)
   2. As child I had a book with ancient sagas/tales.(preterite)
   3. The Müllers had gone (lit. driven) on holiday. (pluperfect)
   4. The bill was already paid. (preterite)
   5. In the evening the barn had not yet been burning (on fire). (pluperfect)
   6. Later the barn was burned down completely. (preterite)

B. 1. I was on holiday in Italy in September. (present perfect)
   2. It was very nice and warm there. (preterite)
   3. I had been in France before and I had visited a friend of mine there. (pluperfect)
   4. I had had a great time with my friend in France. (pluperfect)
   5. In Florence I wanted to visit a museum. (preterite)
   6. The museum was closed, however. (preterite)
   7. The museum had been closed, however. (pluperfect)
   8. There had been a small fire in the night before (pluperfect) and the house was damaged. (preterite)
   9. I visited a park then and ate a pizza. (both present perfect)
   10. Next year I will go/drive to Spain. (future)

Chapter 7

7.2

1. The young man is my son.
2. He has the hair of his mom, but the eyes from my grandfather.
3. Unfortunately, our children have also inherited the stubbornness of their parents.
4. Mr Professor, your wife has called. She asks you, to (please) pick up your daughter from the nursery/kindergarten.

7.3

A. 1. The soup is too spicy.
   2. "Too fast and too dangerous" describes the rollercoaster very well.

B.

1. Er hat ihren unveröffentlichten Artikel schnell gelesen.

ihren	X qualifies a noun
unveröffentlichten	X qualifies a noun
schnell	X qualifies a verb

2. Der Inhalt deines Artikels ist so komplex, dass ich ihn einfach nicht verstanden habe.

deines	X qualifies a noun
komplex	X qualifies a verb
einfach	X qualifies a verb

3. Mein Hut ist neu.

mein	X qualifies a noun
neu	X qualifies a verb

4. Der Hut ist ein neuer.

neuer	X qualifies a noun

The use of an adjective ending on *neuer* implies another instance of the word *Hut*.

5. Ich suche den grünen und roten Stift.

grünen und roten	X qualifies a noun

I am looking for a green and red pen (one single pen, not different green and red pens!).

6. Ich lese oft aktuelle Artikel, um auf dem Laufenden zu bleiben.

aktuelle	X qualifies a noun

7. Das Resultat ist eindeutig, aber leider unerwünscht.

eindeutig	X qualifies a verb
unerwünscht	X qualifies a verb

8. Neulich haben Experten eine alte Fliegerbombe aus dem Zweiten Weltkrieg in unserer Nachbarschaft entschärft.

neulich	X qualifies a verb
alte	X qualifies a noun
unserer	X qualifies a noun

9. Suchen Sie Ihre Brille? Sie liegt auf dem kleinen Tisch.

ihre	X qualifies a noun
kleinen	X qualifies a noun

10. Spätrömische Dekadenz ist ein negativ konnotierter Begriff.

spätrömische	X qualifies a noun
negativ	X qualifies another adjective
konnotierter	X qualifies a noun

7.5

	as	how	than	when	as if
Tu nicht so, als könntest du Französisch verstehen! Ich weiß, dass du kein Französisch gelernt hast.					X
Ich habe keine Uhr. Ich weiß nicht, wie spät es ist.		X			
Das neue Parteiprogramm der Partei ist konservativer als das letzte.			X		
Mein Vater arbeitet als Gesangslehrer, aber er ist als Klempner ausgebildet.	X (both)				
Als wir in Frankreich waren, habe ich eine tolle Oper besucht.				X	
Neil Armstrong betrat als erster Mensch den Mond.	X				
Obwohl Helium nicht so leicht wie Wasserstoff ist, benutzt man es heute in Zeppelinen.	X				

7.6

1. Good advice is expensive (dear).
2. May the better one win!
3. The last will be the first.
4. Expensive wine is expensive, but cheap wine is cheaper. (Only the last form is a comparative form.)
5. It is easier to give good advice than to follow it. (In German this is plural, but the English word "advice" is not used in the plural.)
6. Honesty (lit. honestly) lasts the longest.
7. One does not eat the soup as hot as one cooks it.
8. The meeting tomorrow is too early for me.
9. Seneca the Elder was the biological father of Seneca the Younger.
10. Nature can be cruel, but humans are even crueler.
11. The candle shines the brightest in the dark night.
12. The most pious (well-mannered) man cannot live in peace, if it doesn't appeal to (please) the evil neighbour.
13. Although the K2 is not as high as the Mount Everest, it is much more dangerous for climbers than the Everest.

Practice text – Rumpelstiltskin

Once upon a time there was a miller. He was poor, but he had a beautiful daughter. Now it happened that he came to speak with the king, and in order to give himself a standing (make himself appear important), he said to him: "I have a daughter, she can spin straw into gold". The king said to the miller: "That is an art, if your daughter is as skilled as you say. Bring her to my castle tomorrow, I want to put her to the test."

When now the girl came to him, the king led her into a chamber. The chamber was all full of straw. He gave her a spinning wheel and a reel and said: "Now put yourself to work, and if you haven't spun all this straw to gold through the night to the morning, then you must die." Then he locked the chamber and she stayed alone in it. The poor miller's daughter sat there and didn't know any solution (lit. advice): she didn't know how one is able to spin straw to gold. And her fear became greater and greater, so that she started to cry. There suddenly the door opened and a little man came in and said: "Good evening, mistress (maiden) miller, why do you cry so much?"

"Ach," the girl answered, "I am supposed to spin straw to gold, but I don't understand it." There the little man said: "What will you give me, if I spin it for you?" "My necklace," said the girl. The little man took the necklace, sat in front of the little wheel, whirr, whirr, whirr, three times (he) pulled, the spool was full. Then he put another one on it and whirr, whirr, whirr, three times (he) pulled and the second one was full. And it went on so forth until the morning, and all spools were full of gold.

At dawn the king came and when he saw the gold, he was surprised and happy, but his heart only became even greedier. He brought the miller's daughter into another much larger chamber full of straw and ordered her to spin as well this night, if her life was dear to her. The girl didn't know how to help herself and cried, then the door opened once more and the little man appeared and said: "What will you give me, if I spin the straw to gold for you?"

"A ring from my finger," the girl answered. The little man took the ring, began to spin the wheel and by the morning he had spun all the straw into shiny gold. The king was very happy at the sight, but still didn't have enough of the gold. He brought the miller's daughter into an even larger chamber full of straw and said: "You must spin it this night. If you manage it, you shall become my wife."

As the girl was alone, the little man came again a third time and said: "What will you give me, if I spin the straw once more?" "I don't have anything anymore that I can give," answered the girl. "So promise me your first child, when you are queen." The miller's daughter didn't know how she could help herself differently. She promised it to the little man and he spun the straw into gold once more. And when in the morning the king came and found the gold, he married her and the beautiful miller's daughter became a queen.

Over a year later she brought a beautiful child into the world and she didn't think of the little man any more. There he suddenly stepped into her chamber and said: "Now give me what you have promised." The queen was startled and offered the little man all the riches of the kingdom, if he left her the child. But the little man said: "No, I prefer something alive rather than all the treasures of the world." There the queen started to lament and cry and the little man had pity on her: "I will give you three days", he said, "if you know my name by then, you shall keep your child."

The queen thought the whole night about all names and she sent a messenger into the country, in order to enquire about further names. The little man came the next day and she started with Kaspar, Melchior and Balzer and she said all the names, but with each the little man said: "That is not my name." On the second day she asked in the neighbourhood what the people were called there, and she said the most unusual and weirdest names to the little man: "Are you perhaps called Rippenbiest or Hammelswade or Schnürbein?" But he always answered: "That is not my name."

On the third day the messenger came back again and said: "I have not been able to find any new names, but I came to a high mountain in the forest, where fox and hare bid each other goodnight. There I saw a little house and in front of the house a fire was burning. And around the fire jumped a totally (quite) ridiculous little man, he was jumping on one leg and was screaming:

> "Today I bake,
> tomorrow I brew,
> the next day I'll get the queen's child,
> Ach, how good that nobody knows,
> that my name is Rumpelstiltskin!"
> (In rhyme: Today I bake, tomorrow brew, the next I'll have
> the queen's child, ha!, how glad I am that no one knew, that
> Rumpelstiltskin I am styled.")

You can imagine how happy the queen was when she heard the name, and when shortly after that the little man entered, and asked: "Now, Mrs Queen, what is my name?", she first asked: "Are you called Kunz?" "No." "Are you called Heinz?" "No." "Is your name Rumpelstiltskin?"

"The devil told you that, the devil told you that," screamed the little man, and he stamped his right foot, full of rage, so deep into the earth, that it drove into the earth up to the body, then he grabbed his left foot in rage with both hands and ripped himself asunder in the middle (and he tore himself in two).

Chapter 8

8.1

A. 1. I am not going to the cinema, because I am going to the theatre. (It makes sense to use the going to-future for these sentences, because they sound like plans.)

2. I am not going to the cinema, but I am going to the theatre.
3. I am not going to the cinema, after I've been to the theatre.
4. The prince and the princess are marrying, although they come from different countries.
5. The prince and the princess are marrying, because (since) they come from different countries.
6. In case the article is out of date, we must search for a new one.
7. The prince agrees to the wedding, whereas the princess declines it.
8. I didn't know that that can happen. (In English it sounds awkward the other way round.)
9. We often ask ourselves, whether someone watches over us.
10. By re-interpreting (re-evaluating) known sources, the researcher was able to add something new to the topic.

B.

	Conjunction	Adverbial	Preposition
Während der Arbeit klingelt oft mein Handy.			X
Nachdem ich gegessen habe, gehe ich nach Hause.	X		
Ich esse jetzt zu Ende, **danach** gehe ich nach Hause.		X	
Der Artikel ist fertig, wir müssen **allerdings** die Quellen aktualisieren.		X	
Der Artikel ist fertig, **aber** wir müssen die Quellen aktualisieren.	X		
Da drüben steht ein Baum.		X	
Der Verleger kürzt den Artikel, **damit** er in die Ausgabe passt.	X		

8.2

1. The ring, which belongs to the woman, is (made of) silver.
2. The people, whom I trust, can be counted on one hand.
3. The Christmas address, for which we are waiting, is scheduled for 8 pm.
4. He defeats a boxer, whose weight is (lit. lies) one category above his.
5. I write to the students of the course, who have taken the exam, that the board, which publishes the results, wants to repeat the exam.
6. He uses a writing programme (word processor), which is able to correct the mistakes that he makes.

8.3

1. The rules in the orphanage determine when one has to eat and sleep.
2. It is difficult to understand, to what the author wants to draw our attention.
3. We will have to answer in court for what we have done. (Lit. for that which we...).
4. The kind of distress (lit. tilt) into which the bank has got itself, is unbelievable.

8.4

Main clauses are marked in bold; verbs are underlined; finite verbs have an (f) after them; (sc) - subordinate clause; (nc) - nested clause; (rc) - relative clause; (ic) - infinitive clause

---

Max Weber: Wissenschaft als Beruf (1919)

Ich soll (f) nach Ihrem Wunsch über „Wissenschaft als Beruf" sprechen. Nun ist (f) es eine gewisse Pedanterie von uns Nationalökonomen, an der ich festhalten möchte (f) (rc): daß wir stets von den äußeren Verhältnissen ausgehen (f) (sc), hier also von der Frage (phrase): **Wie gestaltet (f) sich Wissenschaft als Beruf im materiellen Sinne des Wortes? Das bedeutet (f) aber praktisch heute im wesentlichen: Wie gestaltet (f) sich die Lage eines absolvierten Studenten,** der entschlossen ist (f) (rc), der Wissenschaft innerhalb eines akademischen Lebens sich hinzugeben (ic)? **Es ist (f) zweckmäßig,** vergleichend zu verfahren (ic) und sich zu vergegenwärtigen (ic), wie es im Ausland dort aussieht (f) (sc), wo in dieser Hinsicht der schärfste Gegensatz gegen uns besteht (f) (rc): in den Vereinigten Staaten (phrase).

Bei uns – das weiß (f) jeder (nc) – **beginnt (f) normalerweise die Laufbahn eines jungen Mannes als Privatdozent. Er habilitiert (f) sich nach Rücksprache und mit Zustimmung des betreffenden Fachvertreters an einer Universität und hält (f) nun** – unbesoldet (apposition) – **Vorlesungen,** deren Gegenstand er innerhalb seiner venia legendi selbst bestimmt (f) (rc). **In Amerika beginnt (f) die Laufbahn normalerweise ganz anders durch Anstellung als „assistant".** In ähnlicher Weise etwa (phrase, stands in for a main clause), wie das bei uns an den großen Instituten der naturwissenschaftlichen und medizinischen Fakultäten vor sich geht (f) (sc), wo die förmliche Habilitation als Privatdozent nur von einem Bruchteil der Assistenten und oft erst spät erstrebt wird (f) (rc). **Der Gegensatz bedeutet (f) praktisch,** daß bei uns die Laufbahn eines Mannes der Wissenschaft im ganzen auf plutokratischen Voraussetzungen aufgebaut ist (f) (sc).

8.5

1. The chancellor holds a moving speech.
2. Many people searching for protection came to Germany in the summer of 2015.
3. The football match is interrupted due to pouring rain.

Practice text: Hintergründe zum Weltbevölkerungswachstum

Two positive factors of the growing world population

1. People are getting older
We are living longer than ever before thanks to medical advances (lit. medical advance) and better living conditions. This is true for developed (lit. industrial) countries as well as for developing countries. While the average number of children per woman is decreasing almost everywhere in the world, people in many parts of the earth are reaching an older (lit. higher) age.

2. More children survive
Thanks to the industrial revolution and the worldwide advances for example in the health sector and with the nutritional situation, the mortality rate dropped first in the developed countries and later in developing countries as well. But: That more children survive is also a reason for parents to have fewer children. High numbers of surviving children lead to a reduction in births, because parents have to be less worried about the survival of their own children.

Six negative factors of the growing world population

1. Many people were never sexually educated
Sexual education is the basis for young people and adults to protect themselves with contraceptives such as condoms from unwanted pregnancies and sexually transmitted diseases such as HIV. To talk about sexuality, however, is still regarded as breaking a taboo in many countries. To not talk about it is very dangerous, though. This way, myths take hold around the topic sexuality and the own body. That can have serious consequences for girls and women when they become pregnant – often unwillingly. Only those who possess sufficiently qualified information (sufficient knowledge) can go about their lives in a self-confident and self-determined manner.

What DSW does
We have constructed a network of around 400 youth clubs in East Africa. In these (lit. there) young people can find specially trained youth workers (advisors) of the same age, with whom they can talk about sexuality.

We campaign with our political work so that sexual education receives greater significance worldwide.

2. Poverty and lack of prospects impede progress
The population is growing especially in the poorest countries of the world. Many children represent (offer) an opportunity of support in old age and sickness. At the same time, voluntary family planning could strongly improve the development in poor countries. Children in small families are healthier on average, have better chances at education and better possibilities to participate in the working life. That also has a positive effect on the next generation.

Young people in developing countries deserve a better education, good health care support and above all the prospect of a fulfilling work place.

What DSW does
We offer possibilities for job training and further education in our projects and this way (through this) prospects for young people as well.
We educate young people in the basics of economy.
Young people put into practice (implement) their own ideas on how to keep the youth club running. We support them with this.
We campaign for an increase in foreign aid money, so that poor countries receive better chances for development.

Chapter 9

9.0

a) My assistant has booked the hotel room for me.
    X past participle; active voice
b) In school many tests are written.
    X werden   X past participle; passive voice
c) The trust of old people can be misused for illegal activities.
    X werden   X past participle; passive voice; don't count *werden* twice, i.e. for the infinitive box.
d) It is often said that too much television is bad for children.
    X werden   X past participle; passive voice
e) The winters nowadays are becoming warmer and warmer (ever warmer).
    X werden; active voice, become.
f) We will drive (go) to Spain next year.
    X werden   X Infinitive; active voice, future
g) On Tuesday, my dad will be released from prison.
    X werden   X Infinitive   X past participle; passive voice, future
h) Light from cosmic sources is being analysed at the Max-Planck-Institute in Heidelberg.
    X werden   X past participle; passive voice

i)   All confidential data has been deleted.
     X werden   X past participle; passive voice
j)   The politics of this president will have been forgotten in a few years.
     X werden   X Infinitive   X past participle; passive voice, future

9.1

Vorgangspassiv are: c, e, h, i; note that in e the subject of the sentence has changed and is now *ein Haus,* not *Familie Müller.*
   Example b is an *Ersatzpassiv* construction and can be translated in the passive voice.

9.3

A.

A. 1.   Albert Einstein was born in Ulm, March 14th 1879.
   2.   A lot in the field of Natural Sciences is being published in English.
   3.   Debts with other people are often forgotten.
   4.   My debts will only be paid (repaid) in 30 years.
   5.   I definitely won't forget your birthday. (Not passive.)
   6.   The solving of the crime is demanded by the family of the victim.
   7.   Was the house built last year?
   8.   Different prophesies were made by Nostradamus.
   9.   The thief has been arrested by the police.
   10. The answers of the exam had already been known. (There is no form of *werden* in this sentence, so it is not a form of the *Vorgangspassiv,* but it is a *Zustandspassiv* construction.)
   11. The streets will be salted in winter.
   12. Many good tests (lit. works) have been written in the exam.
   13. The exam had only been passed by one student. (Only one student passed the exam.)
   14. Professor X had founded the school for gifted children. (No passive.)
   15. All homework is supposed to be handed in (submitted) by Friday.
   16. The exams had to be corrected in record time.
   17. Some of the results of the study weren't allowed to be published.

B. 1.   preterite; He worked at Mercedes.
   2.   present perfect, passive; He has been asked by her.
   3.   present; He asks his mother about the woman.
   4.   preterite, passive; He was asked by her.
   5.   pluperfect; It had cost £10.
   6.   pluperfect, passive; At Siemens, a lot had been worked.
   7.   present; The pen belongs to her.
   8.   preterite; The pen belonged to her.

9. present perfect; The pen has belonged to her.
10. present, passive; I am being asked.
11. future, passive; I will be asked.
12. preterite; I asked him.
13. present perfect; I have asked him.
14. present; I work on Monday.
15. future; I will work on Monday.
16. present, passive in second clause; He says, that there is work on Monday (lit. on Monday it is being worked).
17. present; He wants to work on Monday.
18. preterite; I had to work on Monday.
19. present prefect; I have had to work on Monday.
20. future; He will have to ask her.
21. present; He is supposed to ask her.
22. preterite; He was supposed to ask her. (Or: He should ask her.)
23. preterite, passive; He had to be asked.
24. pluperfect, passive; He had been driven to Germany.
25. future, passive; He will be allowed to drive to Germany.

Practice text: Die Zäsur des Mauerbaus 1961

The turning point of the construction of the wall

In a special meeting of the Politbureau on Friday, August 11th 1961, the way for the construction of the (Berlin) Wall was paved, which took place under the supervision of Erich Honecker during the night from August 12th to August 13th 1961. Units of the People's Police, of the paramilitary company workers and of the National People's Army erected a 45km long wall made out of barbed wire and concrete right across Berlin. The construction of the Wall not only destroyed relationships across East and West, it also crushed the hopes of many citizens of the GDR of liberalisation and a freer (more liberal) society. Politically, the construction of the Wall meant that the SED had openly admitted the lack of popularity of its politics and the communist ideology, even though the SED never said this out loud (even if this was never said). The option of fleeing the republic (i.e. the GDR) had disappeared for most citizens and the GDR became known internationally as the country that had to imprison (lock up) its citizens. The Wall became a clearly visible symbol of a system that could only be upheld through force. The mere physical presence of the wall was visible from afar due to the barbed wire barriers, the border fortifications, the permanent stationing of Soviet troops in the city, the constant propaganda of the class struggle. All of this made Berliners aware on a daily basis of their situation as a "walled-in" people. Especially doctors and engineers complained. The technical and medical intelligentsia had up to then enjoyed the privilege to be able to visit the West for professional purposes and for further education, a privilege which had now been repealed with a single stroke, and which made many members of this class aware of their powerlessness against the state machinery.

Chapter 10

10.1

1 Some forms, especially *sie, ihr,* but also *ihm* occur in more than one case or number and have more than one translation. *Ihr* is especially tricky, because it the possessive adjective looks the same. It is also possible to confuse *sie* and *Sie* (used for formal speech).
2 1. Sie; 2. Er, ihm; 3. ihr, ihn; 4. Sie, ihnen; 4. es; 6. ihrer; 7. Sie; ihm; 8. Es; 9. Er; er; ihr; 10. Sie; ihn; 11. sie; seiner;

10.2

1. A proper marksman helps himself.
2. The brave man thinks about himself last. (In modern German, *brav* would be translated as "well-behaved.")
3. He showers every day.
4. The research institute moves to Berlin.
5. The actor changes (his clothes).
6. Imagine, I met the queen.
7. Please introduce me to the queen.
8. Are we going to get another dessert?
9. The students are looking forward to the holidays.
10. He has answered his question himself.
11. Do you remember the prehistory (background)?
12. Have you seen my paper weight? (*Briefbeschwerer* is not a complaint letter.)

Practice text: Glück im Unglück (1)

Blessing in disguise

Following the victory over Hitler, the alliance of the Western Allies with the Soviet Union had achieved its goal – and fell apart. The political-ideological differences were too great, especially in Europe, whose east Stalin swallowed up into his empire. Instead of working together, allies became enemies, the Cold War began.

The defeated Germany lay (was) also at the centre of this post-war drama – and, under the leadership of its chancellor Adenauer the western part made a virtue out of necessity (made the best of a difficult situation). The "old one (old guy) from Rhöndorf", as his subjects called him affectionately, was a crafty (experienced) politician. And yet Konrad Adenauer was not exactly a master of nuanced speech. "The simpler you think (your thinking)", he once said, "is often a valuable gift from God". Intellectuals might have shaken (been horrified), but the common people understood. They understood that things were going upwards with Adenauer (were improving under Adenauer) – and upwards meant westwards, put simply (lit. simply thought). They also understood that the Federal Republic of Germany would have probably developed differently without Adenauer. Possibly unified early, but then only according to the conditions of Moscow.

Chapter 11

11. 1

A.

Short	Long	Short	Long
am	an dem	fürs	für das
ans	an das	hinters	hinter das
beim	bei dem	vorm	vor dem
im	in dem	unterm	unter dem
ins	in das	vors	vor das
vom	von dem	übers	über das
zum	zu dem	unters	unter das
zur	zu der	hinterm	hinter dem
hintern	hinter den	durchs	durch das
ums	um das	aufs	auf das
untern	unter den	übern	über den

B. 1.   We have a prime minister instead of a chancellor in England.
   2.   The president steps out of the car.
   3.   Anna stayed two months long in the rehab clinic.
   4.   He bought a house next to his father's house.
   5.   Do you have the book with you?
   6.   We drink a cup of tea after eating.

7. The air is becoming more and more polluted because of the many cars.
8. The entire class sits around a table.
9. We are going to the cinema.
10. This matter lies outside my influence.
11. We meet at the train station.
12. The Roman encampment was this side of the Rhine.
13. His house is located outside of Hamburg.
14. In his book (lit. work) "Beyond Good and Evil" Nietzsche criticises old-fashioned moral conceptions.
15. Peter drives with his car into the car park from Aldi.
16. Peter is driving with his car in the car park from Aldi (is cruising around in Aldi's car park).
17. For heaven's sake don't go outside without your umbrella.

D. Sentence 2: *Der Präsident steigt aus dem Auto aus.* (separable verb *aussteigen*); sentences 8 and 16 could have a *herum* added to the end and sentences 9 and 15 could have a *hinein* added, turning the verbs into separable verbs.

E. The only time the case made a difference in meaning was sentences 15 and 16. This showcases that it is very rare that the case makes a difference in terms of meaning, and if then the difference is not a very significant one.

11.2

1. He is afraid of spiders.
2. He is afraid that a spider bites him. (He is afraid of being bitten by a spider.)
3. We are thinking about buying a new car.
4. We are thinking about buying a new car.
5. Machiavelli writes about the type of ruler that can stay in power for longer.
6. Machiavelli describes what type of ruler can stay in power for longer.
7. In my dissertation I deal with the rule of the Habsburgs in Switzerland.
8. My dissertation is about the way, how the rule of the Habsburgs affected Switzerland. (My dissertation describes how the rule of the Habsburgs affected Switzerland.)
9. The prophet speaks about (the) life in the future.
10. The prophet speaks about how one lives in the future.

11.3

1. You don't trust someone who lied once (lit. The person who lies once, you don't trust that person).
2. Everyone gets what he deserves.
3. Nobody can help someone who does not want to help himself.
4. A hero is someone who does what he can. The others don't do it.
5. That, which we do out of love, we do to the highest degree voluntarily.
6. You can only count on yourself for certain (lit. Every person only counts on himself for certain).
7. Whoever is not with me is against me.
8. Every person shall have the right to free development of his personality insofar he does not violate the rights of others or offend the constitutional order or the moral law.
9. He who (Whoever) is without sin shall throw (cast) the first stone.
10. Who was Kaspar Hauser really? His case is at least one that achieved international attention.

11.4

1. das Wetter; storm; 2. formal; formality; 3. publizieren; publication; 4. entscheiden; decision; 5. zetern; nagging; 6. schön; beauty; 7. der Unfall & fahren; accident driver; 8. mit & arbeiten; (female) co-workers; 9. rot & verschieben; redshift; 10. schwarz & malen; pessimism; 11. der Laut & malen; onomatopoeia; 12. eigen; property; 13. die Maske & bilden; make-up artist; 14. die Macht; authority, power of attorney; 15. exklusiv; exclusiveness; 16. der Mensch; prehistoric man, caveman; 17. abstreiten; denial; 18. akzeptieren; non-acceptance

Practice text: Ablasshandel

Vocabulary tasks, in order:

a) *Erbin* refers to a feminine word, *die Kirche.*
b) acts of repentance
c) judgement
d) a treasure trove or collection of divine grace, prayer, good deeds etc.; thesaurus ecclesiae
e) *rufen*
f) sense of guilt
g) to offset
h) the church saw itself as the heir
i) *vollbringen*

The fire comes before heaven – a long and painful cleansing from the amassed sins. The one who accomplished special deeds was able to shorten the time in purgatory. The certification for this was the indulgence: the exemption from (waiving of) the punishment for the sins. The requirement for this exemption from punishment was the confession of the guilt in the (sacrament of) confession (you can omit one confession here).

Together with confession, the indulgence formed a kind of contract, which becomes effective in God's judgement. Indulgences were handed out by the church for pilgrimages, later against monetary payments as well. The buying of indulgences was popular, but it also caused (evoked) protest: Indulgences were (lit. The indulgence was) a presumption of the church. It was not only Luther's reform movement that started here.

Indulgences came (lit. the indulgence stems) from a time where people were aware that they are imperfect (flawed) and make themselves guilty (commit sins). What could one therefore do, in order to pass (survive) God's judgement? Pre-emptive punishments through acts of penitence? Good deeds that go beyond one's duties (lit. duty)? The sense of guilt of medieval people was expecting a long, painful cleansing fire (lit. fire of cleansing) after death. In the same way as ore is purified in the melt (furnace), purgatory cleanses the soul in order to be able to enter heaven. An indulgence can shorten the time here, because the church possesses a treasure trove of mercies: they are the countless good deeds of Christ and the saints, who all had done far more than was necessary for their own salvation.

The church saw itself as the rightful heir of Christ and all saints. Indulgences were fed from this inheritance. (A passive construction works better here.) The pope enjoyed the privilege to hand out a general indulgence. This was especially attractive, because it did not only mean the shortening of the punishment in purgatory, but also the liberation (release) from any kind of torture in purgatory. At the time of Martin Luther, it could be purchased for money at any place, where (lit. at which) indulgences were declared under the banner of the pope – for example (also) from Johann Tetzel in Jüterbog. The indulgences from Johann Tetzel were especially attractive, as they were handed out for prices that were structured along social status (lit. socially structured prices) and they also applied to the future or to the deceased (people who had already died). Luther's critique started here: the pope and the church do not have access to the souls of the deceased, according to Luther. And what meaning does repentance have, if future sins are already offset?

Chapter 12

12.3

A. Indicative are: 2, 3; subjunctive are: 1, 4, 5, 6

B.

	Reported speech – neutral	Reported speech – doubt	Advice/ suggestion
1. Albert Einstein sagte einst, Fantasie sei wichtiger als Wissen, denn Wissen sei begrenzt.	X		
2. Drum prüfe, wer sich ewig bindet, Ob sich das Herz zum Herzen findet. Der Wahn ist kurz, die Reu' ist lang. (Friedrich Schiller)			X
3. Der Angeklagte behauptet, er habe kein Geld vom Kläger gestohlen.		X	
4. Die Zeitung berichtet, dass die Bundeskanzlerin ihre Teilnahme an dem Wirtschaftsgipfel abgesagt habe.	X		
5. Du hast mir eine kostbare Stunde gestohlen, sie werde dir an deinem Leben abgezogen! (from Die Räuber by Friedrich Schiller)			X
6. Lang lebe der König!			X
7. Der Student schrieb mir, er könne nicht an der Prüfung teilnehmen, weil er krank sei.		X	
8. Ohne eine Unterschrift könne der Scheck nicht eingelöst werden, sagte mir die Frau von der Bank am Schalter.	X		

Practice text: Glück im Unglück (2)

One thing, however, most people did not grasp (understand): that their chancellor said (lit. talked about it) that the country needed soldiers again (indirect speech; a "supposedly" or "allegedly" could be added to strengthen this in English), only a few years after the end of the Second World War, after the total defeat, after the complete moral discreditation through the crimes of the Hitler regime. Adenauer, who had never served as a soldier, swiftly pushed forward with the plans for the development (assembly) of an army. He did not shy away from transferring this work to a small agency, which carried a sort of "code name" (lit. camouflage name), Centre for Home Service.

Already in his first keynote speech as the chairman of the CDU in the British occupation zone on March 24th 1946 he had stated that state and power were inseparably intertwined and that power showed itself in the most obvious and impressive way through the army. This tone (rhetoric) must have indeed appealed to the strategists of the US army. Already early they toyed with the idea of redeveloping Germany's army in order to integrate it quickly into a Western European system.

Chapter 13

13.1

Indicative: 3, 5, 6, 8, 9
Both possible: 1, 7
Subjunctive: 2, 4

13.3

Indicative: 2, 7, 8, 9
Used as reported speech: 6, 10
Subjunctive II: 1, 3, 4, 5, 9, 11, 12

13.5

1. Some politicians lie as if their life depended on it.
2. He runs as if stung by a tarantula.
3. The insect lies down still, as if dead.

13.6

1. When (whenever) it is dark, the emergency lighting goes on.
2. If you mix hydrogen peroxide with dry yeast, you get a surprising reaction.
3. Even if you were the last human being on earth, I wouldn't go on a date with you.
4. I would order the fish, if it wasn't so expensive.
5. Many people cannot afford their mortgages anymore, if the central bank continues to increase the interest rate. (The indicative here emphasises that this is a fact and will definitely happen.)
6. In case I'm not here tomorrow, I ask you to please work on the company vision.

Practice text: Wenn die Haifische Menschen wären

A.

Line	Sentence	Grammar	Translation
1	Wenn die Haifische Menschen wären...	Subj. II	If the sharks were men...
3–4	[Sie] würden bauen.	Subj. II	They would build.
5	Sie würden dafür sorgen, dass...	Subj. II	They would take care, that...
8	Wenn er sich verletzen würde, ...	Subj. II	If it injured itself, ...
8–9	Es würde gemacht.	Subj. II, passive	It would be done (made).
10	Es gäbe Feste.	Subj. II	There would be celebrations. (This is the subj. II form of *es gibt*.)
13–14	Sie würden brauchen.	Subj. II	They would need.
16	Sie könnten finden.	Subj. II	They could find.
17	Sie würden unterrichtet werden,	Subj. II, passive	They would be taught.
17	..., dass es das Größte sei, ...	Subj. I	... that it was the greatest.
17–18	..., wenn es sich aufopfert.	Indicative	..., when it sacrifices itself.
28	Der Unterschied bestehe.	Subj. I	The difference existed.
29	Sie sind stumm und schweigen.	Indicative	They are mute and cannot talk (lit. are silent).
32	Er tötete.	Subj. II	He would kill. (It looks the same as the preterite form.)
41	Sie strömten in die Haifischrachen.	Subj. II	They would stream into the jaws of the sharks. (It looks the same as the preterite form.)
44	Es würde auch aufhören.	Subj. II	It would also cease to be.
47	Sie dürften die kleineren Fischlein auffressen.	Subj. II	They would be allowed to eat the smaller fish.

B.

"If the sharks were men," the little daughter of his landlady asked Mr K., "would they then be nicer to the small fish?" "Certainly", he said. "If the sharks were men, they would let giant boxes be built for the small fish in the ocean, with lots of food inside, plants as well as meat (*Tierzeug* is lit. animal stuff). They would take care that the boxes always had fresh water, and in general they would make all kind of sanitary arrangements. For example, if a little fish (*Fischlein* is a diminutive form) were to injure its fin, they would bandage him immediately, so it would not die and be lost to the sharks before its time (lit. so it would not die away for the sharks before its time). In order for the little fish not to become melancholic, there would be big celebrations from time to time; because happy little fish taste better than melancholic ones.

There would, of course, also be schools in the big boxes. In these schools the little fish would learn how one swims into the jaws of the sharks. They would need geography, for example, so they could find (in order to be able to find) the big sharks that lie around lazily somewhere. The main thing would be the moral education of the little fish, of course. They would be taught that it was the greatest and most beautiful thing, if a little fish sacrifices itself happily, and that they all had to believe in the sharks, especially when they said that they would take care of a beautiful future. One would teach the little fish that this future was assured only if they learned obedience. The would need to beware of all base, materialistic, egoistical and Marxist inclinations, and they would have to notify the sharks immediately, if one of them showed (betrayed) such inclinations.

If the sharks were men, they would of course also wage war against one another, in order to conquer foreign (other) fish boxes and foreign (other) little fish. The wars would be waged by their own little fish. They would teach the little fish that there was a huge difference between them and the little fish of other sharks. The little fish, they would declare, are known to be mute, but they are silent in different languages and hence they cannot possibly understand each other. ("To be silent in another language" is an absurdist joke; note how *sind bekanntlich stumm* is indicative, referring to a fact known by the reader, i.e. fish cannot actually talk.) On every little fish that killed a couple of other little fish during the war, silent in another language, they would pin a small medal made of seaweed and they would award him the title of hero.

If the sharks were men, there would, of course, also be art. There would be beautiful pictures, in which the teeth of the sharks would be portrayed in beautiful colours and their jaws as pure pleasure gardens, in which you can romp about splendidly. The theatres on the floor of the ocean would show how heroic little fish swim enthusiastically into the jaws of the sharks, and the music would be so beautiful that the little fish would stream under the sounds of the orchestra ahead (leading the way) into the jaws of the sharks, dreamily, lulled by the most comfortable thoughts. There would also be a religion, if the sharks were men. It would teach that the little fish only really start to live in the bellies of the sharks. (This last sentence is reported speech.)

If the sharks were men, by the way, it would also stop all little fish being equal, as it is now. Some of them would be given official posts and placed over the others. Those who are a bit bigger would even be allowed to eat the smaller ones. That would only be comfortable for the sharks, as they then would get to eat bigger chunks more often. And the bigger little fish, who have posts, would ensure order among the little fish, would become teachers, officers, engineers in box construction, etc. In short, there would actually only be a culture in the ocean if the sharks were men."

Grammatical questions:

C. a.   lernten, verriete (although the -e is only used for the subjunctive II form), tötete, strömten; the context makes it clear that these are subjunctive II forms.

 b.   There are a couple of indicative forms, which are used to address the reader directly (or the landlady's daughter); they state known facts, such as "they taste better" or "they cannot talk". Then there are also a few subjunctive I forms that are used for reported speech. The use of this shows the dubiousness of the sharks' claims.

Content questions:

c.   The boxes could represent houses or cities, potentially even cages or states.
d.   They would learn in geography how to swim into the jaws of the sharks, and in moral education how to be loyal and obedient fish. This would make it easier for the sharks to feed on them and the sharks could just lie around lazily. The purpose of this education is to ensure that the little fish do what the sharks want them to do.
e.   The sharks would wage war against each other, but their little fish would have to do all the fighting. There would be art and religion, but it would only serve to secure the rule of the sharks and/or to brainwash the fish, so that they sacrifice themselves happily.
f.   Equality would end and a hierarchy would be put in place, in which some slightly bigger fish are given roles, such as officers, engineers, magistrates etc. These fish would support the regime of the sharks and feel important or privileged, but they are essentially still little fish.
g.   There are several hints that the author favours a socialist/communist ideology. First, in line 16 there is the mention of *marxistische Neigungen*, which, if other little fish show this, has to be reported. Second, the mention of the war medals (line 24-25) sounds reminiscent of the Second World War, in particular the Third Reich. Third, the comments about religion paint it in a very negative light (e.g. to support the regime of the sharks, who are clearly not socialists), which fits with Marxist ideology. Finally, the strongest hint is in the passage where little fish are told that they cannot talk to other little fish

(lines 20-23). Since this is ridiculed, it points to all little fish, wherever they are and whatever their language is, being equal, a reference to the international proletariat. The sharks therefore are likely nationalists or fascists, who are opposed to all little fish working together. The last section on the hierarchy of the fish could be interpreted as another sign, but this is not clear, as hierarchies existed in the socialist countries as well.

Chapter 14

14.3

A. 1. The article, which was published in the newspaper "Die Zeit" on August 14th...
2. The writer, who was born in Frankfurt...
3. The man who laughed loudly went out of the room.
4. The thief did not find the jewellery that was hidden in a safe.
5. The child that was raised very badly only gives cheeky answers.
6. The woman whose heart was operated on a few hours ago is still sleeping calmly.
7. The hotel that is completely booked until Christmas has a very good reputation
8. Switzerland, which retains its neutrality, is mediating in the crisis.
9. The child that is always afraid of the dark always comes to the parents during the night.
10. The birds, which are happily tweeting, sit on the trees. (*Dahinzwitschern* is a colloquial form of *zwitschern*.)

B. 1. The university has its origin in a monastery, which is hundreds of years old and located on a mountain. (Since there is a relative clause already following *Kloster*, it makes sense to add the phrase to this clause.)
2. The article, which has been awarded a prize and which is cited very often, is ground-breaking.
3. The international treaties, which have existed so far, play a significant role in world trade.
4. The South Koreans, who are convinced of the importance of technological progress, have a leading position in entertainment technology.
5. Before the fall of the (Berlin) Wall there were two orders that existed separately from each other, East and West.
6. This conclusion was reached by a study that was conducted by an international team of scientists and that was recently published.
7. A new study proves that cocaine that is consumed secretly by humans and released as urine ends up in drinking water.

8. This is a research project that is financed by the EU and other, public sponsoring bodies.
9. The policeman who was as brutal as he was ugly did not dare to arrest Johannes.
10. The cat sneaked away on paws that were as quiet as they were silent in the night that was illuminated by the full moon.
11. Before this, Johannes had been ordered into the palace by the queen, who was powerful, widely feared and sometimes even hated.

Practice text: Flugblatt der Weißen Rose

Flyer I

Nothing is less worthy of a civilised people than to let themselves be "governed" without resistance by an irresponsible clique of rulers that is devoted to dark desires. (First participial phrase.) Is it not the case that every honest German today is ashamed of his government? And who of us can guess the extent of the shame that will come over us and our children, once (when finally) the veil will have fallen from our eyes (lifted from our eyes) and the crimes that are most gruesome and endlessly surpass any measure, are brought to the daylight? (Second participial phrase.)

If the German people have already become so corrupted and decayed (disintegrated) in their deepest being that they, without moving a finger (lit. a hand), in careless trust in a questionable legality of history, give away the highest thing that a human possesses and that raises him above any other creature, namely free will, give away the freedom of mankind to intervene in the course of history themselves and to subordinate the course of history to their rational decision, then they deserve their downfall.

If the Germans, thus without any individuality, have already become such a mindless and cowardly mass, then, yes, then they deserve their downfall.

If everyone waits until the other starts, (then) the heralds (harbingers) of the avenging Nemesis will irresistibly move closer and closer, then even the last victim will have been pointlessly thrown into the jaws of the insatiable demon. Therefore every single being must resist in this last hour, aware of his responsibility as a member of Christian and occidental culture. He must resist as much as he can, to work against the scourge of humanity, against fascism and any system of the absolute state that is similar to it. (Third participial phrase.) Put up passive resistance – resistance – wherever you may be, prevent this atheist war machine from continuing before it is too late, before the last cities are a heap of rubble, like Cologne, and before the last youth of the people has bled to death somewhere for the hubris of an "Untermensch" (inferior person). Do not forget that every nation deserves the government that it tolerates!

We ask you to please copy this paper with as many carbon copies as possible and to distribute it further!

Chapter 15

15.3

1. Max Weber's texts are often difficult to understand.
2. One is not allowed to forget (It must/should not be forgotten) that some of Max Weber's texts were first held as speeches.
3. The insult to our religion cannot be accepted (cannot be put up with).
4. Such statements must be avoided by all means in the future.
5. Careful! The vase is very fragile (can easily be broken).
6. What else can be said about this? (You could skip the "about this".)
7. The rules in regard to periods of rest are easy to comply with (can easily be observed.)
8. You cannot always be a hero, but you can always be a man.

15.4

A. 1. The conclusion of the author cannot be understood.
2. In addition, it must be pointed out, that no reliable information can be read from the set of data.
3. If one is asked a serious question (Being asked a serious question), one should answer honestly. (*Aufrichtig* and *ehrlich* are semantically very close, omitting one doesn't change the meaning.)
4. This false report should be corrected.
5. Where there is need, everything can be dared.
6. The inmate in open prison is given leave from mornings to evenings.

B. 1. It annoys me very much, if someone does not come to a meeting.
2. The fears (concerns) have been proven true.
3. The crimes of the colonial masters have been forgotten.
4. The order of the agenda items is not up to debate.
5. One should feel (be) ashamed of such claims.
6. The verdict has been widely rejected.
7. The process has been perfected by these changes (lit. seen perfection through these changes).
8. The tickets for the concert were sold faster than expected.
9. Even today many researchers are interested (show interest) in the works of the classical period.
10. Where is the exit located?

15.4

1. Our modern world that is dominated by the Internet cannot be imagined without the Hypertext Transfer Protocol as the basic building block of the Internet. (Lit. the Hypertext Transfer Protocol cannot be

thought away from our modern world.) Developed originally by Tim Berners-Lee and his team in Switzerland, it facilitated (made possible) the modern World Wide Web's rapid triumph, which was unprecedented and irrevocable.

2. The solution that should be used in this situation is obvious.
3. The views of religious hardliners, which can be attacked as old-fashioned and patriarchal, cannot (should not/must not) be defended anymore nowadays.
4. A breakthrough in stem cell therapy that has suddenly become possible is being hampered by laws that are behind the times (outmoded).
5. The jacket that was supposedly found by you on the train looks suspiciously like the jacket that I lost.
6. One climber is still missing (lit. being missed). The search team that has been put together for his rescue and that is still searching for him has so far been without success.
7. The problem of law in the New Testament that has been contested for so long and so fiercely seems to me to have been handled.
8. The criminal who must be arrested is armed and dangerous.
9. The theses of Rudolf Sohms's work on church law, which was published in 1892, but is still a moving and fascinating piece of work today, still define the current debate. (Normally you would not move a part of the phrase out of the relative clause, but in this case it makes for an awkward translation if you leave *Rudolf Sohms* in the relative clause.)
10. The strange structure of the sentence has to my knowledge almost never (hardly ever) been looked at, exactly as that of his parallel sentences, which is to be mentioned at once. (The second "sentence" should be inserted here to avoid confusion. In German the capitalisation of *Parallelen* makes it clearer that we're dealing with a noun.)
11. Those who want to topple the government, which is new and democratically elected, belong to the guard that is loyal to the old general.

Practice text – An den Bewohner meines Hauses

A. 1. I don't know how you are called.
   2. Red is a strong colour, which can be removed only with difficulty. (This is an *Ersatzpassiv* construction, but the simpler translation "which is difficult to remove" sounds better.)
   3. Books, I have been told, are not very popular in the empire (Reich), in which you live, Mr X.
   4. I wonder what bookshelves could be used for in the Third Reich.
   5. Have my tortoises and lizards really been killed?

B. 1. I am obliged to continue to pay the mortgage interest as well as my German taxes with assets, which I must earn (acquire) newly (from scratch) abroad.

2. Have the flowerbeds and the stone garden suffered a lot, when the SA-people chased my porter, who was beaten crooked and feeble (lame), through the garden, as he fled into the forest?

C.1. A letter from his mortgage company told Feuchtwanger, that the police of the Third Reich had seized his entire active and passive assets (liabilities) and had transferred them to the Reichsaktiengesellschaft for the confiscation of political enemies (Chairman of the board Minister Göring).

2. The letter told him that the German law of the Third Reich only considered/confiscated active assets of political enemies. Despite the fact that his active assets were worth a multiple of the mortgage, he was still supposed to pay the mortgage interest as well as his German taxes from a new income abroad. The irony, as Feuchtwanger points out, is that now Mr X sits in his house and he still has to pay the interest on the mortgage according to German judges.

3. He was badly beaten and injured. Feuchtwanger cynically recommends a company for cleaning the carpet, in case it has been soiled with blood, and for repairing the floor, in case the SA boots have damaged it.

4. Feuchtwanger was in America at the time when the SA came to his house.

5. He believes that reading is not popular in the Third Reich. He innocently stated (again, this is ironic) that the 140.000 words in Hitler's book "Mein Kampf" were 140.000 violations/offences of the essence of the German language. As a result, his house was confiscated and his butler badly beaten.

6. They were killed because their owner was of a race other than the Aryan race.

7. Because of my statement.

Translation

To the occupant of my house Mahlerstraße 8 in Berlin.

I do not know your name or (lit. and) by what manner you came into possession of my house. I only know that two years ago the police of the Third Reich seized all my property, active and passive assets, and handed it over to the stock company formed by the Reich for the confiscation of the properties of political adversaries (chairman of the board: Minister Goering). I came to know of this through a letter from the mortgagee. They explained to me that under the laws of the Third Reich confiscations of property belonging to political opponents concerned themselves (lit. understood) only with active assets. So although my house and my bank deposits, which had been confiscated, greatly exceeded in value the amount of the mortgage,

I was obliged to continue paying the mortgage interest, as well as my German taxes, from money that I was supposed to earn abroad (Note that this sentence contains several instances of reported speech, underlining the absurdity of the demands in the letter.). Be that as it may, in any case – you, Mr X, now sit in my house and I, in the opinion of the German judges, have to pay the interest.

How do you like my house, Mr X? Do you find it pleasant to live in? Did the silver-grey carpeting in the upper rooms suffer a lot while the SA-men were looting? My concierge fled to these upper rooms, as, with me being in America, the gentlemen had decided to seek compensation from him (take advantage of him). The carpet is very delicate, and red is a strong color, hard to get out (This is a fake passive construction, but can be translated more simply). The rubber tiling in the stairway was also not exactly designed for the boots of SA-men. Should it have suffered too badly, I recommend you contact the Baake company.

I wonder what use you have for the two rooms that contained my library. Books, I have been told, are not very popular in the Reich in which you live, Mr X and whoever concerns himself with them is likely to get into trouble (lit. problems). I, for instance, read your Führer's book and harmlessly (simply, merely) remarked that his 140,000 words were 140,000 offenses against the spirit of the German language. The result of this remark of mine is that you are now living in my house. Sometimes I wonder to what purpose the bookcases could be used in the Third Reich. Please be careful not to damage the wall in case you decide to have them ripped out (The subjunctive I here is as imperative/advice.).

And what have you done with the terrarium? Were my tortoises and my lizards really killed (beaten to death) because their owner was of a "foreign race"? And did the flower beds and the rock garden suffer very much when the SA-men pursued my badly hurt (lit. beaten crooked and lame) concierge through the garden as he fled into the woods?

Don't let my house become rundown, Mr X. Please take care of it a little bit.

With many good wishes for our house,

Lion Feuchtwanger

Chapter 16

Practice text: Conversations with Goethe in the last years of his life

Goethe continued: "I see more and more that poetry is a common good of humanity and it comes forth everywhere and at all times in hundreds and hundreds of people. One of them does it a bit better than the others (lit. other); he swims at the top for a little longer than the others, that is all. Mr von Matthisson doesn't need to think that he is it (the best), and I don't need to think that I am it; instead everybody needs to say that poetic talent isn't such a rare thing. (Goethe uses the subjunctive I here, but it is difficult to render it adequately).

And that nobody really has a reason to be vain about it, if he makes (writes) a good poem. But admittedly, if we Germans don't look out of (look beyond) the narrow circle of our own surroundings, then we come (fall) far too easily into this pedantic arrogance. In need of something exemplary, we must always go back to the ancient Greeks, in whose works the beautiful human is always depicted. Everything else we must only look at historically and we must acquire the good (part) from it, as much as that is possible."

"Therein," Goethe continued, "the Greeks in turn were so great that they went less for the fidelity (accuracy) of a historical fact, but rather how the poet treated it. Fortunately we now have an excellent example with the Philoctetes, a topic (theme) that was dealt with by all three great tragic poets, and by Sophocles last and in the best way. This splendid work of this poet fortunately came to us in complete form; from the Philoctetes of Aeschylus and Euripides only fragments were found (*Ersatzpassiv* with *man*), from which one can sufficiently see how they treated their topic. If time allowed it, I would restore these plays, as I have done with the Phaeton of Euripides, and it wouldn't be an unpleasant or useless task for me. With this topic the task was very easy: in fact, to get Philoctetes with his bow from the island of Lemnos. But the way this happens, that is the part of the poets, and therein each one of them was able to show the power of their imagination and outdo the others. Ulysses is supposed to get him; but should he be recognised by Philoctetes or not, and by what means should he be unrecognisable. Should Ulysses go alone, or should he have companions, and who should accompany him? In Aeschylus('s version) the companion is unknown, in Euripides' it is Diomedes, in Sophocles' it is the son of Achilles. Further, in which state should one find Philoctetes? Should the island be inhabited or not, and if inhabited, should some merciful soul have befriended him or not? And so hundreds other things, which were all at the whim of the poets and by choosing or not choosing them one poet was able to show a higher wisdom than the other. This is where it lies, and this is how today's poets should also do it, and today's poets should not always ask if a topic has already been dealt with or not; while they always search in the south and in the north after unheard incidents, which are often barbaric enough and then simply work as incidents. But admittedly, to take a simple topic (theme) and through masterful treatment turn it into something, that requires intellect and great talent, and that is missing.

Additional practice texts

Text 1: Völker der Welt

1. Ernst Reuter addresses the entire world, which is watching the situation in Berlin during the blockade. He specifically mentions generals, governments (*Kabinette*) and free and democratic countries such as the US, England, France and Italy.

2. According to Reuter, (West) Berlin is a bastion or outpost of freedom that cannot be given up without consequences.
3. He says that relinquishing the city would mean not just giving up on the citizens of Berlin, it would also mean giving up "a world" and "one-self", in other words it would mean a capitulation of the West and its ideals. The subjunctive implies that the people in East Germany (in the Soviet occupation zone) would also be outside and listen to his speech as well, if only they could (i.e. they are oppressed and not allowed to go out and demand freedom and democracy).
4. The only option is for Western countries to stand together with Berlin and keep fighting until the battle is won.
5. It refers to the Soviet Union and their communist ideology; note that at that time Stalin was in power in the Soviet Union.

Text 2: "Ich habe doch nichts zu verbergen"

A. 1. the assumption, which is widespread, but rarely challenged
   2. the phrase, which is meaningless, but can nevertheless be found everywhere
   3. the data set, which is well developed
   4. an identity, which is new and orientated towards the future
   5. rooms, which are extended and open
   6. the tired society (or society of tiredness), which has been analysed by Byung-Chul Han

B. 1. it cannot be made secret again
   2. when it is, in fact, not about the preservation of our secrets

C. Instead the slogan **would have** to be updated (needs to be updated) into "I don't have to do anything" or "I don't have to want anything", which **could** be a suitable description of the tired society.

D. 1. There is a widespread assumption that data protection is "only" a protective shield against infringements by the state, media or large corporations. The subjunctive I shows that the author keeps a criti-cal distance to the statement and that the assumption is not verified, but rather presented as questionable.
   2. The argument means that people believe that they have nothing to hide and that therefore the small and fleeting infringements of their private sphere do not matter to them or are not taken seriously. The author uses the metaphor of a bank with an empty vault, which can be raided again and again with no loss of actual money.

3. The problem is that this type of thinking only looks backwards and not into the future. If, to continue the previous metaphor, the bank would suddenly acquire some funds, it would need a place to store them securely. Similarly, one needs data protection in the future, if personal circumstances change.

4. The role of data protection is less to safeguard existing data sets, but rather to establish safe areas and "rooms" for future developments, which are independent from governments and corporations and which allow the individual to become, what it could become, without constant observation.

5. We need safe, extended and large open spaces (in the Internet) where we can keep our secrets and experiment in privacy. In this case the argument does not work anymore, because it is only looks at the now, where we have "nothing to hide", it doesn't look at what could be and how life could potentially develop.

6. Giving up one's space for experimenting means to give up all kinds of ambition, and to give up on making decisions for oneself. It would mean accepting the current status quo forever.

Text 3: Matthäus 1: 18-25

A. Present tense: fürchte, erwartet, ist, sollst
Preterite: war, zeigte, erwartete, wollte, beschloss, nachdachte, erschien, sagte, erfüllte, erwachte, tat, nahm, erkannte, gebar, gab
Perfect: ist geschehen, hat gesagt
Pluperfect: waren zusammengekommen, hatte befohlen
Future: wird gebären, wird erlösen

B. This is how it was with the birth of Jesus Christ: Maria, his mother, was engaged to Joseph. But before they had come together, it became apparent that she was expecting a child – through the work of the Holy Spirit. Joseph, her husband, who was faithful to the law and did not want to embarrass her (disgrace her), decided to separate from her silently (divorce her). While he was still thinking about this, an angel of the Lord appeared to him in a dream and said: "Joseph, son of David, do not be afraid to take Mary as your wife, for the child that she is expecting is from the Holy Spirit. She will give birth to a son and you are (supposed) to give him the name Jesus, because he will save his people from their sins." All this has happened to fulfil what the Lord has said through the prophet. When Joseph woke up, he did what the angel had ordered him to do and took Mary as his wife. But he did not consummate the marriage until she gave birth to a son. And he gave him the name Jesus.

Text 4: Von den 95 Thesen zum Augsburger Religionsfrieden

Scoring: There is a total of 75 marks in the test (45 in the part 1, 30 in part 2). A result of 40+ marks would mean that you have passed the test and have a thorough understanding of German Reading Skills. A result 52+ marks would be a very good result and a result of 62+ marks would be an excellent result.

Part 1

A. 1. accusative; 2. nominative; 3. accusative; 4. nominative; 5. dative; 6. dative; 7. genitive; 8. genitive

B. 1. Indicative: 1, 4; subjunctive I: 2, 3

C. 1. present tense, passive; 2. future, active; 3. preterite, passive

D.
transnationalen	X qualifies a noun
exklusiv:	X qualifies a verb
rechtsverbindlich:	X qualifies another adjective
geforderte:	X qualifies a noun
exakt:	X qualifies another adjective
zeitlicher:	X qualifies a noun
weithin:	X qualifies another adjective
offen:	X qualifies a verb

E. 1. Bei <u>diesem</u> seit dem Hochmittelalter ausgebauten <u>Heilsinstitut</u>...
the promise of salvation, which had been developed since the High Middle Ages

2. ... dass der Ablass <u>die</u> jedem Christen gebotene stetige <u>Buße</u> aushöhle...
the repentance, which is demanded constantly from every Christian

3. ... gegenüber <u>dem</u> wegen seiner Gottferne verzweifelten <u>Sünder</u> verkünde,
the sinner, who despairs due to his distance from god

4. ... durch den Buchdruck <u>eine</u> für ihn selbst völlig überraschende <u>Verbreitung</u>
a distribution, which was completely surprising for him (himself)

5. ... kraft <u>der</u> ihm übertragenen <u>Schlüsselgewalt</u>
the power (authority), which had been transferred to him

Task F

1. The entire previous clause (*so war...*); 2. Luther; 3. der Stellvertreter Christi

Part 2

Task A

True are: 1, 3, 5, 8, 9, 11, 12, 17, 18 (*marktschreierisch* suggests as much)
  False are: 2, 4, 6 (not as propaganda), 7, 10, 13, 14, 15, 16,

Task B

1. Luther was a mendicant friar (1) and he was not the first theologian to criti-
   cise indulgences (2), but he was the one whose criticism had an unprecedented effect and the reception of this criticism surprised him. (3).
       This was due to two factors: first, he attacked indulgences from within,
   relying on central Christian beliefs and the basic understanding of repentance (4). Second, the book press enabled a much faster and widespread
   distribution of his ideas in Germany and the rest of Europe (5).
2. Luther's theses were a direct attack on the pope (1), because the pope
   claimed to be the one with access to the collective treasure of mercy
   that the church had collected over the years and that he could share it
   as he saw fit (2).
3. After the publication of his theses there was a very lively debate (1). Luther
   had theological discussions with Tetzel and others who were defending
   the Catholic Church. (2). Other aspects were added to the debate (3,
   no need to translate them all). As the debate continued, more and more
   theologians and authors began supporting Luther (4), others took care
   that his works were reprinted and distributed all over Europe (5).

Key vocabulary from chapters 1–16

The vocabulary list contains the majority of words that you encountered in chapters 1–8, including the vocabulary listed under exercises and texts. Obvious cognates are not included, and from chapter 9 onwards, only words that occur frequently in texts – regardless of discipline – have been included; abbreviations, very obscure terms, most prepositions and most pronouns have been left off this list.

Abend, der (-s, -e) – evening
aber – but
abermals – (once) again, one more time
Abfall, der (-s, Abfälle) – rubbish
abgießen (sep.v.) – to drain
von etwas abhängen (sep.v.) – to depend on sth.
Ablass, der (-es/Ablässe) – indulgence [rel./hist.]
absagen – to cancel
abschalten (sep.v.) – to turn off
etwas abschmecken (sep.v.) – to season sth. by taste; *alles* – everything
etwas abschreiben (sep.v.) – to copy something, usually by hand
Abteilung, die (-, -en) – department, section, division
Abwesenheit, die (-, -en) – absence
Achterbahn, die (-, -en) - roller coaster
Akte, die (-, -n) – file, case
aktuell – current, relevant, up-to-date
all dies – all this, but usually translated as "all of this"

allein – alone
allerdings – certainly, indeed, however
allerhand – all kinds of
als – as, when (when used as a conjunction)
als wie zuvor – as before
alsdann – thereupon
Amt, das (-(e)s, Ämter) – office, official position
amtlich – official
Amtssprache, die (-, -n) – official language
ändern – to change, alter, modify
anders – different
Anfang, der (-s, Anfänge) – beginning, start
anfangen (sep.v.) – to begin
angenehm – pleasant, enjoyable, preferable
Angriff, der (-s, -e) – attack, assault
anhänglich – devoted, clingy
anheften (sep.v.) – to pin
ankommen (sep.v.) – to arrive
anmaßen (sep.v.) – to assume/presume to do sth.

anpassen (sep.v.) – to adapt to

anrufen (sep.v.) – to call

Ansehen, das (-s, no plural) – reputation, standing, esteem, prestige

anstatt – instead of

anziehen (sep.v.) – to put on clothes, to tighten

arbeiten – to work

arm – poor

Arzt, der (-es, Ärzte) – doctor, GP

auch – also, as well

auf etwas hinweisen (sep.v.) – to point sth. out, to indicate

aufbauen (sep.v.) – to build (up), assemble, arrange

auffressen (sep.v.) – to eat up

Aufgabe, die (-, -n) – task

aufgeben (sep.v.) – to give up

aufhören (sep.v.) – to stop, end

Aufklärung, die (-, -en) – enlightenment, clearing up, sex education

aufladen (sep.v.) – to charge

aufmachen (sep.v.) – to open

sich aufopfern (sep.v.) – to sacrifice oneself

aufrechterhalten (sep.v.) – to keep up, sustain, perpetuate

sich aufregen (sep.v.) – to get upset, to fuss about sth.

sich aufrichten (sep.v.) – to stand up, get up

aufrichtig – sincere, earnest, honest

aufschauen (sep.v.) – to look up to

aufschließen (sep.v.) – to unlock

aufstehen (sep.v.) – to get up, to get out of bed

aufwärts – upwards

aus – from, out of

Ausbildung, die (-, -en) – (job) training, education, apprenticeship

ausdrucken (sep.v.) – to print out

Ausgabe, die (-, -n) – edition

ausgehen (sep.v.) – to go out; *von etwas ausgehen* – to assume something

Ausland, das (-(e)s, no plural) – overseas, abroad

Ausländer, der (-e, -) – foreigner

auslösen (sep.v.) – to cause, trigger, provoke

ausmachen (sep.v.) – to turn off, to agree on

ausprobieren (sep.v.) – to try, attempt, test

aussagen (sep.v.) – to give testimony, bear witness, predicate

aussprechen (sep.v.) – to pronounce, state, announce, proclaim

ausstatten (sep.v.) – to equip

aussteigen (sep.v.) – to get out, exit

aussterben (sep.v.) – to become extinct

etwas auswerten (sep.v.) – to evaluate sth., interpret sth., analyse sth.

Auto, das (-s, -s) – car

bahnbrechend – groundbreaking

Bauch, der (-(e)s, Bäuche) – belly

bauen – to build

Baum, der (-(e)s, Bäume) – tree

etwas beachten – to pay attention to sth.

beantworten – to answer (synonym of *antworten*)

bedeuten – to mean, imply

Bedingung, die (-, -en) – condition

sich beeilen – to hurry

sich mit etwas befassen – to concern oneself with sth.

befehlen – to command

befolgen – to obey, follow

Begebenheit, die (-, -en) – event, incident

begeistert – enthusiastic

beginnen – to begin, start (synonym of *anfangen*)

begreifen – to grasp, recognise, understand

Begriff, der (-s/-es, -e) – term

begrüßen – to greet

behaupten – to claim, assert, allege
bei – with
jmdm. etwas beibringen (sep.v.) – to teach sth. to so.
Beichte, die (-/-n) – confession
beißen – to bite
Beispiel, das (-s, -e) – example
etwas beitragen (sep.v.) – to contribute sth., add sth.
bekannt – famous, familiar, known
bekanntlich – generally well-known
etwas bekennen – to confess sth.
beklagen – to complain, lament, bemoan
bekommen – to get
Belag, der (-(e)s, Beläge) – covering, film, coat, surface
Beleidigung, die (-, -en) – insult
Bemühen, das (-s, no plural) – effort
sich benehmen – to behave
benutzen – to use
beobachten – to observe
berechnen – to estimate, calculate, charge
Bereich, der (-s/-es, -e) – area, section
bereits – already
Bergsteiger, der (-s, -) – climber
Bericht, der (-(e)s, -e) – report, account
Besatzungszone, die (-, -n) – occupied area
beschädigen – to damage
sich mit etwas beschäftigen – to deal with sth./occupy oneself with sth.
Bescheinigung, die (-/-en) – certification
beschlagnahmen – to confiscate
beschreiben – to describe
beschweren – to weigh down, to burden; *sich beschweren* – to complain
besiegeln – to seal
besiegen – to defeat
besonders/insbesondere – especially
Bestätigung, die (-, -en) – confirmation

bestehen – to exist, pass, consist; *auf etwas bestehen* – to insist on sth.
bestimmen – to decide, determine
Bestimmung, die (-, -en) – order, instruction
besuchen – to visit
beten – to pray
betonen – to emphasise, stress
betrunken (participle of *betrinken*) – drunk
beweglich – mobile, movable
bezwingen – to defeat, conquer, overcome
Bildung, die (-, -en) – education
Birne, die (-, -n) – pear
bisschen – a little, a little bit, a few
blasen – to blow
bleiben – to stay, remain
Blume, die (-, -n) – flower
Boden, der (-s, Böden) – floor, ground
bohren – to drill
böse – mean, evil
Brand, der (-s/-es, Brände) – the fire
Bratwurst, die (-, Bratwürste) – fried sausage
Brauch, der (-(e)s, Bräuche) – custom, tradition
Braut, die (-, Bräute) – bride
brechen – to break
Briefbeschwerer, der (-s, -) – paper weight
Brille, die (-, -n) – (eye) glasses
Brot, das (-s, -e) – bread
Bruchstück, das (-(e)s, -e) – fragment
Brücke, die (-, -n) – bridge
Bruder, der (-s, Brüder) – brother
Buch, das (-(e)s, Bücher) – book
buchen – to book
Büchergestell, das (-s, -e) – book shelf
Bühne, die (-, -n) – stage
Bündnis, das (-ses, -se) – alliance
Büschel, das (-(e)s, -) – bunch

daher – because of this, due to this

dann – then

dank – thanks to (preposition with genitive)

dass – that

Datenschutz, der (-(e)s, no plural) – data protection

davonschleichen (sep.v.) – to sneak away

denken – to think; sich denken – to imagine

deutlich – clear, distinct

Deutsch, das (-s, no plural) – German

Dieb, der (-(e)s, -e) – thief

dienen – to serve

drüben – yonder, over there; usually with *da* or *dort* in front

dunkel – dark, gloomy

dünn – thin

durch – through

durchaus – indeed, quite, definitely, by all means

Durchschlag, der (-(e)s, Durchschläge) – carbon copy

durchschnittlich – on average

durchsetzen (sep.v.) – to enforce, push, assert

dürfen – to be allowed to

Ehebruch, der (-(e)s, Ehebrüche) – adultery

Ehrenamt, das (-s, -ämter) – honorary post or office, can also be related to charity posts

ehrlich – honest

Ei, das (-s, -er) – egg

eigenhändig – herself, with her own hands

etwas einhalten (sep.v.) – to observe, hold, comply with sth.

Eimer, der (-s, -) – bucket

eindeutig – clear, unambigious

eindrucksvoll – impressive

einfach – simple, easy

Einfluss, der (-es, Einflüsse) – influence

einige – some

einladen (sep.v.) – to invite

einlullen (sep.v.) – to lull

Einmaleins, das (-es, no plural) – basics

einschalten (sep.v.) – to turn on

sich für jmndn./etwas einsetzen (sep.v.) – to advocate sth., plead for sth. or so., speak up for sth. or so.

sich einverleiben (sep.v.) – to incorporate, swallow up

entfernen – to remove, to depart

entfernt – distant

enthalten – to contain; *sich enthalten* – to abstain

entlassen – to release, fire

entschärfen – to defuse, disarm, ease

entscheiden – to decide

entwickeln – to develop

Entzugsklinik, die (-, -en) – rehab centre

erben – to inherit

Erde, die (-, -n) – earth

Erdnuss, die (-, Erdnüsse) – ground nut, peanut

erfahren – to experience, find out

erfüllen – to comply, fulfil, satisfy

Ergebnis, das (-ses, -e) – the result

ergreifen – to seize

erhalten – to maintain

erhellen – to illuminate

erinnern – to remind; *sich erinnern* – to remember

erkennen – to recognise

erklären – to explain, state

Erlaubnis, die (-, -se) – permission

etwas jmdm. erlassen – to exempt so. from sth., waive sth. for so.

Erlösung, die (-/-en) – deliverance , redemption, salvation

Ermäßigung, die (-, -en) – discount

Ermordung, die (-, -en) – murder, synonym of *Mord*

erobern – to conquer
erreichen – to reach, achieve
erscheinen – to appear
erschlagen – to kill
erschrecken – to scare, frighten, startle; here: to be startled
jmdn. ertappen – to catch so.
erwarten – to expect
erwerben – to acquire, purchase, earn, gain
essen – to eat
Etikett, das (-s, -e/-en) – label
etwas – something

Fach, das (-s/-es, Fächer) – subject, discipline, field of study
Fähigkeit, die (-, -en) – ability, skill
fahren – to drive
Faktum, das (-s, Fakten) – not very common for: factum, fact
Falschmeldung, die (-, -en) – hoax, false report
fast – almost, nearly
faul – lazy
Fegefeuer, das (-s/-) – purgatory
fehlen – to lack, be missing
feig – cowardly, craven
Feile, die (-, -n) – rasp
Feind, der (-(e)s, -e) – enemy
feindlich – hostile
fertig – finished, complete
festhalten (sep.v.) – to hold on, retain
etwas festlegen (sep.v.) – to define, determine or fix sth.
feststellen (sep.v.) – to assert, determine, state
Fleisch, das (-(e)s, no plural) – meat
fleißig – industrious
fliegen – to fly
fliehen – to flee
Flosse, die (-, -n) – fin
flüchten – to flee
flüchtig – fleeting
etwas fördern – to support something

Forscher, der (-s, -) – scientist, researcher
fortschreiten (sep.v.) – to progress
Fortschritt, der (-s/-es, -e) – progress, advance
fragen – to ask
Frau, die (-, -en) – woman, wife
Freizeit, die (-, -en) – leisure time, free time
fremd – foreign, alien
fressen – to feed upon, to eat (usually only animals)
freudig – cheerful, happily
sich freuen – to be happy, rejoice
fröhlich – happy
fromm – pious, godly
frühmorgens – early morning
führen – to lead
Führung, die (-, no plural) – leadership
sich vor etwas fürchten – to be afraid of sth.

Gabe, die (-, -n) – gift, talent
ganz – whole, complete
Gasse, die (-, -n) – alley, lane, narrow street
gebären – to give birth
Gebäude, das (-s, -) – building
geben – to give; *es gibt* – there is/are
gebildet – educated
Gedanke, der (-n, -n) – thought, idea
gedenken (with genitive object) – to remember, commemorate
Gefahr, die (-, -en) – danger, risk
gefährlich – dangerous
Gefährte, der (-n, -n) – companion
gefallen – to appeal to, like, enjoy
Gegensatz, der (-es, Gegensätze) – contrast, opposition
gehen – to go
gehören – to belong to
Gehorsam, der (-s, no plural) – obedience
gelangen – to end up, reach

gelb – yellow

Geld, das (-s/es, -er) – money

Gelegenheit, die (-, -en) – opportunity, chance

Gelehrte, der (-n, -n) – scholar, savant

gelten als – to be known as, regarded as, to be said to be

genauso – exactly

etwas genießen – to enjoy or savour sth.

genug – enough

in etwas geraten – to get into sth.

gerecht – just, faithful

Gerechtigkeit, die (-, -en) – justice, fairness

Gericht, das (-(e)s, -e) – court, dish

geschehen – to happen

Geschichte, die (-, -n) – history, story

geschickt – dexterous, nimble, skilled

Gesellschaft, die (-, -en) – society, community, company (of people)

Gesetz, das (-(e)s, -e) – law

Gesicht, das (-s, Gesichter) – face

gesund – healthy

Gesundheit, die (-, -en) – health

gewaltig – enormous

Gewicht, das (-s, -e) – weight

gewieft – smart, crafty, experienced

gewinnen – to win

sich an etwas gewöhnen – to get used to sth.

gierig – greedy

glauben – to think, believe

Gläubiger, der (-s, -) – creditor

gleichaltrig – of the same age

Gleichung, die (-, -en) – equation

glücklich – happy, fortunate

glühen – to glow

grausam (ad.) – cruel

Grenzbefestigung, die (-, -en) – border fortification

Grippe, die (-, -n) – flu, influenza

groß – large, big

grün – green

Grund, der (-s/-es, Gründe) – reason, cause, ground

gründen – to found

Gurke, die (-, -n) – pickle

haben – to have

Hähnchen, das (-s, -) – (small) chicken

Haifisch, der (-s, -e) – shark

halten – to hold

hänseln – to tease, pick on so.

hassen – to hate

sich häufen – to accumulate, heap up

häufig – often

Hauptsache, die (-, -n) – the main thing

Hausaufgabe, die (-, -n) – homework

Heil, das (-s/no plural) – salvation

heimlich – secret

heimtückisch – sneaky, malicious

heiraten – to marry

heiß – hot

heißen – to be called; often translated active as "my name is"

Held, der (-en, -en) – hero

helfen – to help, support

Hemd, das (-(e)s, -en) – shirt

etwas hemmen – to hinder or prevent sth.

herab – downwards

herauf – upwards

Herrschaft, die (-, no plural) – rule, reign, authority, dominion

hervorrufen (sep.v.) – to elicit, call forth

Herz, das (-ens, -en) – heart

heute – today

hinfort – hereinafter, henceforth

etwas hinnehmen (sep.v.) – to accept sth., put up with sth.

hoch – high

hoffentlich – hopefully

hohl – hollow, here: narrow or round

hören – to listen, hear

Hose, die (-, -n) – trousers

Hund, der (-s/es, -e) – dog

sich vor etwas hüten – to beware of sth.

Hypothek, die (-, -en) – mortgage

ihr – her, your, their

Inhalt, der (-s, -e) – content

innerhalb – within

sich irren – to err, be mistaken

Jahrhundert, das (-s, -e) – century

jammern – to lament, complain, wail, whine, moan

je... desto... – the (more this)... the (more that)

jede – every

jedenfalls – anyway, in any case, at any rate

jemand – somebody

jetzt – now

jeweils – each

Jungfer, die (-, -n) – mistress, maiden, damsel, spinster

Juristerei, die (-, no plural) – law (another word for *Jura*)

kalt – cold

Kampf, der (-s/-es, Kämpfe) – fight, battle

Kartoffel, die (-, -n) – potato

Kaserne, die (-, -n) – barracks

Kasten, der (-s, Kästen) – box

Katze, die (-, -n) – cat

kaufen – to buy

kennen – to know

Kerze, die (-, -n) – candle

Kind, das (-s/es, -er) – child

Kino, das (-s, -s) – cinema

Kirsche, die (-, -n) – cherry

Klang, der (-(e)s, Klänge) – sound

Klausur, die (-, -en) – exam, test

klein – small

klingeln – to ring

klopfen – to knock

klug – clever

Knochen, der (-s, -) – bone

kochen – to cook

Köder, der (-s, -) – bait

kommen – to come

können – can, be able to

Körper, der (-s, -) – body

Kraft, die (-, Kräfte) – strength

krank – sick

Krieg, der (-(e)s, -e) – war

kühlen – to cool

kündigen – to cancel, fire

künftig (auch: zukünftig) – future, in the future

Kunst, die (-, Künste) – art

sich um etwas kümmern – to take care of sth.

etwas kürzen – to shorten sth.

lächerlich – ridiculous

laden – to load

Laden, der (-s, Läden) – shop

Lage, die (-, -n) – situation, position, status

Land, das (-s/es, Länder) – country, land

langweilig – boring

lassen – to let

laufen – to run, go

lauschen – to eavesdrop, listen to

Läuterung, die (-, -en) – cleaning, catharsis

leben – to live

Leck, das (-s, -s) – leak

lediglich – merely, solely, only

lehren – to teach

Lehrer, der (-s, -) – teacher

Leib, der (-(e)s, -er) – body

leiblich – fleshy, bodily

leichtsinnig – careless, lightheaded

leiden – to suffer

leider – unfortunately

leihen – to lend

Leitung, die (-, en) – supervision, management, leadership, line, cable, pipe

lernen – to learn

lesen – to read

leuchten – to glow, light, shine

Leute, die (-, always plural) – people

Licht, das (-s/es, -er) – light

liegen – to lie, be located

List, die (-, -en) – trick, deception, ploy

loben – to praise

Loch, das (-(e)s, Löcher) – hole

löschen – to delete, erase

Lösung, die (-, -en) – solution

lügen – to lie

lustig – cheerful, funny, happy

machen – to do, make

Mädchen, das (-s, -) – girl

man – one, you

mangelnd – missing, lacking of

Mann, der (-s/es, Männer) – men

Mannschaft, die (-, -en) – team, crew

Maß, das (-es, -e) – measure

Mauer, die (-, -n) – wall

Meer, das (-(e)s, -e) – sea, ocean

mehr – more

melden – to report

Mensch, der (-en, -en) – human, person, in plural often: people

Minderheit, die (-, -en) – minority

mindestens – at least

mischen – to mix

Mißbilligung, die (-, -en) – disapproval

Mitläufer, der (-s, -) – follower

Mitleid, das (-(e)s, no plural) – mercy, pity, sympathy/compassion

Mittel, das (-s, -) – means, appliance, resource, average (math.)

möchten – would like

mögen – to like, may

Möglichkeit, die (-, -en) – possibility, chance, opportunity

Morgen, der (-s, -) – morning

müssen – to have to, must

Muttersprache, die (-, -n) – native language

Nachbar, der (-n, -n) – neighbour

Nachricht, die (-, -en) – news, messsage

nächste – next

Nagelfeile, die (-, -n) – nail file

nehmen – to take

Neigung, die (-, -en) – inclination

nett – nice

neulich – recently

nicht – not

nichts – nothing

nie – never (synonym of *niemals*)

Niederlage, die (-, -n) – defeat

etwas niederlegen (sep.v.) – to abdicate sth.

niedrig – low, base

niemand – nobody

nirgendwo – nowhere

nötig – necessary

nun – now

nur – only

ob – whether, if

obwohl – although

öffnen – to open

ohne – without

Opfer, das (-s, -) – victim, sacrifice

opfern – to sacrifice

Orden, der (-s, -) – medal

passen – to fit

passieren – to happen

Pferd, das (-s/es, -e) – horse

etwas pflegen – to take care of sth., look after sth.

Pfote, die (-, -n) – paw

etwas preisgeben (sep.v.) – to relinquish sth., to disclose

Priester, der (-s, -) – priest
prüfen – to investigate, check, test
Prüfung, die (-, -en) – exam, test

Qual, die (-/-en) – pain, torture
Quelle, die (-, -n) – source, spring
quer und krumm – literally "across and crooked," here: criss-cross

rächen – to avenge
Rachen, der (-s, -) – throat, jaws
Rat, der (-(e)s, no plural) – advice
raten – to guess, advise
Ratgeber, der (-s, -) – advisor
Ratschlag, der (-(e)s, Ratschläge) – advice
Rätsel, das (-s, -) – mystery, puzzle
Rechnung, die (-, -en) – bill, invoice
Regel, die (-, -n) – rule, norm, custom
regieren – govern, rule
Regierung, die (-, -en) – government
reglos – motionless
reiben – to rub
rein – clean, pure, absolute
reinigen – to clean
Reinigung, die (-, -en) – cleaning, purification, dry cleaner
reißen – to tear, rip
reiten – to ride
Reue, die (-, no plural) – repentance, remorse
riesig – huge
Rind, das (-(e)s, Rinder) – cattle (ox/cow)
Ritter, der (-s, -) – knight
rot – red
Rückgang, der (-s/-es, Rückgänge) – decline, drop, fall

Saal, der (-(e)s, Säle) – hall
sagen – to say
Sahne, die (-e, -n) – cream
schadlos – harmless; here: to compensate for sth.
schälen – to peel

sich schämen – to be ashamed
Schatten, der (-s, -) – shadow
Schatz, der (-(e)s, Schätze) – treasure
Schauspiel, das (-s, -e) – play, show
Schein, der (-(e)s, -e) – shine, light, appearance
schenken – to give (as a gift), to gift
sich vor etwas scheuen – to shy away from sth.
Scheune, die (-, -n) – barn
Schieflage, die (-, -n) – tilt, difficult or ailing position
schier – almost, just about
schießen – to shoot
schlafen – to sleep
schlagen – to beat, hit
Schleier, der (-s, -) – veil, haze
schließen – to close, lock
Schlussfolgerung, die (-, -en) – conclusion, deduction, argumentation
Schmach, die (-, no plural) – disgrace, humiliation
schmecken – to taste
schmerzhaft – painful
Schnee, der (-s, no plural) – snow
schneiden – to cut
schnell – fast
schon – already
schön – beautiful, pretty
Schraubenzieher, der (-s, -) – screwdriver
schreiben – to write
Schuld, die (-, -en) – debt, fault, guilt
Schuldbewusstsein, die (-s, no plural) – feeling or sense of guilt
Schüler, der (-s, -) – pupil, student
Schüssel, die (-, -n) – bowl
sich schütteln – to shake, tremble
schweigen – to be silent
schwer – heavy, difficult
Schwert, das (-(e)s, -er) – sword
Schwester, die (-, -n) – sister
sehen – to see
sich nach etwas sehnen – to long for sth.

sein – to be

seit – since, for

selbst – self (himself, herself, itself…)

selbstbestimmt – self-determined

selbstbewusst – self-confident

Senf, der (-(e)s, -e) – mustard

setzen – to place, set; *sich setzen* – to sit down

sichern – to secure, ensure

sie – she, they, you (formal)

Sinn, der (-(e)s, -e) – sense, meaning

sinnfällig – evident, obvious

sitzen – to sit, be positioned

sofort – immediately

sogar – even

sogleich – immediately

sollen – ought to, shall, should, is supposed to

sonst – otherwise

für etwas sorgen – to take care of sth.

sowohl… als auch… – as well as

später – later

spazieren – to go for a walk

Spiegel, der (-s, -) – mirror

spielen – to play

Spinne, die (-, -n) – spider

Spion, der (-s, -e) – spy

Sprache, die (-, -n) – language, speech

sprechen – to talk, speak

Spruch, der (-(e)s, Sprüche) – saying, phrase

Staat, der (-s/-es, -en) – state

Staatsapparat, der (-s, -s) – state machinery

Stacheldraht, der (-s, Stacheldrähte) – barbed wire

Stadt, die (-, Städte) – city

staffeln – to stagger, scale

ständig – constant

stattfinden (sep.v.) – to take place, occur

stechen – to sting

stehen – to stand

stehlen – to steal

Stein, der (-(e)s, -e) – stone

Steinbruch, der (-(e)s, Steinbrüche) – quarry

steinigen – to stone to death

Stelle, die (-, -n) – spot, position

sterben – to die

Steuer, die (-, -n) – tax

Stift, der (-s/-es, -e) – pen, peg

stoßen – to push

Strafe, die (-, -n) – punishment, here: ticket

Streit, der (-s/es, -e) – argument, fight

streng – strict, severe

strömen – to stream

stumm – mute, silent

stur – stubborn

stürzen – to rush, fall, overturn

suchen – to search, seek

Sujet, das (-s, -s) – an object or topic of artistic contemplation/work; subject

Sünde, die (-, -n) – sin

Sünder, der (-s, -) – sinner

Tag, der (-s/es, -e) – day

Tarnmantel, der (-s, Tarnmäntel) – invisibility cape

Tasche, die (-, -n) – bag

Tat, die (-, -en) – action, deed

tauschen – to trade, exchange

teilnehmen (sep.v.) – to participate

teuer – expensive

Teufel, der (-, -s) – devil

Tisch, der (-(e)s, -e) – table

Tochter, die (-, Töchter) – daughter

toll – great, awesome

Tor, der (-en, -en) – fool (do not confuse this with *das Tor* – the gate)

töten – to kill

totschlagen (sep.v.) – to beat to death

tragen – to carry, wear

Traum, der (-(e)s, Träume) – dream

träumen – to dream träumerisch
– dreamily
treffen – to meet
Tresor, der (-s, -e) – the safe, strong
box
Trieb, der (-(e)s, -e) – urge, drive,
desire
trotzdem – regardless, anyway
Tugend, die (-, -en) – virtue
tun – to do
Tür, die (-, -en) – door
Tüte, die (-, -n) – bag

über etwas verfügen – to have sth. at
one's disposal, to possess sth.
überhaupt – actually (can sometimes
be omitted)
überleben – to survive
überlegen – to think, ponder
übernatürlich – supernatural
übersetzen – to translate
übersteigen – to exceed, outstrip
übertragbar   –   transferable,
assignable
übertragen – to delegate (a task), to
transfer
überwachen – to surveil/monitor
übrigens – by the way
um etwas besorgt sein – to care for
sth./worry about sth.
umfassen – to grab, include
umschalten (sep.v.) – to change a
channel, turn a switch
Umstand, der (-(e)s, Umstände) –
circumstance, fact, situation
Umwelt, die (-, -en) – environment
umziehen (sep.v.) – to move
Unannehmlichkeit, die (-, -en)
– inconvenience
unaufhaltsam – inexorable
unbequem – uncomfortable
und – and
unerwünscht – unwanted, undesired
Unfall, der (-s, Unfälle) – accident
unkenntlich – unrecognisable

unnütz – useless
untereinander – amongst themselves
untergehen (sep.v.) – to sink, perish,
disappear
unterhalten – to entertain, sustain; *sich unterhalten* – to have a
conversation
unterrichten – to teach, educate
Unterschied, der (-(e)s, -e)
– difference
Unterschrift, die (-, -en) – signature
unterstützen – to support
untersuchen – to look into, examine
untrennbar – inseparable
Unverwundbarkeit, die (-, -en)
– invulnerability
Urlaub, der (-(e)s, -e) – vacation,
holiday
Urteil, das (-s, -e) – verdict,
judgement

veraltet – obsolete, outdated; *verrechnen* – to miscalculate, offset
Verband, der (-s, Verbände)
– bandage
verbessern – to improve
verbinden – to connect
Verbrechen, das (-s, -) – crime
verdammen – to condemn (more
commonly: to damn, doom)
verdeutlichen – to make clear, illustrate, point out
verdienen – to deserve, earn
verfestigen – to strengthen, intensify, consolidate
verfolgen – to chase, persecute
Vergebung, die (-, no plural)
– forgiveness
vergessen – to forget
verhaften – to arrest so.
Verkehr, der (-s, -e) – traffic
verkommen   –   to   deteriorate,
degenerate
Verlag, der (-s, -e) – publishing
house

verlassen – to leave

verlassen – to leave; *sich auf etwas verlassen* – to rely or count on something

Verleger, der (-s, -) – publisher

verletzen – to injure

verlieben – to fall in love

verlieren – to lose

verloben – to engage (for the purpose of marriage)

verloren – lost; participle of *verlieren*

Verlust, der (-s/es, -e) – loss

vermeiden – to avoid

Vermögen, das (-s, -) – wealth, assets

vermutlich – presumably, probably

vernichten – to destroy, annihilate

veröffentlichen – to publish

verraten – to betray, rat out

verringern – to reduce

verrückt – crazy, mad

verschieden – different

verschmutzen – to pollute

Versorgung, die (-, -en) – supply

verstehen – to understand

verstehen – to understand; *sich verstehen* – to agree, get along; *sich als etwas verstehen* – to see oneself as sth.

versuchen – to try; *jmdn. versuchen* – to tempt so.

vertrauen – to trust

vertraulich – confidential

Verunreinigung, die (-, -en) – impurity

verwandt – related

verwenden – to use, utilise, employ

verwerflich – reprehensible, repugnant

verwirren – to confuse

viel – a lot, many

Vielfalt, die (-, no plural) – diversity, variety

Vogel, der (-s, Vögel) – bird

Volk, das (-(e)s, Völker) – nation, people, population

vollbringen – to accomplish, achieve

voran – ahead

vorantreiben (sep.v.) – to push on/forward, to advance sth.

vorbereiten – to prepare

vorhalten (sep.v.) – to hold in front, to reproach so. with sth.

vorher – before

Vorhersage, die (-, -n) – prediction, forecast

vorkommen (sep.v.) – to exist, happen

vorladen (sep.v.) – to summon, serve

vorstellen (sep.v.) – to introduce, present; *sich vorstellen* – dative pronoun: to imagine; accusative pronoun: to introduce oneself

Vortrag, der (-s/-es, Vorträge) – lecture, speech

etwas wagen – to dare (to do) sth.

wählen – to choose, vote

während – during

Wahrheit, die (-, -en) – truth

Waisenhaus, das (-(e)s, Waisenhäuser) – orphanage

walten – to rule, preside

Wand, die (-, Wände) – wall

warum – why

was – what

wecken – to wake

weder… noch – neither… nor

weg – away

sich weigern – to refuse

Weihnachten, die (-, -) – Christmas

weil – because

weiß – the infinitive of this irregular verb is *wissen*

Weiterbildung, die (-, -en) – further or continuing education

weltbekannt – world famous

wenig – a little, few

wenigstens – at least

wenn – when, if

werben – to advertise

werden – to become
werfen – to throw
wert – worth
Wettbewerb, der (-es, -e) – competition
wie – how, as (when used for comparisons)
wiederholen – to repeat
wiedervereinigen (sep.v) – to reunite
Wirken, das (-s, no plural) – act, effect
Wirtin, die (-, Wirtinnen) – landlady
wissen – to know
Wissenschaftler, der (-s, -) – scientist, researcher, scholar
wo – where
wobei – at which, whereupon, in doing so
Woche, die (-, -n) – week
wohl auch – here: probably as well
wohnen – to live, inhabit
Wohnung, die (-, -en) – apartment
wollen – to want
Wunsch, der (-es, Wünsche) – wish
würzen – to season

zeigen – to point at, to show; *sich zeigen* – to become apparent or clear
Zeit, die (-, -en) – time
Zeitung, die (-, -en) – newspaper
zerbrechen – to shatter, break
Zeuge, der (-n, -n) – witness
Zins, der (-es, -en) – (financial) interest (almost always used in plural)
ziseliert – eloquent, detailed, nuanced
zu – to, towards, too
zufrieden – happy, satisfied
etwas zugeben (sep.v.) – to admit sth.
zügig – quick, rapid
zugreifen (sep.v.) – to access sth, take hold
Zukunft, die (-, no plural) – future
zumachen (sep.v.) – to close
zurück – back
zusammen – together
Zustand, der (-s, Zustände) – state, condition
zustimmen (sep.v.) – to agree, concur
zuverlässig – reliable
zuvor – before/at an earlier time
zwangsläufig – inevitably, unavoidably
Zweifel, der (-s, -) – doubt
Zwiebel, die (-, -n) – onion
zwischen – between

Index

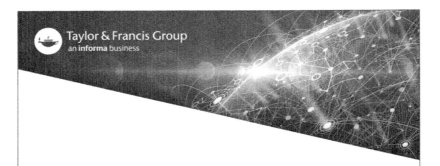

Printed in Great Britain
by Amazon

47911497R00165